ELEVATION ON WASHINGTON AVENUE
SCALE ¼" = 1'-0"
SCOTTISH RITE CATHEDRAL
SANTA FE, NEW MEXICO
HUNT & BURNS, Architects.
Los Angeles, California.
NOTE:
ALL GLASS MARKED "O.G." TO BE OBSCURE GLASS
TILE RIDGE AND HIPS
MISSION TILE ROOF
CONCRETE BRACKETS
SECOND FLOOR LINE
FIRST FLOOR LINE
GROUND FLOOR LINE
PRESENT GRADE
SEE SCALE DETAILS
OPEN

The Santa Fe Scottish Rite Temple

FREEMASONRY, ARCHITECTURE, AND THEATRE

EDITED BY WENDY WASZUT-BARRETT AND JO WHALEY

Essays by

RICK HENDRICKS

KHRISTAAN VILLELA

WENDY WASZUT-BARRETT

Photography by
JO WHALEY

MUSEUM OF NEW MEXICO PRESS
SANTA FE

LOUDER
SLOWER

Contents

Preface

THE SANTA FE SCOTTISH RITE TEMPLE has remained veiled in mystery throughout the decades. Like many other Masonic edifices, it once announced the presence of a secretive society loudly through a monumental building in the heart of a city, hiding in plain sight. Today, many of the country's Masonic buildings are being repurposed, and their collections are being liquidated.

This book evolved from both an anticipated loss and a desire to preserve Santa Fe's heritage when the 1912 Scottish Rite Temple was put up for sale in 2013. It was the jewel box theater with its original scenery collection that initially caused our paths to cross. The building and its artifacts represent a time capsule of Masonic culture and theatrical history that deserves documentation.

Through the heroic efforts of its members, the Santa Fe Scottish Rite Temple is no longer for sale and has been preserved, remaining under the continued stewardship of the Freemasons, who share their building with the community. We wish to thank the Valley of Santa Fe for generously opening their doors and supporting this book.

This volume explores the Ancient and Accepted Scottish Rite of Freemasonry in New Mexico and the significance of its temple in Santa Fe. Rick Hendricks examines the emergence of Freemasonry (chapter 1) and key Masonic figures during New Mexico's territorial period through statehood (chapter 2). Khristaan Villela considers the Moorish revival style, the architectural significance of the building, and use by the Fraternity, both past and present (chapter 3). Wendy Waszut-Barrett examines the theatrical production of Masonic degrees and the significance of the painted scenery collection (chapter 4). Throughout the book, historic images and Jo Whaley's photographs give the reader a glimpse into the secretive world of the Santa Fe Scottish Rite Temple.

We invite you to step inside.

Editor's Note

View of the Scottish Rite Temple from the Federal Building grounds, 2016.

THE ANCIENT AND ACCEPTED Scottish Rite of Freemasonry selected a variety of names for their buildings, with the two most common being *temple* or *cathedral*. There is virtually no difference between the two types of structures, as each was used for meetings, ceremonial activities, and social events. Santa Fe Scottish Rite Masons selected *cathedral* for the name of their building during the initial planning and design phase.

Pressures from both inside and outside the organization affected not only the initial selection of a building's identification, but also subsequent name changes in later decades. The selection to use either *temple* or *cathedral* was seldom based on correct etymological definitions. In many cases, the use of *cathedral* signified the architectural grandeur of the building by those in charge at the time. From an architectural standpoint, some Scottish Rite edifices appeared to be the works of Medieval operative masons, suggesting a link to past Gothic cathedrals. This was often extremely confusing to the general public. Freemasons professed no particular religious affiliation, yet there continued to be a plethora of Masonic temples and cathedrals appearing throughout the country.

In some instances, anti-Masonic sentiment and pressures from local members or religious communities prompted Masonic leaders to seek alternative names to the commonly known *temple* or *cathedral*. By the late twentieth century, the use of Masonic Center became a popular alternative. It was a neutral title that did not suggest Judaic, Islamic, or Christian origins. Many Scottish Rite Valleys accepted the use of *Masonic Center* as they began opening their doors to the public as a venue for theatrical performances, social events, and weddings. Although there was never any Masonic legislation implemented to uniformly change the name of all Scottish Rite buildings to Masonic Centers, it was strongly encouraged by many during the early twenty-first century.

In Santa Fe, the Scottish Rite building was dedicated as a cathedral, yet members continued to refer to it as the Scottish Rite Temple. For the purposes of this book, we have chosen to use Scottish Rite Temple as it most closely embodies the spirit of Freemasonry in the Southwest region. It is a sacred space where men gathered to learn about themselves and others.

Assembly of Freemasons for the Reception of the Masters. Entrance of the Candidate in the Lodge. *Engraving by Johann Martin Bernigeroth, 1745. Courtesy of Arturo de Hoyos.*

1
Freemasonry and the Scottish Rite

RICK HENDRICKS

FREEMASONS ARE MEMBERS OF THE WORLD'S oldest and largest fraternal organization. A member of the modern Fraternity of Freemasons is a speculative Mason, a person who, like a living stone, is being built into a spiritual house.[1] There is no consensus on many aspects of the emergence of speculative Masonry, but many historians believe that speculative Masonry derives from operative masonry.[2] An operative mason is a person who builds buildings out of stone, applying such tools as the square and the compass; the combination of these two symbolic objects is universally recognized as an emblem of Freemasonry. As builders, operative masons knew the secrets of architecture and geometry. They organized into guilds, which had three classes of masons: apprentices (entered apprentices), journeymen (fellow craft), and master masons. These guilds held regular meetings in lodges. Eventually, guilds accepted members who did not work stone, and the original trade organization gradually transformed into the Fraternity that is modern Freemasonry.

Working Tools, *DeMoulin Bros. glass slide, ca. 1900, 3½ × 3½ in. This slide was used as a lecture aid in the Symbolic Lodge to present the working tools of an operative mason. Courtesy of Dan Irick.*

There is general agreement that modern Freemasonry dates from 1717, when four lodges in London gathered at the Goose and Gridiron alehouse in the city's St. Paul's Churchyard section and formed a grand lodge to assist individual lodges in holding regular meetings and to convene an annual assembly.[3] Today, all Masons belong to a local lodge, called the Symbolic Lodge (or Blue Lodge), which confers three degrees: Entered Apprentice, Fellow Craft, and Master Mason. The term *degree* refers to the level of membership or the ceremony necessary to attain that level. A Freemason is said to be "initiated" into the First Degree, "passed" to the Second Degree, and "raised" to the Third Degree. To be considered full-fledged Masons, members have to attain the Third Degree, that of Master Mason. Beginning in the 1840s, Freemasonry—and many other fraternal organizations—in the United States entered a period of rapid expansion, which lasted until the onset of the Great Depression. Unique among fraternal groups, Freemasonry attracted numerous Masonic organizations known as appendant or collateral bodies. Among these appendant bodies are the York and Scottish Rites and the Ancient Arabic Order of the Nobles of the Mystic Shrine (whose members are commonly known as Shriners). Originally, to become a member of the York or Scottish Rite or the Shrine, a man had to be a Master Mason. The term *Scottish Rite* is something of a misnomer because the organization is of French rather than Scottish origin.

The Scottish Rite is the best-known appendant Masonic body. Its origin in the United States dates from the beginning of the nineteenth century in Charleston, South Carolina, the official birth date being May 31, 1801.[4] The Ancient and Accepted Scottish Rite of Freemasonry is an advanced, or high, degree system based on an earlier prototype, presented within the French Rite of Perfection, that used elaborate historical reenactments. This rite was transported from France to the West Indies and then up the Eastern Seaboard. Through the efforts of Etienne Morin, French Freemasonry and the Rite of Perfection arrived in Santo Domingo in the Caribbean in 1763. Morin had been appointed an Inspector General, with authority to expand the Rite in the French West Indies and on the American mainland. Confusion and disparity developed among many early lodges, which were loosely connected through individual interpretations, even though the titles, subjects, and lessons remained constant. To standardize the abundant variations of ritual work, the Rite published and distributed a flyer, announcing creation of the Scottish Rite Supreme Council, known as the Supreme Council, 33rd Degree, the Mother Supreme Council of the World.[5] Its authority derived from Morin's patent and the Grand Constitutions of 1786.

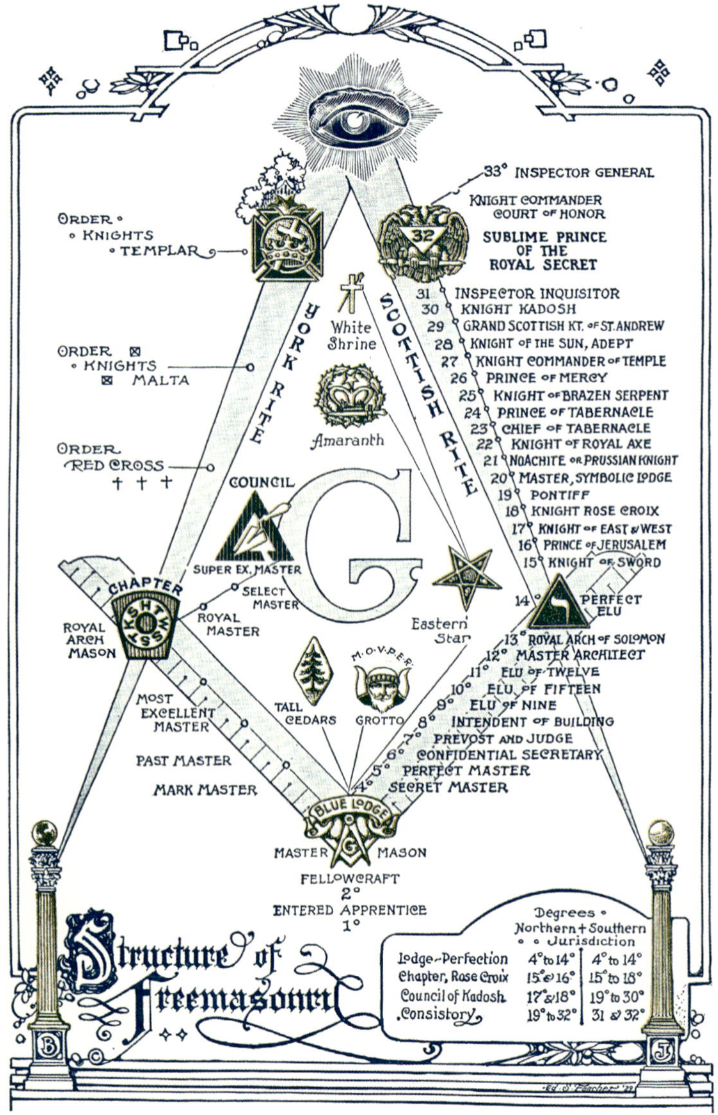

A graphic representation of the structure of Freemasonry, 1929. Collection of the Scottish Rite Temple, Santa Fe.

Assembly of Freemasons for the Reception of the Masters. *The Candidate is placed on the coffin drawn on the floor cloth, representing a symbolic grave. Engraving by Johann Martin Bernigeroth, 1745. Courtesy of Arturo de Hoyos.*

The Rite of Perfection's twenty-five-degree structure was increased to a thirty-two-degree structure, with a possible honorary Thirty-third Degree.[6] Creating a single governing body did not achieve the unity that the fraternal founding fathers anticipated and only briefly provided a collective American Masonic identity. The Mother Supreme Council's demand for nationally recognized unity and individual lodges' demand for regional autonomy created tension. Attempts to establish alternative governing bodies occurred within the first decade of the group's existence. The organization split into two independently governed jurisdictions when a second Supreme Council appeared in 1813, thus dividing the Rite into geographical regions.[7] An 1827 territorial agreement created two Scottish Rite jurisdictions: the Northern Masonic Jurisdiction included the area east of the Mississippi River and north of the Ohio River, including Delaware, and the Southern Masonic Jurisdiction encompassed the rest of the country.

The Scottish Rite confers the Fourth through Thirty-second Degrees: a series of dramatic presentations—morality plays—that build on knowledge gained in the first three degrees and provide insight into Masonic legends, but the addition of a degree production did not appear until the mid-nineteenth century. The Scottish Rite's twenty-nine degrees were "communicated," "conferred," or "conferred in full" to a Masonic candidate. *Communication* carefully emphasized words and linguistic interpretation, whereas a *conferral* emphasized words' contextual environment through visual aids. Full conferrals distinguished later nineteenth-century conferrals and their increasingly complex environments from their earlier nineteenth-century predecessors, utilizing more elaborate scenic environments, with additional theatrical elements that included raised platforms, area dividers, backing flats, costumes, and special effects.

Wendy Waszut-Barrett's chapter 4 on Masonic theatre thoroughly discusses the emergence of degree productions from degree conferrals. The Thirty-third Degree is conferred only to Scottish Rite Masons who have performed outstanding service to the Fraternity or the world.

Lodge Opened in the Master Mason Degree, *DeMoulin Bros. glass slide, ca. 1900, 3½ × 3½ in. This instructional slide depicts King Solomon* (left), *the chief architect Hiram* (center), *and Hiram of Tyre* (right). *Courtesy of Dan Irick.*

Entered Apprentice chart, which assisted Masonic instruction for the First Degree to new initiates in the Symbolic Lodge. Nineteenth-century lithograph, 3 × 4 ft. Collection of Union Lodge No. 4, Wagon Mound, New Mexico.

The Traitor, *production staged at the Santa Fe Scottish Rite, ca. 1930. The setting is used for the second section in the Twentieth Degree. Photograph by T. Harmon Parkhurst. Collection of Chapman Lodge No. 2, Las Vegas, New Mexico.*

NOTES

1. A very similar concept is expressed in the Bible in 1 Peter 2:5 (New Revised Standard Version).

2. David Stevenson, *The Origins of Freemasonry: Scotland's Century, 1590–1710* (Cambridge: Cambridge University Press, 1990), 11, 96.

3. Joseph Fort Newton, *The Builders: A Story and Study of Freemasonry* (Cedar Rapids, IA: Torch Press, 1922), 181.

4. Robert Freke Gould, *The Concise History of Freemasonry* (London: Gale and Polden, 1903), 407–8.

5. John Henry Cowles, *The Supreme Council, 33rd; Mother Council of the World, Ancient and Accepted Scottish Rite of Freemasonry, Southern Jurisdiction, USA* (Louisville, KY: Standard Print, 1931), 420.

6. "History—Ancient and Accepted Scottish Rite," Masonic Union of Strict Initiation Observance (UMSOI), 2008, http://www.umsoi.com/english/history-ancient-and-accepted-scottish-rite/.

7. Mark A. Tabbert, "From a Point to a Line: Twenty Sovereign Grand Commanders," Pietre-Stones Review of Freemasonry, 1996–2017, http://www.Freemasons-Freemasonry.Com/Tabbert2.html.

Masonic parade on Main Street, Las Cruces, New Mexico, ca. 1910. New Mexico State University Library, Archives and Special Collections (00040376).

2
Freemasonry in New Mexico, 1846–1911: Challenges and Opportunities

RICK HENDRICKS

THIS BOOK CELEBRATES the Scottish Rite Temple of Santa Fe. The Scottish Rite came to New Mexico formally on February 1, 1883, with the establishment of Santa Fe Lodge of Perfection No. 1 under the direction of Charles Spaulding of Topeka, Kansas, a deputy of the Supreme Council for the Southern Jurisdiction.[1] Freemasonry in New Mexico, however, was almost four decades old by 1883. Rather than a comprehensive history of Freemasonry in New Mexico, this chapter focuses on some of the challenges the Fraternity faced in the territory and how its members confronted and overcame them. It also examines how Freemasonry functioned in New Mexico and the opportunities it afforded its members as they transformed frontier society.

The timing of the establishment of Freemasonry in New Mexico was fortuitous in that it coincided with the rapid growth of the Fraternity in the United States. Khristaan Villela's chapter, which follows, is a richly detailed architectural history of the temple in Santa Fe. This magnificent building is an outstanding example of the architect's craft and deserves to be studied in its own right, but it belongs to a particular historical context. For that reason, this chapter includes, if not precisely architectural histories, at least some observations about three other major Masonic buildings constructed in the same period as the Scottish Rite Temple in Santa Fe. Those temples were in Las Vegas, Albuquerque, and Las Cruces. Outstanding architects designed these structures, and each was remarkable in its own way.

It is traditional for Masonic histories to include biographical sketches of members of the Fraternity. In honoring that custom, this chapter provides sketches of prominent Freemasons in the early years of the Territory of New Mexico. The men who appear in this section are representative of some of the themes developed in this chapter. Some of these men were active in more than one lodge in New Mexico. Some lived in one town and then settled in another, but a number of these men moved back and forth between communities. A number of them were lawyers and judges and involved in government; others were merchants. These individuals moved all over the territory, another characteristic of early Freemasons in New Mexico. For many men, membership in the Fraternity and seeking out fellow Freemasons eased the process of establishing themselves in a new town.

Beginnings

Freemasonry made its first appearance in New Spain, of which New Mexico formed the northernmost province, toward the end of the eighteenth century in the person of Frenchmen who took up residence in Mexico City and were eventually brought before the Tribunal of the Holy Office of the Inquisition and condemned.[2] Although it is not possible to prove their existence using the documentary record, it is probable that Freemason military lodges or individual Freemasons were part of the Spanish army serving in New Spain. Whether the rank-and-file soldiers serving in the Santa Fe presidio, most of whom were local men, had any association with Freemasonry is probably unknowable, based on surviving documentation. Masonic ideas are more likely to have influenced their officers, many of whom were from elsewhere in New Spain or from Spain, where Freemasonry had more of a presence.

The first Freemasons who came to New Mexico for whom there is documentary evidence arrived late in the long period of Spanish colonial rule in the first decade of the nineteenth century. Among the first Masons in New Mexico was Dr. John H. Robinson, who came to the area on Zebulon Montgomery Pike's exploratory expedition to the Rocky Mountain region in 1806. Robinson left the Pike expedition in February of that year and made his way to Santa Fe.[3]

When Napoleon placed his brother, Grand Master of the Grand Orient of France Joseph Bonaparte, on the throne of Spain in 1808, traditional Spanish limitations on Freemasonry were lifted, allowing it to spread more easily to Spain's American possessions.[4] The role of Freemasonry, or lack thereof, in the movement for the independence of Mexico from Spain that began in 1810 has been hotly debated, but there is no question that during the brief reign of Emperor Agustín de Iturbide, two affiliated Rites came into conflict. The York Rite attracted followers because it espoused the liberal ideas of Great Britain and the United States without mixing Freemasonry with politics. Conservatives of the privileged classes preferred the Scottish Rite and sought to retain the power they had enjoyed during the rule of the Bourbon monarchy. In the absence of political parties in newly independent Mexico, the York and Scottish lodges and their members began to manifest the ideologies of the liberal–conservative divide on the national level in the military, legislative bodies,

Charles Bent, Freemason and fur trader, carved his name on a tree trunk near Fort Garland, Colorado, in 1834. Collection of Montezuma Lodge No. 1, Santa Fe.

Oil painting of Governor Charles Bent, Freemason and first military-appointed civilian governor of New Mexico, 1846–47. Palace of the Governors Photo Archives (NMHM/DCA 007004).

and religious corporations and on the level of newly created entities, such as New Mexico, which became a part of the Mexican nation in 1821.[5]

Many Masons arrived in New Mexico during the period of Mexican rule, which lasted from the advent of Mexican independence from Spain in 1821 until US invasion and occupation, which began in 1846. In 1824 John S. Patton, a former resident of Boone County, Missouri, relocated to Santa Fe, making him one of the earliest arrivals from the United States to settle in the Mexican territory of New Mexico.[6]

Beginning in 1851, Patton was very active in Montezuma Lodge in Santa Fe.[7] He relocated to Mesilla and remained there until his death in 1866. He received full Masonic honors at his funeral, and his obituary noted that he had been a Mason for some forty-five years, which means that he became a Freemason before arriving in New Mexico, probably in Missouri. Dr. Rowland Willard, a physician, was an organizer and Junior Warden of Hyram Lodge No. 3, Saint Charles, Missouri, before departing for New Mexico.[8] Willard was also a member of the York Rite. He traveled to New Mexico in 1825, spending time in Santa Fe before heading south to Chihuahua.

New Mexico politics in the Mexican period aligned closely with the often tumultuous situation in the rest of the country. There is no better example of this than Governor Albino Pérez, who may have been a *yorkino,* or York Rite Mason.[9] Pérez was a native of Valladolid (present-day Morelia), Michoacán, where Masonic lodges existed by the 1820s.[10] He also lived and performed military service in Mexico City and Veracruz, which also had active Masonic lodges. Mexican president Antonio López de Santa Anna, who was a yorkino, dispatched Pérez to New Mexico in 1835 to implement a number of reforms, among them the imposition of taxes, which the local population was unaccustomed to paying. New Mexicans resented Pérez, who in addition to being an outsider was something of a dandy and a married man who took up with a local woman. In 1837 some Nuevomexicanos rebelled against the Pérez government. Pérez attempted to put down the revolt, but the rebels defeated his small force and beheaded him.

Proceedings of the Grand Lodge of Texas indicate that in 1841, doubtless in conjunction with the ill-fated Texan Santa Fe Expedition, there was an attempt to establish a lodge in Santa Fe, as many members of the invading force were Freemasons. Apparently, a dispensation was granted for the institution of a lodge at Santa Fe, but it came to nothing.[11]

Charles Bent, a brother Freemason who was destined to become the first military-appointed civilian governor of New Mexico, had been supplying both the rebel and the government forces. The rebels mistakenly believed that Bent was also a yorkino and a supporter of Pérez, and they locked him up in Taos. He resorted to bribery and bluster to gain his freedom. Bent, a native of Charlestown in what is now West Virginia, was a founding member of Missouri Lodge No. 1 in Saint Louis in 1821.[12] Bent, who was named governor in September 1846, suffered a fate remarkably similar to that of Pérez, and for many of the same reasons. Rebellious Natives of Taos Pueblo and some of their Hispano neighbors trapped Bent in his home in Taos in January 1847 and beheaded him.

One of the rebels' principal grievances was the military occupation of New Mexico that General Stephen Watts Kearny had led in August 1846 and the imposition of a governor who was an outsider, which was true of most of Kearny's appointments to civil offices. In addition, six of eight key appointments went to Freemasons. Kearny's appointments were Charles Bent, governor; Donaciano Vigil, territorial secretary; Richard Dallam, marshal; Francis P. Blair, US district attorney; Charles Blumner, treasurer; and Joab Houghton, Antonio José Otero, and Charles Beaubien, judges of the superior court. Bent, Dallam, Blumner, Houghton, Otero, and Beaubien were Masons.[13] Kearny departed for California, leaving Colonel Sterling Price to put down the rebellion that produced Bent's death. Price, who was governor of Missouri from 1853 to 1857, was a member of Warren Lodge No. 74, Keytesville, Missouri.[14]

In the spring of 1847, a call went out for troops from Missouri. Acting on orders of the governor, Grand Master John Ralls raised a company for service in the war against Mexico. The Third Regiment of Missouri Mounted Volunteers reached Santa Fe in September 1847.[15] Ralls assumed Masonic jurisdiction of New Mexico in the name of the Grand Lodge of Missouri and chartered Missouri Military Lodge No. 86 for the Missouri cavalry unit. It held its first meeting in Independence, Missouri, before departing for the West. It was called an ambulant or traveling lodge because it held its communications (lodge meetings) as the movement of troops and opportunity permitted. On September 18, 1847, the military lodge members met in Santa Fe. On October 8, Colonel Ralls chartered Hardin Military Lodge No. 87 for the First Illinois Volunteers,[16] which also served in New Mexico, arriving in September 1847 and mustering out the following October.[17] The first members of Hardin Lodge were officers and enlisted men of the volunteer company, but many citizens subsequently applied to join, and the lodge grew quickly. Ralls was the first Master of Hardin Lodge, which operated until August 14, 1848.[18]

For about a year, Freemasons in New Mexico were without a lodge. They petitioned the Grand Lodge of Missouri, which granted a charter on May 8, 1851, to Montezuma Lodge No. 109 (No. 1 on the New Mexico register) to do Masonic work. Under the authority of this charter, the new lodge was instituted on August

Kit Carson's .54-caliber Hawken rifle, presented to Montezuma Lodge No. 1 in 1868. Collection of Montezuma Lodge No. 1, Santa Fe.

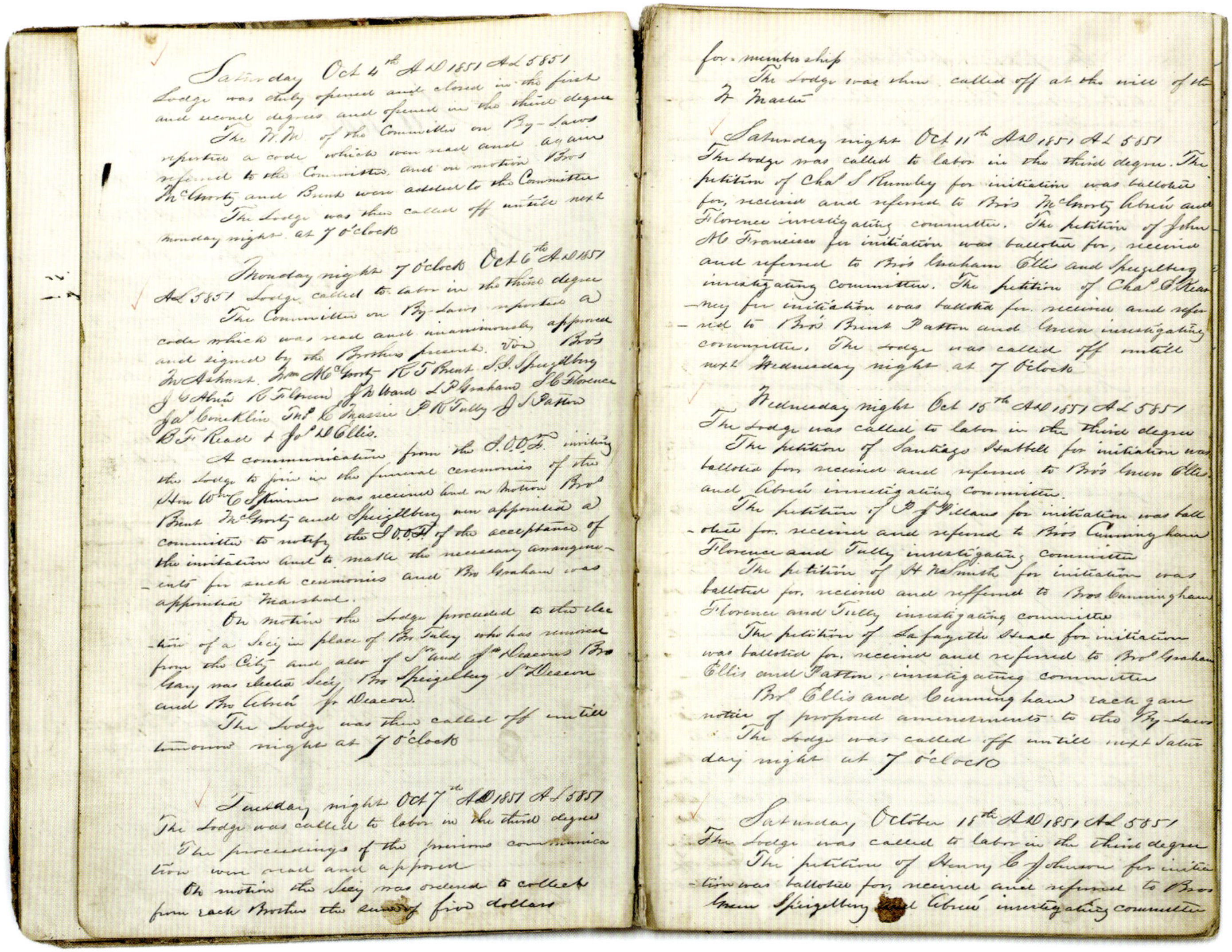

Saturday Oct 4th A.D 1851 A.L 5851
Lodge was duly opened and closed in the first and second degrees and opened in the third degree
The W.M. of the Committee on By-Laws reported a code which was read and again referred to the Committee, and on motion Bros McGroty and Brent were added to the Committee
The Lodge was then called off untill next monday night at 7 o'clock

Monday night 7 o'clock Oct 6th A.D 1851 A.L 5851 Lodge called to labor in the third degree
The Committee on By-Laws reported a code which was read and unanimously approved and signed by the Brothers present. Viz Bros M Ashurst. Wm McGroty R T Brent. S.A. Spiegelberg J G Abreu R F Green J R Ward L P Graham S C Florence Jas Conklin Ths C Massie P R Tully J S Patton B F Read & Jos D Ellis.
A communication from the I.O.O.F. inviting the lodge to join in the funeral ceremonies of the Hon Wm C Skinner was received and on motion Bros Brent McGroty and Spiegelberg were appointed a committee to notify the I.O.O.F. of the acceptance of the invitation and to make the necessary arrangements for such ceremonies and Bro Graham was appointed Marshal.
On motion the Lodge proceeded to the election of a Secy in place of Bro Tuley who has removed from the City and also of S and J Deacons Bro Gray was elected Secy, Bro Spiegelberg S Deacon and Bro Abreu J Deacon.
The Lodge was then called off untill tomorrow night at 7 o'clock

Tuesday night Oct 7th A.D 1851 A.L 5851
The Lodge was called to labor in the third degree
The proceedings of the previous communication were read and approved
On motion the Secy was ordered to collect from each Brother the sum of five dollars for membership
The Lodge was then called off at the will of the W Master

Saturday night Oct 11th A.D 1851 A.L 5851
The Lodge was called to labor in the third degree. The petition of Chas S Rumley for initiation was balloted for, received and referred to Bros McGroty Abreu and Florence investigating committee. The petition of John McFrancisco for initiation was balloted for, received and referred to Bros Graham Ellis and Spiegelberg investigating committee. The petition of Chas S Kearney for initiation was balloted for received and referred to Bros Brent Patton and Green investigating committee. The Lodge was called off untill next Wednesday night at 7 o'clock

Wednesday night Oct 15th A.D 1851 A.L 5851
The Lodge was called to labor in the third degree
The petition of Santiago Hubbell for initiation was balloted for received and referred to Bros Green Ellis and Abreu investigating committee.
The petition of D J Pillans for initiation was balloted for. received and referred to Bros Cunningham Florence and Tully investigating committee
The petition of H N Smith for initiation was balloted for. received and referred to Bros Cunningham Florence and Tully investigating committee
The petition of Lafayette Head for initiation was balloted for. received and referred to Bros Graham Ellis and Patton, investigating committee
Bros Ellis and Cunningham each gave notice of proposed amendments to the By-Laws
The Lodge was called off untill next Saturday night at 7 o'clock

Saturday October 18th A.D 1851 A.L 5851
The Lodge was called to labor in the third degree
The petition of Henry C Johnson for initiation was balloted for, received and referred to Bros Green Spiegelberg and Abreu investigating committee

Montezuma Lodge No. 1 minutes book, 1851–59. Collection of Montezuma Lodge No. 1, Santa Fe.

22, 1851.[19] Present for the first lodge meeting were Worshipful Master Merrill Ashurst; Senior Warden William McGroty; Junior Warden Robert T. Brent; Secretary Pinkney R. Tulley; and Brothers R. Frank Green, Love, Tuley, Francis A. Cunningham, Jesús Gil Abréu, Sylvester C. Florence, John Grenier, and Murray F. Tulley. Visiting were L. A. Wingfield and Mosely. At the time, Montezuma Lodge was only the second Masonic lodge in the West. The Grand Lodge of Missouri had granted a charter, on October 17, 1846, to Multnomah Lodge No. 84 of Salem, Oregon, and that lodge was instituted on September 11, 1848.[20]

By August 1852, Montezuma Lodge had fifty members.[21] The number of members of a given lodge is not, however, an accurate measure of either the number

Military personnel in Masonic group portrait, including Kit Carson (center), December 26, 1866. Seated, left to right*: Colonel D. H. Rucker, Kit Carson, Brevet Brigadier General James H. Carleton.* Standing, left to right*: Colonel E. H. Bergmann, delegate Charles P. Clever, Colonel Nelson H. Davis, Colonel Herbert M. Enos, surgeon Basil K. Norris, and Colonel J. C. McFerran. Photograph by Nicholas Brown, Palace of the Governors Photo Archives (NMHM/DCA 009826).*

of Freemasons or the influence of the Fraternity in a given area. The most famous New Mexico Freemason, frontiersman Christopher "Kit" Carson, was initiated into the Entered Apprentice Degree at Montezuma Lodge on March 29, 1854. He was passed to the Fellow Craft Degree on June 17, 1854, and raised to Master Mason on December 25, 1854. When Bent Lodge No. 204 in Taos received its charter on December 15, 1859, Carson demitted to the new lodge, where he served as Junior Warden. Bent Lodge surrendered its charter in 1864, and the following year Carson returned to Montezuma. Following Carson's death in 1868, Major J. Thompson, a Mason and friend of Carson's, had Carson's .54-caliber Hawken rifle delivered to the lodge.[22] A close Carson associate, Ceran St. Vrain, a Taos trader and erstwhile trapper, was initiated on March 22, 1853, passed on April 16, 1853, and raised on January 28, 1855, in Montezuma Lodge. He demitted from Montezuma Lodge on April 7, 1860, and joined Brothers Kit Carson, Peter Joseph, Ferdinand Maxwell, John M. Francisco, A. S. Ferris, and others to form Bent Lodge No. 204 in Taos, under a charter from the Grand Lodge of Missouri dated June 1, 1860.[23] The lodge did not survive the Civil War, surrendered its charter in 1865, and ceased work.[24]

Visiting

Visiting is a core concept of Freemasonry, and from the time of its inception, men with affiliations in other lodges registered as visitors at Montezuma Lodge and participated in its activities but never formally became members. Freemasons from all over the United States recorded their names in the visitors' books of Montezuma Lodge. On occasion in the early years, foreign Freemasons recorded their presence as visitors. The first record of a foreign visitor was that of George Murison on December 27,

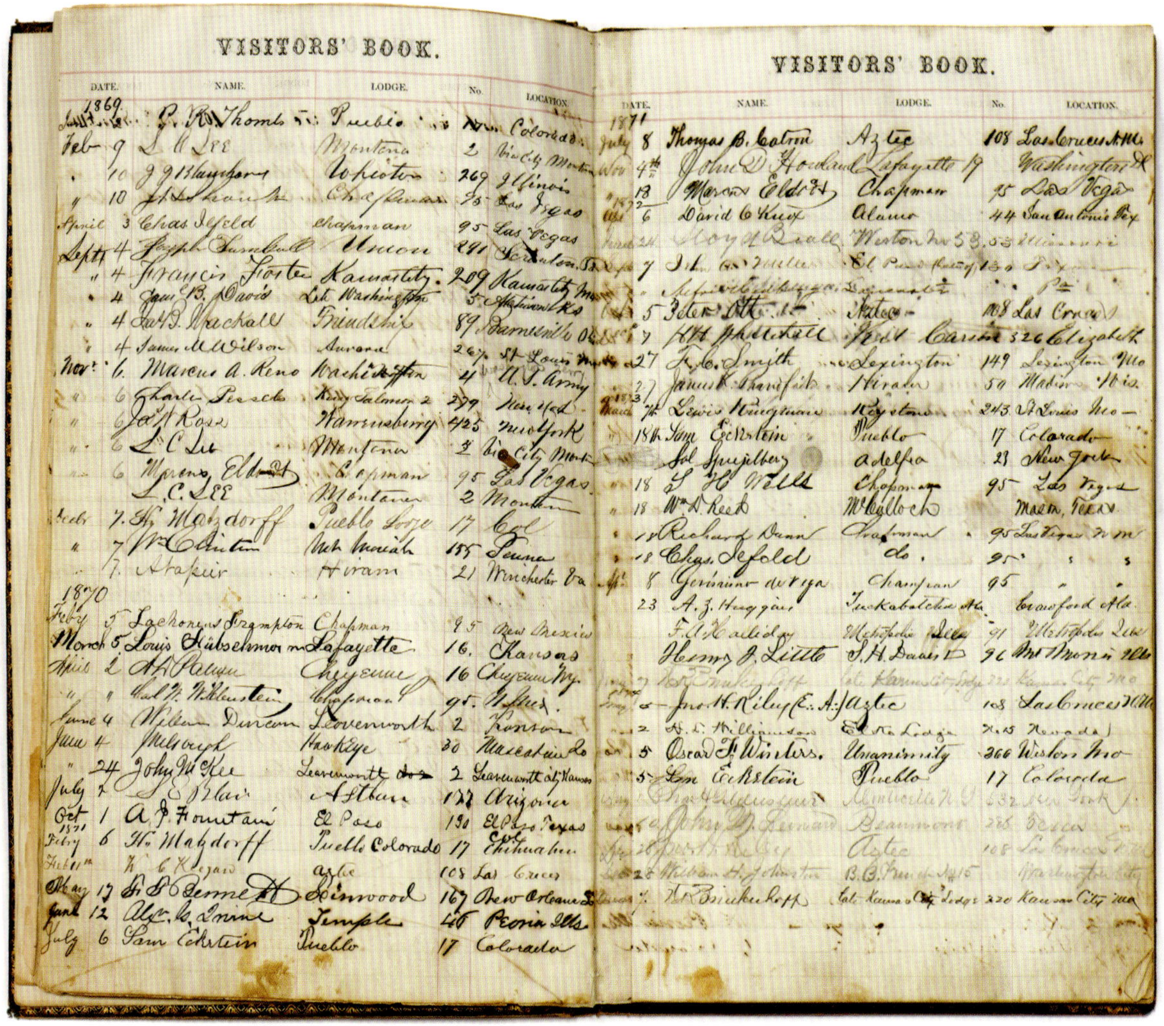

Montezuma Lodge No. 1 visitors' book, 1869–71. Collection of Montezuma Lodge No. 1, Santa Fe.

1878. Murison was a member of Lodge Incorporated Kilwinning No. 182, Montrose, Scotland.[25] Another foreigner registered as a visitor on August 10, 1881.[26] He was Adolf Friedheim, who gave his affiliation as Brüdertreue Lodge, Hamburg, Germany. Beginning in 1885, lists of imposters and "scoundrels or unworthy brothers who had let their membership lapse or had fallen below Freemasonry's proper moral code of conduct" circulated widely.[27]

Montezuma Lodge in Santa Fe was the mother lodge of Freemasonry in New Mexico and the greater Southwest. For almost a decade, it was the only Masonic lodge in present-day New Mexico, Colorado, and Arizona. Many members had to travel hundreds of miles to attend regular communications, and transportation was limited because there were no railroads and few stagecoaches. Moreover, armed conflict between Native Americans and the US military was frequent, and there was considerable crime and generalized violence throughout the Southwest. Today, Montezuma Lodge shares quarters with Cerrillos Lodge No. 19, which was formerly located in the village of Cerrillos. The building is directly northwest of the Scottish Rite Temple in Santa Fe.

Former location of Cerrillos Lodge No. 19, village of Cerrillos, New Mexico, 1975. Photograph by Alice Bullock, Palace of the Governors Photo Archives (NMHM/DCA HP.2014.14.157).

The Catholic Church versus the Masons

The Masonic community in New Mexico faced a unique challenge. Santa Fe was the seat of a Catholic bishopric, and New Mexico was overwhelmingly Roman Catholic.[28] This was significant because the Catholic Church was historically hostile to Freemasonry. Bishop Jean-Baptiste Lamy arrived in Santa Fe in August 1851, coincidentally the same month that Montezuma Lodge was instituted.

From all appearances, Bishop Lamy maintained very cordial relations with several prominent Freemasons in Santa Fe; most notable was his friendship with the Spiegelberg family. Their close relationship came about when Lamy cared for Levi Spiegelberg after encountering him in the summer of 1852 while crossing the prairie on his return to Santa Fe from the East.[29] Levi was ill, and Lamy nursed him back to health. With Willi Spiegelberg's wife, Flora, Lamy could converse in his native French, and the two shared an interest in gardening.[30] The Jewish Spiegelbergs were among several non-Catholics who donated money for the construction of Saint Francis Cathedral and hosted a celebration for Lamy when he was elevated to archbishop.

In 1863 Lamy was providing rooms for and taking his meals with three prominent Freemasons—General James Henry Carleton, Judge Kirby Benedict, and territorial treasurer William Osterton—at his home in Santa Fe.[31] Osterton was a young German who was secretary of Montezuma Lodge, as well as recording secretary of the Historical

Bishop Jean-Baptiste Lamy, ca. 1866–71. Palace of the Governors Photo Archives (NMHM/DCA 007625).

Spiegelberg Brothers store, East San Francisco Street, Santa Fe, before 1882. The Spiegelbergs were Freemasons and prominent Jewish merchants. They had a Masonic lodge room above their store. Palace of the Governors Photo Archives (NMHM/DCA 150156).

Society of New Mexico. He was found dead in his room on the morning of February 23, 1863, having dined with Lamy and his brother Freemasons the night before. At his funeral the following day, Worshipful Master Benedict led the Masonic rites.

There is no evidence that Lamy personally made anti-Masonic pronouncements. That does not imply, however, that he rejected Catholic positions on Freemasonry. In 1875, the year Lamy was elevated to the position of archbishop of Santa Fe, a group of Italian Jesuits in Las Vegas, New Mexico, began publication of *Revista Católica*, a Spanish-language newspaper printed every Saturday, which gave voice to Catholic opposition to Freemasonry. Lamy was a great admirer of the Jesuits, and they could not have routinely published material to which the archbishop objected.

The inaugural issue in January stated its purpose as "maintaining and encouraging the faith and piety of the Mexican population, safeguarding them from the dangers of Protestantism."[32] If the vigor with which the Jesuits attacked Freemasonry is any indication, they could have easily added the Masons as a threat to the local population. In the early years of publication, *Revista Católica* took on prominent citizens who were Freemasons, especially men who promoted nonreligious public education, such as Samuel B. Axtell, William G. Ritch, and Maximilian Eugene Frost, owner and publisher of the *Santa Fe New Mexican*.

New Mexico presented Catholics with the opportunity to establish free public schools of their own, since the territorial legislature had levied a tax to support public schools. County boards of school supervisors were charged with establishing public schools. French priests or Italian Jesuits dominated the boards in at least half the counties, and in some places Catholic schools became the only schools.[33]

Prominent Freemasons such as Frost, Ritch, and Axtell attacked Catholic education through the newspapers, charging that the ignorance of the people of New Mexico was the fault of Catholic priests. *Revista Católica* provided a counterpoint by expressing the opinions of Italian Jesuits and French secular clergy. Ritch expressed the view that New Mexico's schools should be American rather than sectarian and stated that it would be the teachers' responsibility to instill in their students an understanding of their rights and duties as US citizens.

Colonel Maximilian Frost (1852–1909), Second Regiment, New Mexico Militia. Palace of the Governors Photo Archives (NMHM/DCA 007224).

In 1880 Lamy's vicar general and fellow Frenchman Augustin Truchard informed the New Mexico press that when Frost's *Santa Fe New Mexican* claimed that using public funds for sectarian schools went against the law, the newspaper was expressing "the masonic doctrine about public schools." Truchard stated that nothing could make the priests accept a school system that the Catholic Church condemned.

Catholic anti-Masonic attitudes fell heavily on Miguel Antonio Otero and his family. Otero was one of the most successful men in New Mexico. In addition to amassing a fortune reckoned in the millions of dollars, Otero held important political positions, such as delegate of the Territory of New Mexico to the US Congress from 1855 to 1861. When he died unexpectedly in Denver in May 1882, the vicar general of the Diocese of Denver, Jean-Baptiste Raverdy, denied him the rites of a Catholic burial because Otero was a Freemason, much to the consternation of his widow.[34] Brother Masons and an Episcopalian minister conducted the burial services. Newspapers all over the Midwest reprinted the story in the days following Otero's death.

The Roman Catholic Church already had a long history of antagonism toward Freemasonry when *Revista Católica* began publication. Beginning in 1738 with Pope Clement XII's bull *In eminenti apostolatus*, which prohibited Catholics from becoming Freemasons under threat of excommunication, Roman pontiffs issued condemnations of secret societies, none more roundly or frequently criticized than Freemasons. Papal attacks on Freemasonry occurred twenty more times over the next 165 years. The most problematic for the world body of Freemasonry dated from April 20, 1884, when Pope Leo XIII published an encyclical, *Humanum genus*, which held that mankind was divided into two parts: the kingdom of God on earth and the kingdom of Satan. In the pope's words, Freemasons were "the partisans of evil" who were "boldly rising up against God Himself. . . planning the destruction of [the] holy Church."[35]

The editors of *Revista Católica* printed a Spanish translation of *Humanum genus* in its entirety, in two parts on consecutive Saturdays, the first installment a mere six weeks after Pope Leo XIII issued the encyclical in Rome.[36] Over the next few years, the pages of *Revista Católica* carried other attacks on Freemasonry, with such titles as "Católico y Masón" (Catholic and Mason), "Siguen protestando los Francmasones" (Freemasons Continue Protesting), "Las Amenazas de la Masonería" (The Threats of Masonry), and "El Futuro de la Masonería" (The Future of Masonry).[37]

In response to *Humanum genus*, a Frenchman, Marie Joseph Gabriel Antoine Jogand-Pagès, began writing and publishing under the pseudonym Léo Taxil. Previously, Taxil had flirted with libel by writing an anticlerical book called *The Secret Loves of Pope Pius IX*.[38] Taxil pretended to undergo a very public conversion to Roman Catholicism. He stated that he aimed to redress the damage he had done to the Catholic faith and set about writing about the evils of Freemasonry. He began with a series of publications, the *Révélations Complètes sur la Franc-Maçonnerie*, which included such titles as *Les Frères Trois-Points* (1885), *Les Soeurs Maçonnes* (1886), and *Le culte du grand architecte* (1886). Taxil's writings purported to expose Freemasonry as a sinister, devil-worshipping cult. In 1891 Taxil coauthored *Y-a-t-il des femmes dans la Franc-Maçonnerie?* (Are There Women in Freemasonry?), which introduced the idea

Miguel A. Otero Sr., New Mexico delegate, US House of Representatives, 1855–61. Palace of the Governors Photo Archives (NMHM/DCA 152218).

French poster for an anti-Masonic book by Léo Taxil, 1896. Bibliothèque National de France (btv1b9014879z).

of a secret inner group within Freemasonry, the Palladian Order, known only to elite members and overseen by Albert Pike of Charleston, South Carolina. According to Taxil, the Palladian Order included men and women who engaged in devil worship, ritual sexual debauchery, and many other evil activities.

The Catholic Church fell hard for the Taxil hoax, and the Jesuits in Las Vegas were no exception. Beginning in 1886, *Revista Católica* published a number of articles about Taxil and his anti-Masonic revelations. An article from May 1886, "Número de Masones" (Number of Masons), cited *Les Frères Trois-Points* in revealing supposed Masonic secrets.[39] "M. Leo Taxil," introduced the fraud to unsuspecting readers.[40] In Paris in April 1897, Taxil revealed that his conversion to Catholicism and his anti-Masonic writings were an elaborate hoax. Despite his complete recantation, Taxil's calumnious writings caused irreparable harm to Freemasonry and subjected the Fraternity to vitriolic attacks in New Mexico for years.

Freemasonry as an Integrative Force in Frontier Society

The Freemasons in the military who participated in the annexation of Mexican New Mexico—which began in 1846 with Kearny's invasion and occupation and ended with the incorporation of much of the Southwest into the United States with the ratification of the Treaty of Guadalupe Hidalgo in 1848—were among the first arrivals in what rapidly became a flood of newcomers to the region. The influx of people from the United States transformed predominately Spanish-speaking and Roman Catholic New Mexico into a society where many ethnicities were represented and where Protestants of several denominations, Jews, and a very few local Hispanics mixed in their public and private lives. Another interesting development involved Europeans who, after observing that many of the most prominent Anglo men in New Mexico were Freemasons, joined the Fraternity in the interest of becoming part of the local social and business elite.

Representative of these phenomena was the presence within the Masonic Fraternity of New Mexico of German Jewish merchants such as the Spiegelberg, Jaffa, and Lesinsky families; Swiss watchmaker Jules H. Jeanneret;[41] Protestant attorneys and businessmen such as Thomas B. Catron, an Episcopalian, Albert Jennings Fountain, an Episcopalian, William G. Hayden, a Presbyterian, and physician J. J. Shuler, a Presbyterian; and such ostensibly Catholic Hispanics as Jesús Gil Abréu and the Miguel Antonio Oteros, father and son.

Historian Tomas Jaehn notes that the initial absence of German social organizations in New Mexico led men to become Freemasons.[42] Charles Blumner joined

Montezuma Lodge in the 1850s. Louis Sulzbacher, Emanuel Rosenwald, and Charles Ilfeld were Masters of the lodge in Las Vegas in the 1860s and 1870s. Aaron Schultz was a member of lodges in Las Cruces and Silver City, where Hyman Abraham belonged.

Historian Ralph Emerson Twitchell, who was an active Freemason in Santa Fe, observed:

> The Masonic lodge in those days became something more than a mere civic society. In the absence of American women very generally during the first two decades of the American occupation, there were no social centers, no places of amusement, no homes of the American family, no attractive resort in which to while away an hour—unless, forsooth we mention the Mexican baile, the gambling room, and the saloon. Naturally members congregated at the Masonic lodge room. The Masonic hall became the club room and social center of those who would avoid contact with the dissipations of the country.[43]

Indeed, the sole Protestant church of the period had representatives on the ground—sometimes.

As Mary Ann Clawson has noted regarding the movement in Great Britain and the United States in the Victorian era, "Freemasonry offered a complex of values and assumptions that can be characterised as those of an emergent bourgeoisie—a detachment from inherited social identities, a belief in social mobility, an acceptance of market relations and property-based authority."[44] Precisely these characteristics made it possible for frontier Anglo entrepreneurs in New Mexico to thrive in an alien world with a very conservative and rigid social and business environment.

Freighters on the Santa Fe Trail: Bernard Seligman, Zadoc Staab, Lehman Spiegelberg, and Kiowa Indian scouts. Palace of the Governors Photo Archives (NMHM/DCA 007890).

The Santa Fe Ring

For Mark Twain, the late nineteenth century was the Gilded Age, glimmering on the outside and rotten at its core. Coalitions of wealthy and powerful men, determined to enrich themselves and to amass political power, with little concern for the general public, formed "rings," in the parlance of the day. In New Mexico, men accused of being part of the Santa Fe Ring included government officials, lawyers, ranchers, and land speculators. The most authoritative and thoroughly researched study of the Santa Fe Ring is unquestionably David L. Caffey's *Chasing the Santa Fe*

Ring.[45] Caffey emphatically challenges the notion that many scholars of the territorial period in New Mexico have championed—namely, that the ring was "a predominately Masonic organization," as Philip J. Rasch expressed it. According to Frederick W. Nolan, one of the most respected historians of the period, "most of the members of the Ring were Masons. . . . Joined fraternally as well as by a desire for wealth and power."[46] Michael Wallis stated, "Regardless of ethnic heritage or political stripe, nearly every member of the Santa Fe Ring had something in common: each belonged to a Masonic lodge."[47]

Caffey is clearly skeptical of the very existence of the Santa Fe Ring, but he reports on his exhaustive research into individuals suspected of belonging to such an organization, however loosely it might have been formed. He concludes that of 165 possible members or associates of the Santa Fe Ring, only a dozen were Freemasons. By that measure, the Masonic community did not constitute anything like a majority or even significant portion of Ring members. But of the fourteen men Caffey identifies as core members of the Santa Fe Ring, at least nine were Freemasons.[48] Moreover, many of these men were among the most powerful people in New Mexico, most prominent among them Thomas B. Catron.

Therefore, the nature and extent of Masonic involvement becomes something of a question of one's definition of the Santa Ring. If it was a relatively small group consisting mainly of the core members Caffey names, then it would be correct to say that most of them were Freemasons. If, however, the Santa Fe Ring was much larger, then Freemasons were very much in the minority.

Jaffa, Prager & Co. store, Roswell, New Mexico, 1887. Left to right*: George H. Haggley, Sidney Prager, H. S. Prager, Nathan Jaffa, Horace Clarkson, Dr. Sutherland, Pat Garrett, and F. P. Gayle. New Mexico State University Library, Archives and Special Collections (RG86-102-241).*

Freemasons as Leaders in New Mexico Society

The following table presents known Masonic affiliations of twenty-five chief executives of New Mexico in the period from the US invasion and occupation in 1846 to the advent of statehood in 1912. The first four individuals were active-duty US Army officers; only one of them, Sterling Price, was a Freemason. This situation is unexpected given that Freemasonry in New Mexico had a clear military origin. The other twenty-one governors were civilians, some of whom occupied the governorship in an interim capacity. Of these, thirteen were Freemasons. Beginning with interim governor William G. Ritch in 1875 through Miguel Antonio Otero Jr. in 1906, eight consecutive governors were Freemasons.[49]

Masonic Affiliations of Chief Executives of New Mexico

Governor	*Term*	*Known Masonic Affiliations*
Stephen W. Kearny	1846–1847	None
Sterling Price	1847–1848	Warren Lodge No. 74, Keytesville, Missouri; Warren Lodge No. 23, Warren, Alaska[50]
John M. Washington	1848–1849	None
John Munroe	1849–1851	None
Charles Bent	1846–1847	Missouri Lodge No. 1, Saint Louis, Missouri
Donaciano Vigil	1847–1848	None
James S. Calhoun	1851–1852	Yes
William Carr Lane	1852–1853	Vincennes Lodge No. 15, Vincennes, Indiana[51]
David Meriwether	1853–1855	None
Abraham Rencher	1857–1861	None
Henry Connelly	1861–1866	None[52]
Robert Byington Mitchell	1866–1869	None
William Anderson Pile	1869–1871	None
Marsh Giddings	1871–1875	None
William G. Ritch	1875	Representative of Grand Lodge of Wisconsin to Grand Lodge of New Mexico;[53] Montezuma Lodge No. 1 and Santa Fe Commandery Knights Templar, Santa Fe, New Mexico[54]
Samuel Beach Axtell	1875–1878	Amador Lodge, Jackson, California;[55] Lodi Lodge No. 256, Lodi, California[56]
Lewis Wallace	1878–1881	Fountain Lodge No. 60, Covington, Indiana;[57] Montgomery Lodge No. 50, Crawfordsville, Indiana
Lionel Allen Sheldon	1881–1885	Scottish Rite, Santa Fe, New Mexico; Royal Arch Mason, Crown Chapter, No. 72, Pasadena, California;[58] Shriner
Edmond G. Ross	1885–1889	Topeka Masonic Lodge No. 17, Topeka, Kansas[59]
L. Bradford Prince	1889–1893	Cornucopia Lodge No. 563, Whitestone, New York;[60] representative of Grand Lodge of New York to Grand Lodge of New Mexico;[61] representative of Grand Lodge of New Mexico to Grand Lodge of New York
William Taylor Thornton	1893–1897	Yes[62]
Miguel Antonio Otero	1897–1906	Montezuma Lodge No. 1, Santa Fe, New Mexico
Herbert James Hagerman	1906–1907	None
George Curry	1907–1910	None
William Joseph Mills	1910–1912	Chapman Lodge No. 2, Las Vegas, New Mexico

Another measure of the influence of Freemasons on the political affairs of New Mexico is the participation of members of the Fraternity in the constitutional convention of 1910. Of the ninety-seven delegates to the convention whose biographies appeared in the convention book, twenty-six were Freemasons, thirty-nine were Anglo non-Masons, and thirty-two were Hispanics, none of whom were members of the Fraternity.[63]

Las Vegas and Las Cruces

Chapman Lodge No. 95, named for Colonel William Chapman, met for the first time at Fort Union on March 28, 1862, under a dispensation from the Grand Lodge of Missouri.[64] Records of the Grand Lodge of Missouri indicate that Chapman Lodge had done work in 1862 and petitioned for a charter, but the request was not granted because of irregularities in the work. On May 25, 1866, the Grand Secretary of the Grand Lodge of Missouri received instructions to issue a charter to Chapman Lodge as soon as its Master and Wardens were qualified for the work. The lodge held its last communication at Fort Union on July 27, 1867.[65] The next communication took place on August 14, 1867, in Las Vegas, about thirty miles south of Fort Union.

On December 21, 1867, members passed a resolution recommending the purchase of a lot on Main Street in Las Vegas, and a committee was appointed to make plans for construction of a lodge hall. The structure remains at 500 West National Avenue (formerly Main Street) opposite the San Miguel County Courthouse in Las Vegas. The dedication of the hall took place on January 16, 1869.

In 1884 Chapman Lodge relocated to 400 Railroad Avenue in East Las Vegas, where it remained for eleven years. On November 26, 1894, the cornerstone was laid for a new temple, built in the Richardsonian Romanesque style following the design of Isaac Rapp (who was also a Mason), at 518 Douglas Avenue in East Las Vegas. The temple was dedicated on June 24, 1895.[66] Chapman Lodge moved to this building, and there it remains. It is now the oldest Masonic temple in New Mexico.[67]

Chapman Lodge No. 2, Las Vegas, New Mexico, ca. 1912. Constructed in 1895, the building was designed by architect Isaac Rapp. Collection of Chapman Lodge No. 2, Las Vegas.

The closing of Bent Lodge during the Civil War meant that a new lodge organized by Masons in Las Cruces, in Doña Ana County, was one of only three lodges in New Mexico. The Grand Lodge of Missouri granted a dispensation on June 4, 1866, and Aztec Lodge organized on December 29 with nine members.[68] The Grand Lodge of Missouri chartered it on October 19, 1867, as Aztec Lodge No. 108. The number 108 had first designated the Masonic Lodge at New Madrid, Missouri, which had been chartered in 1849 and closed during the Civil War. From its inception until the summer of 1871, Aztec Lodge met in a rented hall in Las Cruces.[69] The consecration of that first hall took place on November 15, 1867. Among the furnishings of the hall was a pair of Middle Chamber columns, a gift of Montezuma Lodge. In the early years of the lodge, many officers and soldiers from US Army posts in New Mexico attended meetings, and some joined the lodge.

By 1871 Aztec Lodge needed larger quarters. Henry Lesinsky, a prominent Jewish merchant, built a two-story building in Las Cruces and leased the second floor to Aztec Lodge for one dollar for a term of ninety-nine years. Construction was complete in time for a grand celebration on July 4, the proceeds of which enabled the lodge to purchase a blue carpet for the hall. An organ purchased for $106 and transported over the Santa Fe Trail made musical accompaniment a part of future installation ceremonies at the lodge.[70] In 1872 the lodge acquired a tract of land for a Masonic cemetery. Prior to the establishment of this burial ground, the only cemetery was the Catholic cemetery. On October 20, 1877, the lodge was chartered under the jurisdiction of the Grand Lodge of New Mexico, which had been organized in August.

The first occasion of a communication at the Grand Lodge of New Mexico held in Las Cruces was in 1889. Following ceremonies at the lodge hall, there was a banquet at the Rio Grande Hotel. Colonel Albert Jennings Fountain and Henry Stoes took charge of local arrangements, and the event included what was described as "royal entertainment." The bill for the meeting came to $640, a rather astounding sum for the time.[71] By the next year, Aztec Lodge membership had reached thirty-five. By 1910 the lodge had sixty-one members.

The following year, the US government purchased the property upon which the lodge sat. A site for a new temple was acquired for $2,500, and a contract for construction was agreed upon, setting costs at $14,000.[72] Furnishings and incidentals added another $4,500. The lodge obtained a loan of $7,500. Numa Reymond, who at the time was living in Switzerland, paid $5,000 toward the total cost, and members supplied a further $6,400 in voluntary subscriptions. In short order, the temple was fully paid for.

Henry Lesinsky, Freemason and prominent Jewish merchant. Undated photograph. Arizona Historical Society Library and Archives (70126).

The Grand Lodge

Four New Mexico lodges called for a convention in Santa Fe on August 6, 1877, to form a grand lodge. A total of 165 delegates from three lodges—Montezuma No. 109 of Santa Fe, Chapman No. 95 of Las Vegas, and Aztec No. 108 of Las Cruces—gathered at Montezuma Lodge, on the second floor of a building at the northwest corner of the Santa Fe Plaza, and formally organized the Grand Lodge of New Mexico

Masonic apron of Solomon J. Spiegelberg. Collection of Montezuma Lodge No. 1, Santa Fe.

on August 7.[73] Governor Samuel Beach Axtell called the convention to order. The first officers of the Grand Lodge were Grand Master William Washington Griffin, an employee of First National Bank in Santa Fe; Senior Grand Warden William Logan Rynerson, a leading lawyer and territorial district attorney from Las Cruces; Junior Grand Warden George William Stebbins, deputy internal revenue collector in Las Vegas; Grand Treasurer William Spiegelberg of Santa Fe; and Grand Secretary David Jefferson Miller.

Having adopted a constitution and bylaws, the Grand Lodge ordered charters issued to the four lodges that had joined together: Montezuma, Chapman, Aztec, and Union. A fifth lodge, Silver City No. 465, did not participate and sent no delegates to Santa Fe for the convention. Silver City also refused to surrender the charter it had received from the Grand Lodge of Missouri and did not join the newly formed Grand Lodge of New Mexico.

The convention lasted four days and ended on August 10. It included a reunion and banquet. Many prominent Freemasons and non-Masons from throughout New Mexico attended. The banquet took place in the dining room of La Fonda hotel. During the evenings of August 9 and 10, the degree of Master Mason was conferred upon Colonel Maximilian Frost and Captain Frederick Freeborn Whitehead, who was stationed in Santa Fe as the officer in charge of purchase and issue of provisions for the military district of New Mexico.

The Grand Lodge of New Mexico's first regular communication convened in Montezuma Lodge in Santa Fe on January 6, 1879. Subsequently, regular grand communications took place annually. Additional lodges were then constituted. One of them was White Mountain Lodge No. 5. It received its charter on July 5, 1880, in Globe City, Arizona. At the time, there was no Grand Lodge in Arizona, but when the Grand Lodge of Arizona was organized in 1882, Globe City Lodge joined it.[74] Temple Lodge No. 6 in Albuquerque received its charter on November 11, 1880.

Masonic apron of Grand Master Maximilian Frost. Collection of Montezuma Lodge No. 1, Santa Fe.

Controversy in Silver City

Founded in 1870, Silver City in Grant County quickly became in important mining and smelting center. Local Masons requested a dispensation for a lodge, which the Grand Lodge of Missouri granted on May 1, 1873. Silver City Lodge No. 465 received a charter on October 16, 1873.[75]

On April 25, 1880, the Grand Master of the Grand Lodge of New Mexico, Colonel William L. Rynerson, issued an edict declaring Silver City Lodge No. 465 to be clandestine, meaning that it was working without a valid charter. He forbade all Masonic intercourse—that is, any type of communication involving sharing the secrets of Freemasonry—with its members.[76] This edict stemmed from the fact that the Silver City Lodge had declined to take part in the formation of the Grand Lodge of New Mexico in 1877. The Grand Master's edicts also arrested the charter of Silver City Lodge.

Almost all the Masonic Grand Lodges in the United States, Canada, England, Scotland, Ireland, and other English-speaking countries recognized the Grand Lodge of New Mexico as a legal and sovereign Masonic grand body.[77] A notable exception was the Grand Lodge of Missouri, which refused to grant such recognition and standing to the Grand Lodge of New Mexico in acknowledgment of the rights and prerogatives of the lodge at Silver City.

The position of the Grand Lodge of Missouri constituted a challenge to the Grand Lodge of New Mexico, which exerted its sovereign jurisdiction by granting a charter to a new lodge in Silver City, Alpha Lodge No. 7, in 1881. Grand Master Simon Bolivar Newcomb of Las Cruces granted a dispensation to Alpha Lodge on August 8, 1881. On March 20, 1882, Silver City Lodge No 8. received a charter from the Grand Lodge of New Mexico. The members of this lodge came from Alpha

Lodge No. 7 and Silver City Lodge No. 465, which finally surrendered its charter to the Grand Lodge of New Mexico. The Grand Lodge of Missouri then recognized the Grand Lodge of New Mexico as a free and sovereign independent grand body within its own territorial limits. This instance marked an "important occurrence in Masonic Jurisprudence. It established the fact that a Grand Lodge could be legally formed within any political subdivision by three lodges"[78] as long as Masonic laws and regulations were complied with. So even within the world of Masonry, New Mexico had to fight for its rights and privileges, perhaps for many of the same reasons it struggled for statehood.

A Permanent Home for the Grand Lodge

The New Mexico Grand Lodge of Freemasons met in Albuquerque on January 26, 1891, in regular annual communication.[79] Grand Master F. H. Kent, assisted by Deputy Grand Master Albert J. Fountain, presided. Sixteen out of eighteen lodges were present. In addition to conducting the routine business of the organization, such as the presentation of committee and financial reports, participants discussed choosing a permanent location for the Grand Lodge. They unanimously decided to locate the Grand Lodge in Albuquerque, doubtless influenced by the willingness of the local lodge to donate a very valuable downtown lot, measuring 60 by 100 feet, as the site of a Masonic temple for the Grand Lodge. A building committee made up of all past Grand Masters was appointed to study and report on construction plans and financing. That night, approximately one hundred Masons gathered in the dining room of the highly regarded San Felipe Hotel at Fifth Street and Gold Avenue.

The Santa Fe delegation representing Montezuma Lodge No. 1 at the annual communication included Philip E. Harroun, son of Dr. William Smith Harroun; Marcus Eldodt, a successful merchant; and Ralph Emerson Twitchell, district attorney of the First Judicial District. At the time, Twitchell was Junior Warden of Montezuma Lodge. Another member of Montezuma Lodge present for the assembly in Albuquerque was Colonel Max Frost, the first Master Mason raised by the Grand Lodge of New Mexico at its organization in September 1877. In the intervening years, he served as Master of Montezuma Lodge; High Priest of Santa Fe Chapter No. 1 and Eminent Commander of the Knights Templar Commandery in Santa Fe; and Grand Senior Warden, Deputy Grand Master, and Grand Master of the Grand Lodge of New Mexico. He was also master of the Scottish Rite Lodge in Santa Fe and a Thirty-second-Degree Mason. Frost always served as an officer in some Masonic body from the time he was raised to Master Mason. Because of his study of all things Masonic, he developed a reputation as an expert on Masonic law and jurisprudence. People sought out his opinions and considered them authoritative. Beginning in about 1885, Frost chaired the committee on foreign correspondence of the Grand Lodge.

The register of the Grand Lodge of New Mexico in August 1877, when it was organized, listed 172 members divided among four lodges. In July 1905 the population of New Mexico was estimated at three hundred thousand.[80] As of August 31, 1906, there were 1,628 members in twenty-six lodges. One year later there were eighteen hundred Master Masons and thirty lodges—twenty-six chartered and four under a year of dispensation.

House of the Temple, Washington, DC. Designed by John Russell Pope, the building was dedicated in 1915. ©Bettmann/Getty Images.

Halcyon Days of Freemasonry

The 1920s are usually considered the heyday of Freemasonry in the United States. According to historian Mark A. Tabbert, by the end of the decade, 12 percent of the adult male population belonged to Masonic bodies; the dues this large membership contributed made possible the construction of truly grandiose temples and lodges.[81] Yet, leaving aside the size of the membership, an examination of Masonic buildings reveals that during the first decades of the twentieth century, from 1900 to 1919, fifty-one historically significant temples and lodges were constructed. Included in this number are the House of the Temple in Washington, DC, and the Masonic Temple and Murat Shrine in Indianapolis. Temples in Albuquerque, Las Cruces, and Santa Fe also belong to this period. Another fifty-one date from the 1920s. These include many of the most impressive, such as the massive temples in Detroit and Dayton.

The laying of the cornerstone for the new Masonic temple, the property of Temple Lodge No. 6, took place in Albuquerque on August 2, 1910.[82] New Mexico's last territorial governor, William Joseph Mills, was in the city on April 21, 1911, to celebrate the dedication of the new temple with his fellow Masons.[83] The temple was described as "one of the most pretentious Masonic structures in the southwest." At the time, only El Jebel Temple in Denver and the Masonic building in Los Angeles were larger and cost more to build. The Albuquerque temple was sure to "serve as a lasting monument to the energy, aggressiveness and perseverance of the craft in Albuquerque, and marks a never to be forgotten epoch in the history of Masonic lore in New Mexico and the entire southwest."[84]

The design of the temple was the work of the Denver architectural firm of Baerresen Brothers, whose masterwork was the Moorish revival El Jebel Temple.[85] The Albuquerque temple occupied a site at 625 Central Avenue NW, at the corner of Central and Seventh Street, and measured 97 by 142 feet. The structure consisted of two stories, with a large attic or third floor and a basement. Based on the Parthenon,[86] the imposing front entrance featured six massive pillars, which were "suggestive of the strength and permanency of the Masonic craft."[87] Wide steps led up to heavy doors that provided entry to the main hall on the first floor. Doors off the main hall led to various compartments on the first floor and stairs to the basement and upper floors. Part of the main hall on the first floor was set up as a lounge and smoking room. Wooden bannisters lined the stairs to the second floor. On the southeast side of the first floor were four large rooms for the exclusive use of the Grand Lodge of New Mexico. Adjacent to these rooms were an office and large vault for the Grand Secretary. An armory on the west side was for the exclusive use of Pilgrim Commandery No. 3 Knights Templar. There were also lockers for the storing of uniforms and paraphernalia. Next to the armory was a women's parlor.

Masonic Temple Lodge No. 6, Albuquerque, New Mexico, ca. 1911. Center for Southwest Research, University Libraries, University of New Mexico (#000-885(5)-0019).

The focal point of the temple was a large lodge room on the first and second floors that measured 54 by 77 feet. The room could accommodate a stage, extending from the east side of the wall, with no interference with the original configuration of the space. With the addition of a stage, the room could host theatrical presentations. At the west end of the room was a balcony with space for two hundred theater seats. The ground floor of the room could hold seven or eight hundred, so with the balcony seating, the capacity was one thousand people. Massive beams in the form of a cross separated the ceiling into sections. The windows on the north side of the room contained stained-glass sections with Masonic emblems, symbolizing the various affiliated organizations housed in the temple: a five-pointed star for the Order of the Eastern Star; a square and compass for the Symbolic Lodge; a keystone for the Royal Arch Chapter; a cross and crown, the insignia of the Knights Templar; and a half moon and crescent for the Shrine. One of the windows bore the Scottish Rite emblem, even though when the temple was constructed, the organization had no affiliation in Albuquerque, although several members lived in the city.

The most challenging degree work took place in the large lodge room: "[It is] large enough for the most pretentious carnival that the Shriners may ever care to put on. An oasis may be built in the middle of the room with desert all around over which the novices eager for the honors at the Shrine may walk, leading real camels without creating any disturbance or congesting the population intent on watching the festivities."[88] A smaller lodge room, the large banquet room, and the large lodge room all contained extended balconies suitable for choral group performances.

The small lodge room, located on the second floor and measuring 60 by 40 feet, was designed for degree work. Next to it were rooms for the Red Cross

Commandery and chapter work. Adjacent to the small lodge room were offices and a vault for use by the secretary of Temple Lodge.

The basement held two banquet rooms—one seating 100 and the other seating 400; the combined capacity could be increased by 150 or 200. Kitchens, pantries, and other rooms were conveniently located to provide quick and efficient service to diners. The basement housed a coal-fired heating plant, coal bins, and additional storage rooms. A rear entrance to the basement provided access to the banquet room halls. In the gentlemen's club rooms were billiard and pool tables, box ball alleys,[89] and other amusement devices. The firm Baerresen Brothers of Denver designed the building. Architects Harold William and Viggio Egede Baerresen, immigrants from their native Denmark, were both Masons.[90] E. A. Gertig acted as general contractor, having secured the $50,000 construction contract for most of the temple.[91] W. W. Strong was the supervising manager of the project. Among the organizations that initially made their headquarters in the new temple were Temple Lodge No. 6, AF & AM; Pilgrim Commandery No. 3, Knights Templar; Ballut Abyad Temple AAONM 8, Adah Chapter No. 5, OES; and the Grand Lodge of New Mexico.[92]

Postcard showing Aztec Lodge No. 3, Las Cruces, New Mexico, ca. 1920. New Mexico State University Library, Archives, and Special Collections (00010132).

Five weeks after the dedication of the Albuquerque Temple, an enthusiastic gathering of Freemasons took place in Las Cruces. As in Albuquerque and Santa Fe, a new, elaborate Masonic temple was nearing completion. Dr. Edward Dundas McQueen Gray, president of the University of New Mexico, delivered a powerful address on May 26, 1911, at the Elks Lodge.[93] The meeting was held there because the Masonic Hall, which the new Masonic temple would replace, could not hold the large number of Freemasons in attendance. Gray chose for his subject "The Spirit of Freemasonry," and his lecture, "which was listened to with rapt attention, dealt with the subject in a powerful manner."[94] During the evening, a class of thirteen Master Masons who had recently joined Aztec Lodge served dinner to visiting Masons from the region and other members of the lodge. A choral group called the Masonic Double Male Quartet provided the evening's entertainment, and prominent local Masons delivered addresses.

The Bascom French Company of Las Cruces got the contract for the new Masonic temple, which called for construction on a site adjoining one that the US government had recently purchased for a new federal building. The two-story building in the Spanish mission style measured 40 by 124 feet. The design was the work of Henry C. Trost of Trost and Trost Architects and Engineers of El Paso, Texas, one of the most famous architectural firms in the Southwest.[95] Trost and Trost designed a number of Masonic temples in the region, including the five-story El Paso Temple, built at cost of $112,000 and completed in 1913.

The first floor of the Las Cruces Temple was divided into ten offices that could be rented individually or all together. The upper floor, which was exclusively for lodge purposes, featured a lodge hall measuring 28 by 58 feet, a dining room, a billiard room, a reading room, a kitchen, and rooms for the storage of paraphernalia required for degree work. The Trost design had an estimated total cost of $20,000. Lodge members provided a large portion of this amount. One of them, Numa Reymond, donated $5,000. On Monday, April 8, 1912, the members of Aztec Lodge No. 3 dedicated their new temple in Las Cruces.[96]

Biographical Sketches of Notable New Mexican Freemasons

John William Ralls

John William Ralls was born on November 18, 1807, in Sharpsburg, Kentucky.[97] The family moved to Ralls County (named for his father), and John was orphaned at an early age. He served in the state militia in the Black Hawk War in 1832 and became a lieutenant colonel in 1837. As Grand Master of the Grand Lodge of Missouri in 1846, he issued a dispensation to Missouri Military Lodge No. 86 on June 12, 1847. Ralls was named colonel of the Third Regiment of Missouri Volunteers, which assembled at Independence and marched over the Santa Fe Trail to Santa Fe, where they were assigned to the forces of General Sterling Price. While in New Mexico, Ralls assumed Masonic jurisdiction of the territory for the Grand Lodge of Missouri.

Ralls returned to Kentucky, where he became an apprentice in a court of record. Returning to Missouri, he clerked in the state house of representatives, and in 1850 he was admitted to the bar. Ralls died in 1882. He was a member of the Baptist Church.

Hugh N. Smith, ca. 1854–59. Collection of Montezuma Lodge No. 1, Santa Fe.

Hugh N. Smith

Hugh N. Smith was born in Kentucky around 1820. He attended Transylvania College (now Transylvania University in Lexington, Kentucky) and then practiced law. In 1846 he enlisted in the army. In the war with Mexico, he served under the command of Colonel Alexander Doniphan in New Mexico.[98] After the war, Smith stayed in New Mexico and returned to the practice of law.

Brother Mason and governor Charles Bent appointed Smith New Mexico's first attorney general, and he served in that capacity until 1848, when he was elected to represent New Mexico in the US Congress.[99] Addressing Congress on April 4, 1850, Smith argued that he should be admitted to that body and that it should establish a civilian government in New Mexico. He noted that under Mexican rule there had been a local assembly and that New Mexico had been represented in the national legislature in Mexico City.[100] Smith's arguments were to no avail. Congress refused his request, stating, "It is inexpedient to admit Hugh N. Smith, esq., to a seat in this House as a delegate from New Mexico" because New Mexico lacked a formal, recognized government.[101] Smith returned to Santa Fe and was reconfirmed as attorney general in February 1859, but his second term was brief.[102] He died suddenly on September 12, 1859, after an illness brought on by an "apoplectic fit." Smith, who was master of Montezuma Lodge in 1854 and again in 1859, was buried with full Masonic honors in Santa Fe.

The Spiegelberg Brothers

Simon Jacob, Levi, Emanuel, Lehman, and Willi Spiegelberg were natives of Prussia who settled in New Mexico. Arriving in New Mexico in 1846, Simon Jacob acted as sutler for Sterling Price's troops.[103] That same year he set up a modest mercantile business in Santa Fe and in so doing became the first Jewish merchant in New Mexico. Beginning with Levi in 1848, five brothers followed Simon Jacob to Santa Fe. Brother Elias died soon after arriving, but the others became successful in their business, Spiegelberg Brothers, which sold groceries and dry goods on the south side of the Plaza across from the Palace of the Governors.

The Spiegelberg brothers, ca. 1865–70. Photograph by Napoleon Sarony, University of Arizona Libraries, Special Collections (SJA006 box 5).

Joab Houghton

Joab Houghton was born in New York in 1811. Houghton came to New Mexico in 1844 and served as US consul in Santa Fe.[104] He entered into a partnership with Eugene and Thomas Leitensdorfer. They operated the most successful mercantile operation in Santa Fe from 1846 to 1848 when the business failed. Following the US occupation, General Kearny appointed Houghton as the first chief justice of the Territory of New Mexico, even though he lacked legal training. He was best known for sentencing Antonio María Trujillo to death following a trial in the aftermath of the 1847 Taos Rebellion, although the execution was never carried out.[105]

Houghton's term as chief justice ended in 1851, and he began to practice law in Santa Fe. President Andrew Jackson appointed him associate justice of the supreme court of the territory, a position he held from 1865 to 1869.[106] A trained civil engineer, Houghton drew the plans for the territorial capitol.[107] In 1874 he moved to Las Vegas, New Mexico, where he died on January 31, 1876.

Joab Houghton, ca. 1855–56. Collection of Montezuma Lodge No. 1, Santa Fe.

Houghton was Master of Montezuma Lodge in 1855 and 1856 and Deputy District Grand Master between 1855 and 1864.[108] In 1866 Houghton was demitted from Montezuma Lodge and became the first Master of Aztec Lodge No. 108 in Las Cruces.[109] Houghton was an Episcopalian.

Thomas Benton Catron

Thomas B. Catron, ca. 1917. Palace of the Governors Photo Archives (NMHM/DCA 013309).

Thomas Benton Catron was born on a farm near Lexington, in Lafayette County, Missouri, on October 6, 1840.[110] He graduated from the University of Missouri in 1860 and served four years in the Confederate army during the Civil War. Catron registered as a visitor at Montezuma Lodge on August 6, 1865.[111] Beginning in 1866, he worked briefly as a law clerk for Judge Kirby Benedict. He was appointed district attorney for the Third Judicial District in January 1866, even though he was not admitted to the bar until June 1867. He settled in Mesilla and became one of the first members of Aztec Lodge No. 108.[112] In 1868 he won election to the lower house of the New Mexico territorial legislature. Governor Robert B. Mitchell appointed Catron attorney general of the territory in 1869.
He again visited Montezuma Lodge on July 8, 1871, this time as a member of Aztec Lodge.[113]

He resigned as attorney general and moved to Santa Fe when President Ulysses S. Grant named him a US attorney in 1872. He held the post for six years and resigned. Catron became the most important figure in the Republican Party in New Mexico, winning election to the territorial council six times between 1884 and 1909.[114] He was New Mexico's delegate to Congress from 1895 to 1897. After statehood, Catron became New Mexico's first US senator, serving from 1912 until 1917.

Catron was one of the most active land speculators in US history. By the end of the nineteenth century, he was one of the largest landowners in the country.[115] He had at least a partial interest in numerous land grants, perhaps as many as thirty-four, which amounted to millions of acres in New Mexico. Unlike the robber barons from the eastern US to whom he has been compared, however, Catron was not a successful businessman, and statehood did not eliminate his financial difficulties.

He died following a long illness on May 15, 1921.[116] Montezuma Lodge conducted the funeral services. Catron's body lay in state in the Scottish Rite Temple from 10 a.m. until 3 p.m. on May 17. At 3:30 Catron's remains were escorted from the temple to the Catron mausoleum at Fairview Cemetery, where Masonic burial services were held.

Harper Samuel Cunningham

Harper Samuel Cunningham was born near Zanesville, Ohio, in 1846.[117] He saw service in the Civil War as a teenager. He moved to Kansas about 1881 and then relocated to Oklahoma. Cunningham organized the Scottish Rite in Oklahoma. In 1890 Albert Pike appointed him Deputy for the Supreme Council of the Scottish Rite of Oklahoma.[118] Cunningham received the honorary Thirty-third Degree. He was also a member of the Knights Templar Commandery in Oklahoma.[119]

Cunningham served on the Oklahoma Territorial Council and as attorney general in the administration of territorial governor Cassius M. Barnes (1897–1901).[120] Oklahoma became a state in 1907, and Cunningham was elected to serve in the first senate. He was reelected to the state senate but resigned and moved to New Mexico.

In February 1911 Cunningham traveled to California to consult with Los Angeles architects Sumner Hunt and Silas Reese Burns Jr., founders of the firm of Hunt and Burns, about the Scottish Rite Temple in Santa Fe. He was staying at his daughter's home in Long Beach when he died from stomach and liver ailments. He was sixty-four years old.[121] At the time of his death, Cunningham was serving as Inspector General of the Scottish Rite Masonry in New Mexico, a position he had held in Oklahoma.

Sovereign Grand Inspector General Harper S. Cunningham, ca. 1860s. Collection of the Scottish Rite Temple, Santa Fe.

Miguel Antonio Otero

Miguel Antonio Otero was born in Valencia, New Mexico, in 1829 (see page 26). A graduate of Pingree College in New York, he studied law in Saint Louis and was admitted to the bar in 1851. Otero practiced law in Albuquerque and was a member of the New Mexico territorial house of representatives from 1852 to 1854. In 1854 he became attorney general of New Mexico Territory and served as a delegate to Congress from the territory from 1855 through 1861. Thought to be a millionaire, he was one of the most successful merchants and bankers in New Mexico. He was the father of Miguel Antonio Otero Jr., who was governor of New Mexico from 1897 to 1906. Otero was a member of Montezuma Lodge in Santa Fe.

Albert Jennings Fountain

Colonel Albert Jennings Fountain affiliated with Aztec Lodge on June 3, 1876, having demitted from El Paso Lodge No. 130 of El Paso, Texas.[122] He served as Master of Aztec Lodge in 1881, 1888, and 1889 and as Deputy Grand Master of the New Mexico Grand Lodge in 1882 and 1890. The Twelfth Annual Communication of the Grand Lodge was held in Las Cruces on January 27–29, 1890.

Major Albert J. Fountain with his staff, New Mexico, 1883. Seated, left to right: *Captain Eugene Van Patten, Fountain, and Captain Salazar.* Standing, left to right: *Lieutenant Pedregon, Lieutenant Fountain, and Lieutenant Botello. Palace of the Governors Photo Archives (NMHM/DCA 013148).*

Fountain was born on Staten Island, New York, in 1838. After receiving a public school education, he graduated from Columbia College. Fountain studied law in San Francisco and was admitted to the California bar just before the Civil War began. In August 1861 he enlisted in the First California Volunteer Infantry and received a commission as a lieutenant. After the war, he served in the volunteer cavalry under General James Henry Carleton's command in New Mexico. Fountain subsequently served in Mexico under Benito Juárez, who commissioned him as a colonel. He settled in El Paso, serving as collector of internal revenue for the Western District of Texas. In 1868 he was elected to the Texas State Senate, representing counties in the western part of the state. Subsequently he became president of the senate.

In 1875 Fountain returned to New Mexico and campaigned against the Apache leader Victorio. He organized the First Battalion of New Mexico Cavalry, serving with a commission as a major. In 1885 Fountain participated in the campaign against Geronimo. President Grover Cleveland appointed him special counsel and aide to US Attorney Thomas Smith in the prosecution of land fraud cases. In 1888 he became speaker of the lower house of the New Mexico territorial legislature. President Benjamin Harrison appointed him assistant US attorney for New Mexico in 1889.

In 1895 the Southeastern New Mexico Cattle Association hired Fountain as special counsel to assist in the prosecution of cattle thieves. While serving in that capacity, he—accompanied by his nine-year-old son, Henry—traveled to Chaves County to attend a session of district court. The court handed down indictments against several alleged cattle thieves. When the term ended, the Fountains headed back to Las Cruces. On February 1, 1896, they disappeared about 5 miles south of Luna's Well, south of White Sands. Aztec Lodge spent around $3,000 in an attempt to locate them, including bringing in famous lawman Pat Garrett to investigate, but the Fountains were never found.[123] Lodge member Numa Reymond footed most of the considerable expense, but other New Mexico lodges and the Grand Lodge also contributed to the case, which remains unsolved.

Henry Lesinsky

A Jewish native of Prussia, Henry Lesinsky (see page 32) was initiated in Collingwood Lodge (established in 1856) in Collingwood, Australia, a suburb of Melbourne.[124] Lesinsky had gone to Australia after the discovery of gold there in 1851. He was passed in Aztec Lodge on March 4, 1863, and raised there on April 14, 1868.[125] Lesinsky was proprietor of a large general mercantile establishment, which enabled him to acquire one of the largest fortunes in southern New Mexico. He also had mining interests in Arizona. Lesinsky subsequently sold his mercantile business to Numa Reymond, who later sold out to Martin Lohman. Lesinsky built the two-story building at the southeast corner of the intersection of Griggs and Main Streets in Las Cruces. Aztec Lodge held a ninety-nine-year lease on the second story for a nominal annual rent of one dollar. The lodge used the premises until the construction and dedication of a new Masonic temple at the southwest corner of Griggs and Church Streets. Lesinsky served the lodge as treasurer in 1870, as secretary in 1871, and again as treasurer in 1872. He eventually sold his large mercantile business, worth more than a million dollars, and relocated to New York City, where he died in 1924.[126]

Martin Lohman

Martin Lohman, another pioneer Jew in southern New Mexico, was born on October 29, 1854, in Saint Louis. His parents, John F. and Elizabeth Lohman, were natives of the Kingdom of Hanover (in present-day Lower Saxony, Germany) and came to the United States in 1830.[127] Lohman spent his childhood and youth in Saint Louis, where he received a public school education and attended Saint Louis University. Lohman settled in Las Cruces in 1876.

In 1882 Lohman and Numa Reymond bought out the firm of H. Lesinsky & Co., General Merchandise. Lohman and Reymond built up one of the largest mercantile trades in New Mexico. In 1887 Lohman purchased Reymond's interest in the business and continued to operate it alone. A liberal Republican, Lohman was active in helping members of his party win elected office. He received an appointment as superintendent of public instruction for Doña Ana County and served one term. He was also elected to the New Mexico Constitutional Convention, which convened in Santa Fe in September 1889. At the convention, he served as chairman of the committee on corporations.

Martin Lohman, 1905. Center for Southwest Research, University Libraries, University of New Mexico (#000-021-0105).

Robert Black

Robert Black was a native of Cambridge, Massachusetts.[128] In 1872 Black moved to Silver City, where he became a contractor and builder. In 1859 he enrolled in Harvard College, and he remained in Cambridge until he was twenty-seven. He left Massachusetts and spent one year in Denver. He moved to Silver City to build a quartz mill. He worked as a contractor and builder until 1883, when he sought public office. He later returned to his construction work and built many of the important buildings in Silver City. Black installed the first woodworking machinery in New

Mexico and constructed the first complete planing mill, which he had shipped in sections from Boston.

Silver City incorporated in 1878, and Black was elected the town's first mayor, serving two terms. In 1880 he was elected representative to the territorial legislature for the five southern counties; he held that position for two years. On May 1, 1883, the railroad to Silver City was completed. Black, who was mayor at the time, had the honor of driving the silver spike. In the territorial legislature, Black championed public schools, a cause that his brother Freemasons strongly supported. His business, Black and Company, built the first proper school in Silver City, a two-story brick structure.[129] He served as president of the school board of Silver City for more than twenty-one years.

Black played a major role in the establishment of the New Mexico Normal School in Silver City (present-day Western New Mexico University) in 1893. He was also a member of the board of trustees of the New Mexico College of Agricultural and Mechanic Arts (present-day New Mexico State University). Black was a member of Silver City Lodge No. 8 and took the degrees of the Commandery Knights Templar and of the Shrine in Albuquerque. He was a member of the Eastern Star. Black was an Episcopalian.

Nathan Jaffa

Nathan Jaffa. University of Arizona Libraries, Special Collections (SJA006 box 5).

Nathan Jaffa was born in Germany in 1863 and moved to Trinidad, Colorado, in 1878. In 1881 he moved to Las Vegas, New Mexico, where, at only eighteen years of age, he managed Jaffa Bros. Mercantile Co. In 1884 he relocated to Albuquerque. He operated a business there until 1886, when he moved to Roswell. In partnership with W. S. Prager, he organized Jaffa, Prager & Co., which he operated for many years. He held the position of vice president of the Bank of Roswell until 1890, when he organized Citizens Bank.

Jaffa was a Chaves County commissioner from 1895 to 1897, the first Republican elected to county office. When Roswell organized as a village, Jaffa was chairman of the board of trustees; he held the same position when Roswell became a city. In the 1890s Governor William A. Thornton appointed him regent of the New Mexico Military Institute. He was president of the board for a number of years. He gave up that position in 1907 when President Theodore Roosevelt appointed him secretary of the Territory of New Mexico. President William Howard Taft reappointed him, and he served as secretary until statehood. He was a member of the board of regents of the University of New Mexico from 1912 to 1925, serving as chairman for several years. Jaffa was mayor of Santa Fe from 1924 to 1926, when he ran unsuccessfully as the Republican candidate for state treasurer, suffering a narrow defeat. Jaffa served on the state tax commission from 1928 to 1930.

Jaffa died on September 12, 1945, at the age of eighty-one.[130] At the time, he was working as city clerk of Las Vegas. Jaffa, who was Jewish, was buried at Montefiore Cemetery in Las Vegas, with the Grand Lodge of New Mexico providing Masonic funeral rites. Nathan Jaffa was a Thirty-third-Degree Mason, Past Grand Master of the Masons of New Mexico, Past Grand High Priest of the Royal Arch Masons of the state, and Past Exalted Ruler of the Elks Lodge of Roswell.

NOTES

1. Ralph E. Twitchell, *The Leading Facts of New Mexico History*, vol. 5 (Cedar Rapids, IA: Torch Press, 1917), 325–27. The lodge began conferring the degrees in 1905, when under the direction of Max Frost. Three years later Aztlan Chapter, Rose Croix No. 1, was instituted under Frost's direction. In 1908 the Coronado Council of Kadosh and New Mexico Consistory No. 1 were instituted. The first reunion took place in 1909.

Other appendant organizations were established in New Mexico. The Grand Royal Arch Chapter was organized in 1898, the first Royal Arch Chapter having been instituted in Santa Fe in 1865. The Grand Commandery of the Knights Templar was organized in 1901. The Shrine received its charter in 1887 and located its temple in Albuquerque.

2. Felipe Ávila Marcué, "La francmasonería en México," *Ciencia UANL* 17, no. 65 (January–February 2014): 1.

3. Ray Vaughn Denslow, *Territorial Masonry: The Story of Freemasonry and the Louisiana Purchase, 1804–1821* (Washington, DC: Masonic Service Association of the United States, 1925), 22; William R. Denslow, *10,000 Famous Freemasons* (Independence: Missouri Lodge of Research, 1957), vol. 3, 345. Numerous Masonic sources state that Pike was a Freemason, a member of Lodge No. 3 in Philadelphia, but it was his father, also named Zebulon, who was initiated in this lodge on February 19, 1782, when Zebulon Montgomery was three years old. In 1791 Pike Sr. petitioned the Grand Lodge of New Jersey for a warrant for a traveling lodge in the army. At this time, Pike Jr. was only twelve. Robinson joined Lodge No. 13 in Virginia, later affiliated with Western Star Lodge No. 107 of Kaskaskia, Illinois, and finally became a member of Louisiana Lodge No. 109 in Saint Genevieve, Missouri.

4. Nicolas K. Laos, *Freemasons, World Order, and Mind Wars: The Great Reality of Memphis-Misraim Masonry* (New York: Algora Publishing, 2016), 76.

5. The practices of the two lodges in Mexico had a few differences. The York Rite had seven degrees, and the Scottish Rite had thirty-two. The York Rite adopted the Virgen del Pilar as its patron, while the Scottish Rite opted for the Virgen de Guadalupe. With those few exceptions, the two Rites shared the beliefs common to all Masons. What emerged as perhaps the most significant difference between the York and Scottish Rites was the fact that Joel R. Poinsett, a supporter of and advisor to the Mexican Scottish Rite, was negotiating the international boundary between Mexico and the United States and trying to obtain a favorable result for his government.

6. *Rio Grande Republican* (Las Cruces), June 27, 1885. Patton died on March 13, 1866.

7. Minutes book of Montezuma Lodge, 1851–59. Montezuma Lodge is currently located directly northwest of the Scottish Rite Temple.

8. Joy Poole, ed., *Over the Santa Fe Trail to Mexico: The Travel Diaries and Autobiography of Dr. Rowland Willard* (Norman: Arthur H. Clark Company / University of Oklahoma Press, 2015), 210n69; *History of St. Charles, Montgomery, and Warren Counties, Missouri* (Saint Louis, MO: National Historical Company, 1885), 335–36.

9. Douglas C. Comer, *Ritual Ground: Bent's Old Fort, World Formation, and the Annexation of the Southwest* (Berkeley: University of California Press, 1996), 210. Comer cited Taos lawyer and Freemason Francis Cheetham's article "Governor Bent, Masonic Martyr," 359. Cheetham stated, "This fact has not yet been established."

10. Rick Hendricks and Robert D. Martínez, "A Brief Genealogy of New Mexico Governor Albino Pérez," *New Mexico Genealogist* 53, no. 3 (September 2014): 132; Ramón Alonso Pérez Escutia, "El origen y protagonismo de la masonería en Michoacán, 1821–1831," *Tzintzun: Revista de Estudios Históricos* 61 (January–June 2015): 55, 58.

11. Twitchell, *Leading Facts*, 311n1031.

12. Albert G. Mackey, *Encyclopedia of Freemasonry* (Altenmünster, Germany: Jazzybee Verlag, 2013); Francis T. Cheetham, "Pioneer Freemasons in the Winning of the Southwest," unpublished manuscript, 25.

13. Paul Gordon, "Freemasons on the Santa Fe Trail," *Wagon Tracks* 26, no. 3 (February 2012): 14.

14. George E. Dille, Josephine Kaye Dille, and Earl Kaye Dille, *The Dille Family: Three Hundred Years in America, 1664–1964* (Marceling, MO: Walsworth, 1970), 74.

15. David Clapsaddle, "Four Foot Soldiers on the Trail: An Illinois Odyssey," Santa Fe Trail Research, n.d., https://www.santafetrailresearch.com/research/four-foot-soldiers.html (accessed January 26, 2017).

16. Max Frost, "Sixty Years of Free Masonry in Territory of New Mexico," *Santa Fe New Mexican*, October 19, 1907.

17. "Are Military Lodges Irregular?" *The New Age Magazine* 25, no. 9 (September 1917): 406; Clapsaddle, "Four Foot Soldiers on the Trail."

18. "The Beginnings of Freemasonry in New Mexico," *The New Age Magazine* 24, no. 6 (June 1916): 287.

19. Minutes book, Montezuma Lodge No. 1, Santa Fe, New Mexico, 1851–59.

20. W. B. Dale Boudreau, "The Origin of Freemasonry in Washington," https://freemason-wa.org/grand-lodge-of-wa/history-of-washington-freemasonry/ (accessed September 4, 2017).

21. Minutes book, Montezuma Lodge, 1851–59.

22. J. Morrow Hall, *Seven Score and Ten: 150 Years of Freemasonry in New Mexico* (Santa Fe: Montezuma Lodge No. 1, 2001), 15.

23. Gordon, "Freemasons on the Santa Fe Trail," 13.

24. Bent Lodge reorganized and received a charter from the New Mexico Grand Lodge on October 20, 1909, with a new lodge number, 42, replacing the original 204.

25. Visitors' book, Montezuma Lodge No. 1, Santa Fe, New Mexico, 1852–1923.

26. Ibid.

27. Mark A. Tabbert, *American Freemasons: Three Centuries of Building Communities* (New York: New York University Press, 2005), 108.

28. Roger Finke and Rodney Stark, *The Churching of America, 1776–2005: Winners and Losers in Our Religious Economy* (New Brunswick, NJ: Rutgers University Press, 2005), 121; Carroll Davidson Wright, *Census Reports Eleventh Census: 1890, Issue 9* (Washington, DC: US Government Printing Office, 1894), xx. Information gathered for the 1890 census indicated that communicants made up 68.85 percent of the population of New Mexico, which numbered 160,282. Of these, 77 percent were Catholics.

29. Paul Horgan, *Lamy of Santa Fe* (New York: Noonday Press / Farrar, Straus and Giroux, 1993), 163–64.

30. Ibid., 359, 412; Sheri Goldstein Gleicher, "The Spiegelbergs of New Mexico: A Family Story of the Southwestern Frontier," *Southwest Jewish History* 1, no. 2 (Winter 1992): 1, http://swja.arizona.edu/content/spiegelbergs-new-mexico-family-story-southwestern-frontier.

31. "Death of Wm. Osterton" and "Death of William Osterton," *New Mexican*, November 28, 1863.

32. *Revista Católica*, January 2, 1875; Gerald McKevitt, *Brokers of Culture: Italian Jesuits in the American West, 1848–1919* (Stanford, CA: Stanford University Press, 2007), 205.

33. Clarke Garrett, "French Missionary Clergy Confront the Protestant Menace in New Mexico, 1851–1885," *Proceedings of the Western Society for French History* 33 (2005): 302–4.

34. "Rites of Sepulture Refused," *Indianapolis Journal*, June 3, 1882.

35. Libreria Editrice Vaticana, "Humanum Genus, Encyclical of Pope Leo XIII on Freemasonry," April, 20, 1884, http://w2.vatican.va/content/leo-xiii/en/encyclicals/documents/hf_l-xiii_enc_18840420_humanum-genus.html, l.

36. "Carta Encíclica de Leo XXI, Papa," *Revista Católica*, June 1, 1884, 256–61; "Carta Encíclica de Leo XXI, Papa," *Revista Católica*, June 8, 1884, 268–72.

37. "Católico y Masón," *Revista Católica*, June 1, 1884, 255–56; "Siguen Protestando los Francmasones," *Revista Católica*, July 20, 1884, 340; "Las Amenazas de la Masonería," *Revista Católica*, September 7, 1884, 425–26; and "El Futuro de la Masonería," *Revista Católica*, April 5, 1885, 161–62.

38. Stefan-Ludwig Hoffmann, *The Politics of Sociability: Freemasonry and German Civil Society, 1840–1918* (Ann Arbor: University of Michigan Press, 2007), 142.

39. *Revista Católica*, May 30, 1886, 257–58.

40. *Revista Católica*, August 15, 1886, 388.

41. Rick Hendricks, *The Casads: A Pioneer Family of the Mesilla Valley* (Los Ranchos de Albuquerque, NM: Rio Grande Books, 2012), 65–66.

42. Tomas Jaehn, *Germans in the Southwest, 1850–1920* (Albuquerque: University of New Mexico Press, 2005), 114–15.

43. Twitchell, *Leading Facts*, 318–19.

44. Mary Ann Clawson, *Constructing Brotherhood: Class, Gender, and Fraternalism* (Princeton, NJ: Princeton University Press, 2014), 73.

45. David L. Caffey, *Chasing the Santa Fe Ring: Power and Privilege in Territorial New Mexico* (Albuquerque: University of New Mexico Press, 2014), 151–52.

46. Frederick W. Nolan, *The Lincoln County War: A Documentary History* (Santa Fe: Sunstone Press, 2009), 47.

47. Michael Wallis, *Billy the Kid: The Endless Ride* (New York: W. W. Norton, 2008), 188–89.

48. Caffey, *Chasing the Santa Fe Ring*, 241–45. The members of Caffey's core who were Freemasons were Henry Martyn Atkinson, Samuel Beach Axtell, Thomas Benton Catron, Stephen Benton Elkins, Maximilian Eugene Frost, William W. Griffin, LeBaron Bradford Prince, William Logan Rynerson, and Henry Ludlow Waldo.

49. A copy of the bylaws, adopted on December 1, 1862, was printed by P. M. Prichard of Saint Louis, Missouri. Members listed in the accompanying register provide an example of how pervasive Freemasonry was among important territorial officials, military officers, and leading New Mexico citizens: Jesús Gil Abréu, a member of the well-known Abréu family of northern New Mexico, son of Mexican governor Santiago Abréu; Jacob Ambers of Santa Fe, a leading merchant and Santa Fe Trail trader; Merrill Ashurst, a leading lawyer and a member of the territorial supreme court; Captain George T. Beall, a medical officer in the army; Joseph M. Bell, a lieutenant in the army; Kirby Benedict, lawyer and member of the territorial supreme court; Charles Blumner, one-time territorial treasurer; Robert T. Brent, affiliated from Hardin Military Lodge and killed by Indians; Colonel Horace Brooks; Brigadier-General James Henry Carleton, commander of the Department of New Mexico; Brigadier-General of Volunteers Christopher Carson, whose rifle was left as an heirloom to the lodge; New Mexico surveyor general Charles H. Clark; James Conklin, father of Charles M. Conklin of Santa Fe; assistant adjutant-general of the Department of New Mexico Cyrus H. DeForrest; Albert Elsberg, prominent merchant and Santa Fe Trail trader; Julius Freudenthal, merchant and Santa Fe Trail trader; US district attorney Joseph E. Garey; James Madison Giddings; John Greiner, secretary of New Mexico Territory; William W. Griffin, surveyor (and later president of First National Bank of Santa Fe) and first Grand Master of the Grand Lodge of New Mexico; Lafayette Head, pioneer, trapper, and first lieutenant governor of Colorado; Joab Houghton, lawyer and member of the territorial supreme court; William Thomas Maguder, captain in the US Army (afterward a captain in the Confederate army); David J. Miller, for thirty years chief clerk in the US surveyor general's office in Santa Fe and Grand Secretary of the New Mexico Grand Lodge; Henry O'Neill, merchant and Santa Fe Trail trader; Miguel Antonio Otero, Santa Fe delegate to the US Congress, Santa Fe Trail trader, and father of New Mexico governor Miguel Antonio Otero Jr.; Albert Henry Pfeiffer, colonel of the New Mexico Volunteers during the Civil War; Levi Spiegelberg, merchant and Santa Fe Trail trader, founder of the mercantile firm Spiegelberg Brothers, which did business in New Mexico for forty years; Thomas Sheridan Tucker, printer who, with William Henry Manderfield, began publication of the *Santa Fe New Mexican*; Pickney R. Tulley, merchant and Santa Fe Trail trader; Charles Emil Wesche, an officer in the New Mexico Volunteers and prominent citizen of Las Vegas.

50. *Masonic Voice Review* 27, no. 1 (July 1862): 190. A Sterling M. Price was expelled from this lodge on April 14, 1854.

51. William C. Carson, *He Moved West with America: The Life and Times of Wm. Carr Lane: 1789–1863* (Bloomington, IN: Archway Publishing, 2016), 91, 201. Lane became a Freemason in 1814, advancing to Master Mason. After 1815 he never changed his original lodge affiliation or regularly attended meetings. He did, however, participate in public Masonic activities.

52. "Death of Ex-Governor Henry Connelly," *Santa Fe Weekly Gazette*, August 18, 1866.

53. Grand Lodge of Wisconsin, *Transactions of the Grand Lodge of Free and Accepted Masons of the State of Wisconsin, at Its Annual Communication* (Milwaukee: Grand Lodge, 1885), 71, 44, 90.

54. J. W. Raynolds, *Report of the Secretary of the Territory, 1903–1904, and Legislative Manual, 1905* (Santa Fe: New Mexican Printing, 1905), 500.

55. *Trestleboard* (Amity Lodge No. 442, San Diego) 97, no. 6 (June 2010): 11.

56. Grand Lodge of California, *Proceedings of the Grand Lodge of Free and Accepted Masons of the Jurisdiction of California, at its 62nd Annual Communication* (San Francisco: Shannon-Conmy Printing, 1911), 19.

57. T.E.C., "Famous Freemason: Bro. Lew Wallace," Midnight Freemasons, January 22, 2012, http://www.midnightfreemasons.org/2012/01/famous-freemason-bro-lew-wallace_13.html.

58. Royal Arch Masons, *Proceedings of the Grand Chapter of Royal Arch Masons of the State of California at Its Fifty-Sixth Annual Convocation* (San Francisco: Shannon-Conmy Printing, 1910), 564.

59. James Marples, "Edmund G. Ross, a Masonic Profile in Courage," *Scottish Rite Journal*, March 1998, http://srjarchives.tripod.com/1998-03/marples.htm.

60. "History," Queens Masonic District, 2017, http://queensmasons.com/index.php?option=com_content&view=category&layout=blog&id=52&Itemid=155&lang=en.

61. Grand Lodge of New York, *Proceedings of the Grand Lodge of Free and Accepted Masons of the State of New York, 112th Annual Communication* (New York: Press of J. J. Little and Company, 1893); L. Bradford Prince, *Historical Sketches of New Mexico: From the Earliest Records to the American Occupation* (New York: Leggat Brothers, 1883).

62. "Governor Thornton Dead; Power for Law and Order," *Santa Fe New Mexican*, March 17, 1916.

63. Territorial Archives of New Mexico, series I, Records of the Secretary of the Territory, misc. papers, Constitutional Convention of 1910 and Statehood, Constitutional Convention Book, New Mexico State Records Center and Archives, Santa Fe.

64. "A Short History of Chapman Lodge A.F. & A.M.," Chapman Lodge, n.d., http://chapmanlodgeno2.org/history.htm (accessed January 8, 2017). The number of the lodge, 95, was the number of Acacia Lodge at Cape Girardeau, Missouri, which became extinct during the Civil War.

65. Henry Allen was the first Worshipful Master, Frank Phelps was Senior Warden, Charles S. Hopkins was Junior Warden, S. K. Hodges was Secretary, Pro Tem, B. C. Leonard was Treasurer, G. W. Cook was Senior Deacon, M. Coffman was Junior Deacon, and L. C. Farnaghy was Tyler.

66. *Las Vegas Daily Optic*, March 28, 1933; Knights Templar of Colorado, *Proceedings of the Grand Commandery, Knights Templar of Colorado* (Denver: W. F. Robinson Printing Company, 1898), 121. Rapp was a member of one of the two lodges in Trinidad, Colorado, and a member of Oriental Commandery 18.

67. Chapman Lodge, "A Short History of Chapman Lodge."

68. Aztec Lodge No. 3 AF & AM, *Seventieth Anniversary, 1867–1937* (Las Cruces, NM: Aztec Lodge, 1937), 7.

69. Ibid., 12–13.

70. Ibid., 17.

71. Depending on the method of calculation, $640 in 1889 would be worth approximately $15,000 to $17,000 in 2015 dollars. See https://www.measuringworth.com or http://www.westegg.com.

72. Aztec Lodge, *Seventieth Anniversary*, 24.

73. Gordon, "Freemasons on the Santa Fe Trail," 17n47. In 1907 the New Mexican Printing Company occupied this building.

74. "History of the Grand Lodge of Arizona," Grand Lodge of Arizona, 2015, http://www.azmasons.org/history (accessed October 15, 2016).

75. Frost, "Sixty Years of Free Masonry."

76. *Thirty-four* (Las Cruces), April 28, 1880.

77. Frost, "Sixty Years of Free Masonry."

78. Ibid.

79. "Masonic Grand Lodge," *Santa Fe New Mexican*, January 27, 1891.

80. Miguel Antonio Otero, *Report of the Governor of New Mexico to the Secretary of the Interior* (Washington, DC: US Government Printing Office, 1905), 141.

81. Tabbert, *American Freemasons*, 168; "Membership Totals since 1924," Masonic Service Association of North America, 2015, http://www.msana.com/msastats.asp (accessed January 8, 2017); Art DeHoyos and S. Brent Morris, eds., *Freemasonry in Context: History, Ritual, Controversy* (Lanham, MD: Lexington Books, 2004), 315. The Masonic Service Association of North America provides different percentages, but the trends are the same. According to the association's calculations, the number of Freemasons in the United States peaked in 1959 at 4,103,161, but as percentage of base male population, it peaked in 1929 with a membership of 3,295,125, representing 8 percent of the population. The percentage was 7.6 in 1960 and trending downward; the downward trend has continued.

82. "Handsome New Masonic Temple Rapidly Nearing Final Completion Point," *Albuquerque Morning Journal*, February 3, 1911.

83. Ibid.

84. Ibid.

85. "Masonic Temple, Albuquerque, NM," Denver Public Library, n.d., http://digital.denverlibrary.org/cdm/ref/collection/p15330coll22/id/62129.

86. V. B. Price, *Albuquerque: A City at the End of the World* (Albuquerque: University of New Mexico Press, 1992), 54.

87. *Albuquerque Morning Journal*, April 22, 1911.

88. Ibid.

89. "The History of Holcomb & Hoke Manufacturing Company," J. H. Fentress Antique Popcorn Museum, 2015, http://antiquepopcornmuseum.com/history.php (accessed October 20, 2016). In box ball bowling, touted as a modified version of bowling, players used small balls to knock down five pins set horizontally across a wooden alley. Portable lanes came in three sizes, which made possible fast and easy installation in venues large and small. Ironically, the popularity of box ball alleys began to wane because of market saturation around 1910, the year before the completion of the Albuquerque Temple.

90. National Register of Historic Places Registration Form, Mosque of the El Jebel Shrine, Denver, Colorado, National Register #97001235, section 8, page 17, https://npgallery.nps.gov/pdfhost/docs/NRHP/Text/97001235.pdf (accessed October 15, 2016).

91. Edward J. Mehren, Henry Coddington Meyer, and John M. Goodell, eds., *Engineering Record, Building Record and Sanitary Engineer*, vol. 61 (New York: McGraw, 1910), 52.

92. Rose Marie Walker, "Temple Fire Damage Listed At $250,000," *Albuquerque Tribune*, April 17, 1967. A fire that broke out on the night of Saturday, April 15, 1967, completely destroyed the Albuquerque Masonic Temple.

93. "Dr. Gray's Address Well Received," *Albuquerque Morning Journal*, May 27, 1911.

94. Ibid.

95. "Masonic Temple Las Cruces, New Mexico," Henry C. Trost Historical Organization, 2017, http://www.henrytrost.org/buildings/masonic-temple-las-cruces/ (accessed October 16, 2016); "Masonic Temple El Paso, Texas," Henry C. Trost Historical Organization, 2017, http://www.henrytrost.org/buildings/masonic-temple-el-paso/ (accessed October 16, 2016).

96. "Masons Dedicate New Temple," *Rio Grande Republican* (Las Cruces, NM), April 9, 1912. The masthead incorrectly indicates that April 9 was a Friday; it was a Tuesday.

97. Denslow, *10,000 Famous Freemasons*, vol. 4, 4.

98. *Santa Fe Gazette*, September 24, 1859; T. Edward Shumaker, "Hugh N. Smith, New Mexico's First Attorney General," Office of the State Historian, n.d., http://newmexicohistory.org/people/the-death-of-hugh-smith-attorney-general-of-new-mexico#_edn4 (accessed January 22, 2017).

99. *Santa Fe Gazette*, September 24, 1859.

100. US Congress (31st, 1st session: 1849–1850), House, "Hugh N. Smith, Delegate from New Mexico: 31st Congress, First Session: Rep. No. 220" (Houston, TX: Rice University, April 4, 1850), June 7, 2010, https://scholarship.rice.edu/jsp/xml/1911/27089/1/aa00317a.tei.html.

101. Ibid.

102. *Santa Fe Gazette*, September 24, 1859.

103. Gleicher, "Spiegelbergs of New Mexico," 3–4.

104. "Death of Ex-Chief Justice Houghton," *Daily New Mexican*, February 1, 1876.

105. Robert J. Tórrez, "Rebellion of 1847 Treason Trials," http://newmexicohistory.org/events/rebellion-of-1847-treason-trials (accessed October 28, 2016).

106. Arie Poldervaart, "Black-Robed Justice in New Mexico, 1846-1912," *New Mexico Historical Review* 22, no. 1 (January 1947): 46–47.

107. "Death of Ex-Chief Justice Houghton," *Daily New Mexican*, February 1, 1876.

108. Hall, *Seven Score and Ten*, 13.

109. Aztec Lodge, *Seventieth Anniversary*, 13, 15.

110. US Congress, "Catron, Thomas Benton (1840–1921)," Biographical Directory of the United States Congress, n.d., http://bioguide.congress.gov/scripts/biodisplay.pl?index=c000253 (accessed January 7, 2017).

111. Visitors' book, Montezuma Lodge, 1852–1923.

112. Aztec Lodge, *Seventieth Anniversary*, 13.

113. Visitors' book, Montezuma Lodge, 1852–1923.

114. US Congress, "Catron, Thomas Benton (1840–1921)."

115. David Correia, *Properties of Violence: Law and Land Grant Struggle in Northern New Mexico* (Athens: University of Georgia Press, 2013), 48.

116. "Thomas B. Catron Dies after Long Illness; Funeral to Be Held in Santa Fe on Tuesday," *Albuquerque Morning Journal*, May 16, 1921.

117. State of Oklahoma, *Journal of the Proceedings of the Senate, Regular Session of the Third Legislature of the State of Oklahoma* (Oklahoma City: Warden Printing, 1911), 844–46.

118. Supreme Council for the Southern Jurisdiction, *Transactions of the Supreme Council of the 33rd Degree for the Southern Jurisdiction of the United States of America, October 1882* (Washington, DC: Joseph L. Pearson, 1882), 149.

119. Knights Templar of the United States of America, *Proceedings of the Grand Encampment of Knights Templar of the United States of America* (Washington, DC: Grand Encampment, 1898), 54.

120. State of Oklahoma, *Journal of the Proceedings of the Senate*, 844–46.

121. "Harper Cunningham, Noted New Mexico Mason, Dies," *Los Angeles Herald*, March 11, 1911.

122. Henry Stoes, "Biographical sketches of members of Aztec Lodge," Freemasons Aztec Lodge No. 3 records, 1867–1967, Rio Grande Historical Collections, New Mexico State University, microfilm.

123. Aztec Lodge, *Seventieth Anniversary*, 23.

124. "Admiral Collingwood Lodge," Freemasons Victoria, 2017, http://www.freemasonsvic.net.au/our-lodges/lodge-directory/admiral-collingwood-lodge/ (accessed January 7, 2017).

125. Henry Stoes, "Biographical sketches of members of Aztec Lodge."

126. Natalie Ornish, *Pioneer Jewish Texas* (College Station: Texas A&M University Press, 2011), 178.

127. Helen Haines, *History of New Mexico: From the Spanish Conquest to the Present Time, 1530–1890: With Portraits and Biographical Sketches of Its Prominent People* (Santa Fe: New Mexico Historical Publishing Company, 1891).

128. George B. Anderson, *History of New Mexico, Its Resources and People*, vol. 2 (Los Angeles: Pacific States Publishing, 1907), 496.

129. Helen M. Calkins, *Public Schools of Silver City (New Mexico): A History of the School from 1874 to 1928* [1928?], 21.

130. "Nathan Jaffa, Former Mayor of Santa Fe, Dies at Vegas," *Santa Fe New Mexican,* September 13, 1945; "Henry and Nathan Jaffa," Jewish Virtual Library, 1998–2017, https://www.jewishvirtuallibrary.org/jsource/judaica/ejud_0002_0011_0_09940.html (accessed January 7, 2017).

Scottish Rite Cathedral, Santa Fe, Washington Avenue elevation. Hunt and Burns architectural blueprint, ca. 1910. Photograph by Martin Stupich for the HABS Collection, Library of Congress, Washington, DC.

3
History and Architecture of the Santa Fe Scottish Rite Temple

KHRISTAAN VILLELA

SANTA FE, NEW MEXICO, is famous for its brown and round Spanish Pueblo revival–style architecture, epitomized by structures like the Palace of the Governors and the Cristo Rey Church.[1] The city is also peppered with buildings in other historical styles, from territorial structures inspired by nineteenth-century neoclassicism to craftsman-style bungalows.[2] But the Scottish Rite Temple is undoubtedly one of the most striking buildings in Santa Fe.

Cristo Rey Church, Santa Fe, 1940. Designed by Mason John Gaw Meem. Palace of the Governors Photo Archives (NMHM/DCA HP.2007.20.93).

View of the newly completed Scottish Rite Temple from the Federal Building, 1912. To the right is a home that archaeologist and Scottish Rite Mason Sylvanus G. Morley renovated in 1910. The curved road, now Paseo de Peralta, traces the path of a burro racetrack laid out for the erroneous celebration of Santa Fe's 333rd birthday in 1883. (We now know that Santa Fe was founded around 1610, not 1550.) Photograph by Jesse Nusbaum, 1912. Scottish Rite Temple Collection, Palace of the Governors Photo Archives (NMHM/DCA HP.2016.53.007).

View of the Scottish Rite Temple from the Federal Building grounds, 2016.

The structure's architects, the Los Angeles–based firm of Hunt and Burns, discussed below, drew inspiration from the buildings of the Alhambra, the fortified hilltop in Granada, Spain (completed circa AD 1350). The buildings of the Alhambra, along with the Great Mosque at Córdoba and the Giralda Tower in Seville, were touchstones of Moorish architecture. *Moor* is a general and not always complimentary term for the Islamic inhabitants of the Iberian Peninsula and Northwest Africa. Beginning in AD 711, much of Spain was conquered by Arab and Berber Islamic forces that crossed the Strait of Gibraltar from Northwest Africa. For the next seven hundred years, Spain's inhabitants were subjects of a mosaic of Christian and Islamic kingdoms. Over the centuries, the Islamic states were gradually defeated, a process that culminated in the surrender in 1492 of Muhammad XII, the last ruler of the Emirate of Granada, an incident commemorated in a painting hanging above the theater proscenium of Santa Fe's Scottish Rite Temple.

The Alhambra of Granada, Spain, inspired many Moorish revival–style buildings, including the Santa Fe Scottish Rite Temple. Photograph © trofotodesign, stock.adobe.com.

The Moorish revival was one of many Euro-American revivals in architecture and design from the mid-1700s to the early 1900s. Others included neoclassicism, Gothic revival, Egyptian revival, and lesser-knowns such as Maya revival and Pueblo Indian deco. Many Moorish revival buildings feature pointed and horseshoe arches, windows, and doorways; arcades; courtyards; and multifoil window tracery; as well as decorative brickwork, stucco exteriors, onion domes, and towers, some evoking minarets. In interiors, Moorish revival buildings are characterized by complex painted and plaster, geometric and vegetal designs intended to convey a feeling of richness in pattern and texture.[3] Moorish revival architecture was primarily a phenomenon of nineteenth-century Romanticism in Europe and the United States and was an expression of Orientalism. As Edward Said argued in 1978, Orientalism was a discourse; a body of thinking, writing, and speaking; and a group of strategies that allowed Westerners to describe, imagine, and even control the Orient and those who dwelled there.[4]

The Orient in question here consists primarily of areas relatively close to Europe and peoples who were not Christian or whose cultures were perceived as exotic and foreign: the people of Turkey, the Middle East, Egypt, North Africa, and, closest at hand, Islamic Spain. Lands farther east, such as the Indian subcontinent, China, Korea, and Japan, were not part of this story. Many writers trace the beginnings of Orientalism to the era of the Napoleonic Wars (1803–15), when French forces invaded territories where "exotic" Oriental peoples lived or had once lived. Napoleon Bonaparte's invasion of Syria and Egypt (1798–1801), then both part of the Turkish Ottoman Empire, led to the wide exposure of Islamic culture, art, and architecture in European intellectual circles. In Egypt, French armies were followed

David Roberts's watercolors of the Alhambra and other monuments of Islamic Spain inspired the Santa Fe Scottish Rite Temple architects. Left: Gate of Justice, Alhambra, Granada, *ca. 1834. © Victoria and Albert Museum, London (2008BU4557-01).* Right: The Giralda, Seville*, 1833. © The Metropolitan Museum of Art, New York. Art Resource, NY (Art544186).*

Bonaparte Visiting the Pesthouse in Jaffa, *by Antoine-Jean Gros, 1804. The image shows a dramatic scene from Napoleon's campaign in Egypt and Syria (1798–1801). The horseshoe and pointed arches are hallmarks of Islamic architecture. Musée du Louvre, RMN-Grand Palais/Art Resource, NY (Art151573).*

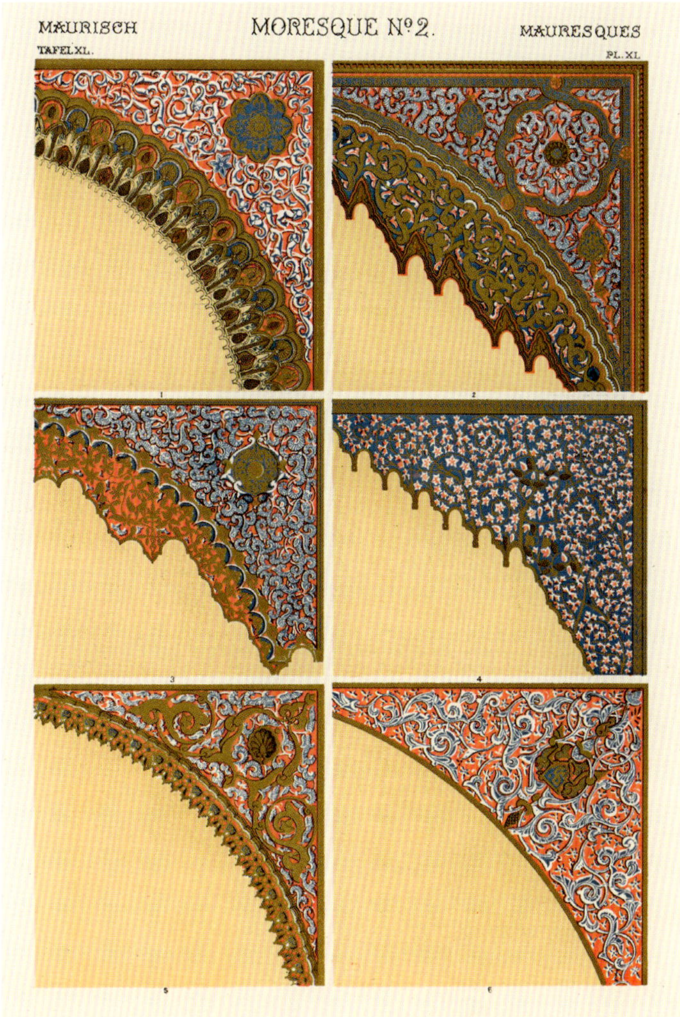

British artist Owen Jones made highly accurate drawings of the Alhambra in the 1830s. His Grammar of Ornament *(1856) made the images widely available to architects and designers in Europe and the United States. Collection of the Scottish Rite Temple, Santa Fe.*

by corps of scientists, archaeologists, and artists eager to discover, record, and collect the antiquities of one of France's shortest-lived colonies.

Aside from the discovery of the Rosetta Stone, which led to the decipherment of Egyptian hieroglyphic writing, the signal accomplishment of Napoleon's Egyptian campaign and his Commission des Sciences et Arts d'Égypte was the publication of the monumental, twenty-three-volume *Description de l'Égypte*, published between 1809 and 1823.[5] While it was not the first publication to include detailed descriptions and accurate drawings of Egyptian antiquities, as well as views of contemporary Egyptian cities and people, it was by far the most influential, establishing the exoticism of the Orient in the minds of many Europeans.[6] *Description de l'Égypte* amplified Romantic-period visions of the Orient, as exemplified by Samuel Taylor Coleridge's 1816 poem "Kubla Khan" or Percy Bysshe Shelley's "Ozymandias" (1818). As was the case for Egypt, Napoleon's failed Peninsular War (1807–14) led to a renewed European interest in the Islamic arts and culture of Spain and Northwest Africa.[7]

In English-language literature, the most notable contributions to the awareness of Spain's Islamic heritage were Washington Irving's *The Alhambra* (1832) and Richard Ford's *Handbook for Travellers in Spain and Readers at Home* (1845). In the visual arts, painters such as Antoine Jean Gros and Eugène Delacroix created both historical and romantic canvases with Orientalist themes and settings.[8] The traveler-artists David Roberts and John Frederick Lewis popularized the monuments and people of Moorish Spain and Northwest Africa for English-speaking audiences when their images were widely reproduced.[9] Roberts's later images of the archaeological and cultural heritage of Egypt and the Middle East, published in 1855–56 in *The Holy Land, Syria, Idumea, Arabia, Egypt, and Nubia*, were also broadly disseminated.[10] While Roberts's and Lewis's images and Irving's descriptions fueled Euro-American interest in Moorish culture and architecture, the British architect Owen Jones's studies of the Alhambra provided detailed plans and images of the complex's buildings and decorations.[11]

Architects and patrons favored Moorish revival architecture for buildings associated with leisure activities, such as theaters, public entertainment venues, hotels, and structures at world's fairs.[12] London's Alhambra Theater (1856; demolished 1936) and El Paso's Alhambra Theater (1914) were important examples of theaters inspired by Spain's Moorish architecture. The New York Crystal Palace, constructed in 1853 for the Exhibition of the Industry of All Nations, was a Moorish revival–style building (see page 61). At the 1893 World's Columbian Exposition in Chicago, Spain's building combined elements of Gothic and Moorish revival and evoked the towers of the Alhambra. Other Moorish revival and Orientalist structures at the fair included the Algerian Theater; the Persian Theater; the Algerian, Tunisian, and Turkish Villages; the Streets of Cairo; and the Moorish Palace, complete with a restaurant, a garden with palm trees, a wax museum, and "Dancing Girls in the Harem."[13] These structures were all intended to evoke exotic, far-off locations and to transport visitors to an Orientalist fantasy.[14] Architecture's power to evoke foreign locales is also why the Moorish revival style was frequently used for Jewish synagogues in Europe and the United States. The style visually represented Judaism's origins outside Europe, in the Middle East, which was the Orient.[15] Notable surviving examples include the Dohány Street Synagogue in Budapest, Hungary (1854–59) and the Central Synagogue in New York (1872).

Freemasons and other fraternal groups in the United States also selected Moorish revival architecture for their theaters and meeting halls. Although fraternal groups built structures in many nineteenth-century revival styles, some were more inclined toward Moorish revival. The Shriners International, formerly known as the Ancient Arabic Order of the Nobles of the Mystic Shrine (AAONMS), was founded by Freemasons in New York in 1871. The Shriners devised rituals based upon an Orientalist understanding of Islam and thus appropriated symbols and language from the Islamic world and the Middle East in general.[16]

Shriners wear red fezzes, tokens of an exotic, appropriated Islamic identity, and meet in lodges called temples or mosques. Given their ritual, dress, and invented history, it is no surprise that many Shrine temples were built in the Moorish revival style. As with Scottish Rite Freemasonry in the United States, membership in the Shrine rose rapidly in the early to mid-twentieth century, and many Shrine temples not only are large but also include sizable theaters used by members during ritual ceremonies. The Al Malaikah Temple in Los Angeles, built in 1906, was one of the earliest Shrine temples built in the Moorish revival style.[17] Other extant examples include the Medinah Temple in Chicago (1912; now a Bloomingdale's department store), the Mecca Temple in New York (1923; now New York City Center concert hall), and the Zembo Shrine Mosque in Harrisburg, Pennsylvania (1930). Aside from the Shriners, other Freemasons also looked to the Alhambra for inspiration. The Grand Lodge of Pennsylvania (Philadelphia Masonic Temple, 1873) and the Grand Lodge of Utah (Salt Lake Masonic Temple, 1927) both feature lodge rooms decorated in Moorish revival style.[18] In Indianapolis, Indiana, the Prince Hall Masonic Temple used by Central Lodge No. 1 was built in 1916 in the Moorish revival style.

Central Synagogue, New York City, 1872. Many European and North American synagogues were built in the Moorish revival style to call attention to the Middle Eastern origins of Judaism. Collection of Central Synagogue.

Moorish revival–style architecture was common for buildings used for public entertainment and fraternal organizations. Clockwise, from upper left*: Crystal Palace, New York, 1853 (Beinecke Rare Book and Manuscript Library, Yale University, 1109535); Al Malaikah Temple, Los Angeles, 1906; Medinah Shrine Temple, Chicago, 1912; Zembo Shrine Mosque, Harrisburg, Pennsylvania, 1930 (courtesy of Khristaan Villela).*

The Mecca Temple in New York (1923; now New York City Center concert hall), originally a Shrine Temple, shows Moorish revival features in the horseshoe arches above the door. A dome adds to the building's Orientalist fantasy. New-York Historical Society (PR181_b-04_9146-01).

The Oriental Hall (1896) at the Philadelphia Masonic Temple, with its opulent architectural ornamentation, was inspired by the Alhambra. Such rooms were exotic interpretations of standard lodge rooms, used to either communicate or confer degrees. The Masonic Library and Museum of Pennsylvania.

Building Santa Fe's Scottish Rite Temple

From its inception, the Santa Fe Scottish Rite Temple was a touchstone in the debate over what architectural style was most appropriate for Santa Fe. A short article in the "Society" section of the *Santa Fe New Mexican* on November 16, 1912, the day before the grand opening of the Scottish Rite temple, noted that the Alhambra was a symbol of the beauty and romance of Old Spain. The columnist said that several people had described the new temple as entirely foreign to Santa Fe, in connection with the question of modeling all buildings in the city after Mexican or Spanish precedents. But the writer disagreed and noted that Moorish-style architecture could be considered the grandsire of New Mexico architecture. The Scottish Rite Temple exterior color drew attention even before the building debuted. The same article noted that the entire building was tinted in the soft pink of the original Alhambra.[19] Painted sections inside the tower, as well as early colored photo postcards, show

Concept drawing of the Santa Fe Scottish Rite Temple by Hunt and Burns Architects, Los Angeles, California, ca. 1910. Collection of the Scottish Rite Temple, Santa Fe.

that the building was a much more muted shade than it is today. The minutes of the Santa Fe Scottish Rite Board of Directors relate that three shades of Venetian red were considered for the exterior color. Just two months before the grand opening, the darkest of the three shades was selected; the color was described as "slap dash pink."[20] The building was replastered and repainted in 1950, when the second half of the courtyard was completed, and again in 1960.[21] The most recent repainting took place in 2010. Regarding the color of the temple, we should recall that the Spanish name Alhambra derives from an Arabic word that means "the red one."

Was Moorish revival–style architecture entirely foreign to Santa Fe? How did New Mexico's Scottish Rite Freemasons fix upon a Moorish revival–style building for their grand new temple? And how could the building's architectural style relate to the question of Santa Fe's identity? Above we discuss how the nineteenth-century phenomenon of Orientalism was a lens used by writers and artists in Europe and the United States to imagine an exotic East, based upon little credible information and freighted with centuries of stereotypes about how people in Turkey, the Middle East, Egypt, and North Africa dressed, spoke, and lived, including what kinds of buildings they inhabited. But a particular Orientalist discourse emerged from both the Spanish conquest of Mexico in 1521 and the later settlement of the western United States in the 1800s. Richard Francaviglia writes in *Go East, Young Man: Imagining the American West as the Orient* that almost from the beginning of the European invasions of the

Americas more than five hundred years ago, the newcomers used Oriental imagery, stories, and frames of reference to describe and explain the people, places, and landscape of the New World.[22] The Native peoples of the Americas were often equated with the Islamic Moors. Apart from the large number of words of Arabic origin in Spanish (such as *albóndiga*, *adobe*, *almohada*, and Guadalupe), Islamic influence can be clearly traced in the art and architecture of Spain and its former overseas colonies. Examples of Moorish, or *mudéjar*, elements in Spanish colonial arts include tile work, ceramics, and complex wooden ceilings in the *artesonado* style.[23] Some early Mexican churches built for the natives, such as San José de los Naturales in Mexico City (circa 1527) and the Capilla Real de Naturales in Cholula (1540), were modeled after Spanish hypostyle mosques, such as the famous example at Córdoba.[24] The argument was that the natives were pagans, like the Moors, and as such they might relate to Christianity better if they could worship in spaces that resembled their former temples. Obviously, imagining that Mexico's native peoples could be converted to Christianity based on analogies to Islamic architecture and culture was a strategy doomed to fail.

Another chapter in the story of how the Orient was transposed onto American soil unfolded in the wake of the Mexican-American War (1846–48), when Americans from the eastern United States began settling in the Southwest and West. Not only did many of the invaders and settlers consider the Mexican and Native peoples they encountered foreign, but also the landscape was alien. The deserts reminded

Left and opposite (detail): *Stereoscopic card of the New Mexico Building, designed by Isaac Rapp for the 1904 Louisiana Purchase Exhibition, Saint Louis, Missouri. Before the development of the Spanish Pueblo revival style in the 1910s, mission revival was considered an appropriate architectural style to represent New Mexico. Courtesy of Khristaan Villela.*

many immigrants of the Holy Land. Many southwestern people were dark-skinned, like Arabs, and some, like the Navajos, were even nomadic or seminomadic, as are some Arab peoples. The Spanish colonial and northern Mexican architecture, constructed of adobe bricks, was also exotic and brought to mind buildings in Northwest Africa, Egypt, and the Middle East, or at least descriptions of such structures in romantic novels like *One Thousand and One Nights*.[25]

The Scottish Rite Temple and the Spanish Pueblo Revival Style

As noted above, while we can find buildings in many historical styles in Santa Fe, the most common are those of the Spanish Pueblo revival style. The history of the Scottish Rite Temple is entwined with the development of interest in this kind of adobe architecture. Much has been written about how this style came to be closely identified with the image of Santa Fe, most notably Chris Wilson's *The Myth of Santa Fe* (1997) and biographies of the most significant proponents of the architectural style, Isaac Hamilton Rapp and John Gaw Meem, both Freemasons.[26] Buildings that looked like Pueblo Indian dwellings or Ancestral Puebloan ruins were constructed both in the Southwest and elsewhere, such as for the World's Columbian Exposition in Chicago (1893). Mary Coulter's Hopi House at the Grand Canyon (1904) was modeled after the Hopi village of Old Oraibi and actually built by Hopi laborers. In Morley, Colorado, Isaac Rapp designed a warehouse for the Colorado Supply Company (1908) that used elements from San Estevan Church at Acoma Pueblo. But none of these structures were advanced as elements in a coordinated program to forge an identity for the city. The first evidence that Santa Fe's tastemakers and boosters were considering how architecture could be used to promote the city's unique identity was Rapp's design for the New Mexico Building at the Louisiana Purchase Exposition, held in Saint Louis in 1904.

As recounted by Wilson, at the turn of the twentieth century, many people associated New Mexico with the greater Hispanic Southwest and with the California mission style of architecture.[27] The use of mission revival–style architecture to promote California and the greater southwestern identity began with the California Building at the 1893 World's Columbian Exposition.[28] The New Mexico Building at the 1904 fair, with its white stucco walls, red tile roof, arcaded porch, and curved gable parapets, exemplified the style.[29] The mission revival style was identified with a romantic image of Native American and Spanish colonial life before the United States annexed those territories.

Harper S. Cunningham poses with a Scottish Rite Class at the Masonic Hall on Water Street in Santa Fe, 1909. The Masonic emblem that hung from the center of the proscenium arch now hangs in the auditorium at the Scottish Rite Temple. The scenery collection shown in this image, from McAlester, Oklahoma, was used to confer Scottish Rite degrees from 1909 to November 1912. Collection of the Scottish Rite Temple, Santa Fe.

The Scottish Rite Temple

The Scottish Rite of Freemasonry first met in Santa Fe in 1882.[30] By the early years of the twentieth century, the Scottish Rite Masons were meeting in lodge rooms on the south side of the Santa Fe Plaza built by Montezuma Lodge No. 1. The Scottish Rite in Santa Fe was incorporated on November 5, 1908, and the group immediately recognized the need for a permanent and dedicated space for lodge meetings and other functions. The Board of Directors appointed Maximilian Frost, Richard H. Hanna, and Samuel G. Cartwright to a building committee, and they reported on November 17 that a suitable building site had been located at the corner of what is now Washington Avenue and Nusbaum Street.[31] When the Scottish Rite Freemasons planned a grand new building for their rituals in Santa Fe in 1908, they turned to Rapp, who not only was a member but also had already worked for fraternal organizations. In 1894 he designed the Masonic temple in Las Vegas, New Mexico, a structure in the Richardsonian Romanesque style. And on July 13, 1908, the *Santa Fe New Mexican* reported that Rapp had been awarded the contract for the new Santa

Isaac Rapp's concept drawing for the Santa Fe Scottish Rite Temple, published in the Santa Fe New Mexican *on September 20, 1909. A Moorish revival–style building was proposed after Rapp's neoclassical design was deemed too costly. Fray Angelico Chavez History Library, New Mexico History Museum.*

Rapp adapted his original design for the Santa Fe Scottish Rite Temple for the Las Animas County Court House and Jail, Trinidad, Colorado, built in 1912. The photo shows what the corner of Washington Street and Paseo de Peralta would have looked like had the design been built. Denver and Rio Grande Railroad Company Collection (20005291), History Colorado.

Fe Elks Club building, another structure in the California mission style (finished in 1911). The plan for the Scottish Rite building went through at least two style iterations and a change of venue before creation of the Moorish fantasy inaugurated in 1912. The *Santa Fe New Mexican* reported on December 12, 1908, that the Scottish Rite Masons had purchased a fine lot on Washington Avenue and that a building would be constructed in the mission style, with all the modern conveniences inside. We should not be surprised by the choice of mission style, given Rapp's previous work. But for unknown reasons, Rapp's proposal for the Scottish Rite Temple, published as a concept drawing on the front page of the *Santa Fe New Mexican* on September 20, 1909, was for a neoclassical-style building, similar in form to his designs for the old New Mexico State Capitol (1903) and the New Mexico Governor's Mansion (1908). For the next year, negotiations with Rapp continued and proceeded alongside a fund-raising effort for the new structure. But by the end of 1910, the Rapp project had been deemed too costly, and in mid-January 1911, the Scottish Rite Board of Directors reached a settlement with the architect that canceled his contract and scuttled the neoclassical design.[32]

How did the Scottish Rite Temple go from mission revival style to neoclassical revival to Moorish revival? Enter Edgar Lee Hewett. By the time of the events detailed here, Hewett (1865–1946) had been living in and around Santa Fe for more than a decade. He was the dynamo behind the founding of the School of American Archaeology (1907) and the Museum of New Mexico (1909). But before he was an archaeologist, he was the first president of the New Mexico Normal School in Las Vegas (1898), now New Mexico Highlands University.[33] His office was in Normal Hall (later Springer Hall), a Romanesque revival–style building designed by Isaac Rapp. We can imagine that Hewett knew Rapp from the Springer Hall project, which was completed the same year he started at the Normal School. Ten years later, both Hewett and Rapp were residents of Santa Fe. They were united not only through Springer Hall at the Normal School but also by Freemasonry. Both men became Freemasons in Montezuma Lodge No. 1 in 1908, and they both joined the Scottish Rite in the class initiated on April 26, 1909. Santa Fe's Masonic groups counted as members a large number of the community's most influential figures, including Hewett and Rapp and also archaeologist Sylvanus G. Morley, photographer Jesse L. Nusbaum, and, later, architect John Gaw Meem.[34]

Toward the end of January 1911, the Scottish Rite Board of Directors authorized General Harper S. Cunningham to travel to Los Angeles to have plans prepared for a temple conforming "to the lines of the sketch heretofore obtained by Brother Cunningham."[35] Cunningham was the Sovereign Grand Inspector General of the

Edgar L. Hewett (center)*, a member of the Aleph Class (1909) of the Santa Fe Scottish Rite, suggested the Moorish revival style for the new temple. Hewett was the founder of the School of American Archaeology, and the images were taken at the school's dig at Quiriguá, Guatemala. Palace of the Governors Photo Archives (NMHM/DCA 007331).* Left: *Scottish Rite Mason Jesse Nusbaum with a Mayan at Quiriguá. Photograph by Charles Lummis, Palace of the Governors Photo Archives (NMHM/DCA 013607).* Right: *Writer Charles Lummis with his son Quimu at Quiriguá, ca. 1910. Photograph by Jesse Nusbaum, Palace of the Governors Photo Archives (NMHM/DCA 060952). Lummis probably suggested to Hewett that the Santa Fe Scottish Rite approach the Hunt and Burns architecture firm in Los Angeles.*

Scottish Rite in New Mexico, the order's chief executive. Before moving to Santa Fe, he was a leading Mason in Oklahoma, and he was involved in the Santa Fe Scottish Rite building plan from its inception. Cunningham traveled to Los Angeles, and by February 1 the architectural firm of Sumner Hunt and Silas Burns was contracted to design Santa Fe's Scottish Rite Temple. On that date, Hunt wrote a letter to Jesse Nusbaum, reminding him that they had met when Hunt had visited Santa Fe about a year previous and had spent the day "tramping over the town and looking at the old buildings."[36] He stated further that through the interest of Hewett, they had been commissioned to make the plans for the new Scottish Rite Temple, and he asked Nusbaum to make photographs of the proposed site on Washington Avenue, across from the Federal Building. We presume that Hunt met Hewett when he visited Santa Fe in late 1909 or early 1910. A letter Hunt wrote to Hewett just a week later, on February 17, 1911, seems to prove that the Moorish revival–style plan for the Scottish Rite Temple was Hewett's idea:

My dear Mr. Hewett:
I am writing to thank you for your very kind endorsement of me to your friend, General Cunningham. He has been in town now for some little time. I am sorry to say that he has been quite sick, and we have been working for him, getting along as fast as we could under the circumstances of his sickness. I think this morning we have everything settled and he seems exceedingly pleased and has approved our plans and told us to go ahead with our working drawings.

I am intensely interested in the scheme—think your suggestion is splendid. Think the type of architecture admirably adapted, not only of course to your location, but also to the building for which we are using it. We shall give the thing our very best attention and endeavor to make it as good as I understand you told the General we are capable of doing.[37]

The cornerstone-laying ceremony for the Santa Fe Scottish Rite Cathedral, 1911, with the Federal Building in the background. Scottish Rite Temple Collection, Palace of the Governors Photo Archives (NMHM/DCA HP.2016.53.005).

Hewett was a leading intellectual in Santa Fe at the time, and Hunt likely sought him out at the Museum of New Mexico headquarters in the old Palace of the Governors. After all, we know that he spent the day with Nusbaum, who was a museum employee. Or Hunt may have been introduced to Hewett through the Los Angeles–based writer Charles F. Lummis. Lummis championed the idea of the greater Hispanic Southwest as expressed by the mission style of architecture. With Sumner Hunt, in 1894 Lummis founded the California Landmarks Club, which helped restore the famous missions of San Luis Capistrano, San Fernando, San Diego, and San Luis Rey. Hunt also collaborated with Lummis to design nineteen floats representing the history of California for the first Los Angeles Fiesta in 1894.[38] And Hunt designed the roof for Lummis's Los Angeles home, El Alisal. Lummis was an early supporter of Hewett's and a leader of the Archaeological Institute of America's Los Angeles Society. He was involved in all the meetings that led to the founding of the School of American Archaeology in 1907 and in the decision to situate it in Santa Fe, under Hewett's direction. Hunt's letter to Hewett mentions Harper Cunningham's illness in Los Angeles. Cunningham never lived to see the project completed. He died on March 10, 1911, and was buried beneath the main stairs of the Scottish Rite Temple.[39]

Although there were numerous delays in raising funds and planning the construction, the cornerstone of the Scottish Rite Temple was laid on August 24, 1911, amid great ceremony, under the auspices of the Most Worshipful Grand Lodge of New Mexico, by Grand Master Edward L. Medler, assisted by Past Grand Masters John J. Kelly, John W. Poe, and William S. Harroun and Grand Secretary A. A. Keen.

Santa Fe Masons and the general public alike gathered for the laying of the cornerstone of the Scottish Rite Temple, August 24, 1911. The Federal Courthouse is visible in the background. Scottish Rite Temple Collection, Palace of the Governors Photo Archives (NMHM/DCA HP.2016.53.004).

The *Albuquerque Journal* described the event as taking place with "Andalusian skies overhead and surrounded by buildings whose mission style recalled the glories of Old Spain." The article said that the building was to be a replica of the Court of the Lions of the Alhambra: "The nearest approach to the Spanish Alhambra to be seen in this country and it will prove a most suitable addition to this land of Spanish romance."[40] A time capsule was laid; it included a pamphlet on Santa Fe by Colonel Ralph E. Twitchell, also a Mason. The ceremony concluded with an address by former New Mexico governor and Scottish Rite Mason L. Bradford Prince. Construction on the temple continued for the remainder of 1911 and through 1912.

The fireproof building was constructed of concrete that was hand-mixed onsite and poured daily. Scaffolding rose, and the cement was carried in buckets and rolled in wheelbarrows. In the basement and elsewhere, one can track the progress of the temple construction by mapping the daily cement pours as they rise up the walls. There was a special preview in late October 1912, when the press and public viewed a test of the scenery machinery. Representatives of the Sosman & Landis Studio of Chicago, which produced the stage drops, were present.[41] Machinery changed the sets so quickly, the *Santa Fe New Mexican* reported, that it reminded the writer of the magic in *One Thousand and One Nights.*[42] In the end, the building cost $165,095, nearly $4 million in 2017 dollars.[43]

The Santa Fe Scottish Rite Temple encased in elaborate scaffolding during construction, 1912. Photograph by Jesse Nusbaum, Scottish Rite Temple Collection, Palace of the Governors Photo Archives (NMHM/DCA HP.2016.53.011).

The New Mexico Museum of Art, which opened in 1917, was adapted by Rapp after a design originally built in San Diego for the New Mexico Building at the Panama California Exposition, 1915. Scottish Rite Mason and Museum of New Mexico staff member Jesse Nusbaum oversaw the construction. Palace of the Governors Photo Archives (NMHM/DCA 016757).

Pueblo Spanish Revival Style Triumphant

The same year the Scottish Rite Temple opened also saw the founding of the Santa Fe city planning board. The group was organized to investigate ways to raise the city's economy out of a thirty-year slump. The commission soon hit upon the idea of promoting the city's ancient adobe architecture as an essential expression of civic identity.[44] The fact that an architectural style based on Santa Fe's adobe buildings quickly gained traction tells us that the Scottish Rite Temple's Moorish revival style was a less popular choice for New Mexico's capital city.

Among the main players in this story were Hewett and the men he hired at the Museum of New Mexico and School of American Archaeology, later the School of American Research. One of Hewett's first hires was Sylvanus G. Morley, who moved to Santa Fe in 1909 after working on Hewett's southwestern archaeological projects for the previous two summers. Morley purchased the old Roque Lobato House (now 311 Bishop's Lodge Road) in 1910 and set about remodeling it, in part to prove that Santa Fe's old adobe homes could be adapted for modern life. He later put the argument to paper in an article published in Twitchell's quarterly *Old Santa Fe* (January 1915).[45] But perhaps the most important event in the history of the Santa Fe architectural style was the New-Old Santa Fe Exhibition, curated by Morley, which made a strong case for the value of Santa Fe's traditional architecture and its potential to attract tourism.

The Southwest Museum, Los Angeles, ca. 1915. Architects Hunt and Burns worked closely with Charles Lummis on the design of the Southwest Museum. Los Angeles Public Library, Security Pacific National Bank Collection (LAPL00031160).

An article in the *Santa Fe New Mexican* on November 19, 1912, just two days after the Scottish Rite Temple opened, led with the headline "New-Old Exposition Is a Decided Hit" and noted that the exposition had opened the previous evening in the Palace of the Governors and that it featured models of Santa Fe–style architecture and proposals for homes and projects to give several areas of the city the Santa Fe treatment. In *The Myth of Santa Fe*, Wilson advances that it was the Scottish Rite Temple, rather than any Spanish Pueblo revival–style structure, that initiated the city's search in the early twentieth century for a unique architectural identity.[46] Francaviglia argues that Santa Fe had been considered partly Moorish because of the relationship of its adobe architecture with traditional building techniques of the Moorish world, especially in Northwest Africa.[47]

Ralph E. Twitchell, a Scottish Rite Mason, attorney, and New Mexico's most prominent historian of the early twentieth century, expressed this sentiment in a promotional pamphlet he wrote in 1912 for the Santa Fe Railway: "Something of that intangible air of mystery that the Moors brought from the far East to Granada was transplanted to American soil by the conquistadores." He continued to say that New Mexico's landscape "must have reminded them of their Iberian home."[48] His point is well taken, since the history of Santa Fe representing itself with Spanish

The Santa Fe Scottish Rite Temple was completed just in time for the first Fall Reunion, held November 18–20, 1912, only one day after the building was dedicated. Photograph by Jesse Nusbaum, Palace of the Governors Photo Archives (NMHM/DCA 061379).

The original blueprint for the front entrance. Photograph by Martin Stupich for the HABS Collection, Library of Congress, Washington, DC.

Sixty members of the 1912 Dedication Class pose on the steps of the new Santa Fe Scottish Rite Temple. Sylvanus G. Morley was a member of the Dedication Class. Photograph by Jesse Nusbaum, Palace of the Governors Photo Archives (NMHM/DCA 061385).

Pueblo revival–style architecture appears to be tied solely to the New-Old Santa Fe Exhibition and the efforts of men like Hewett, Morley, and Nusbaum. But as the story of the Scottish Rite Temple shows, Spanish Pueblo revival style was not the only possibility for architecture that was Spanish but not California mission style. After it was rejected by the Santa Fe Scottish Rite, Isaac Rapp adapted his design for the Scottish Rite Temple for the Las Animas County Courthouse in Trinidad, Colorado (1912).

Once Santa Fe committed to the Spanish Pueblo revival style, Rapp was the architect of choice, completing important projects such as the Gross, Kelly and Company Warehouse in the Santa Fe Railyard (1914), the New Mexico Building at the Panama California Exposition in San Diego (1915), the New Mexico Museum of Art (1917), and the 1920 renovation of La Fonda hotel.[49] After the Scottish Rite Temple, Sumner Hunt went on to design many important projects in Los Angeles, particularly the Southwest Museum, which Charles Lummis had founded. Like the Santa Fe Scottish Rite Temple, the Southwest Museum is in the Moorish revival style. The groundbreaking took place the same day the Santa Fe Scottish Rite Temple was dedicated.

The Scottish Rite Temple, view from the southeast, 2016. Twenty-nine steps—one for each of the Scottish Rite Masonic Degrees—lead up to the Santa Fe Scottish Rite Temple entrance.

Scottish Rite Temple, Then and Now

The Main Entrance

The main entrance to the Scottish Rite Temple is reached by climbing twenty-nine steps from street level, with one step for each of the degrees presented in this branch of Freemasonry, from the Fourth through the Thirty-second Degrees.[50]

Since the building opened, the front steps have been an important location for photographing Santa Fe's Scottish Rite Masons. Beneath the steps is a crypt housing the remains of Harper Cunningham and his wife. As related above, although he died before the cornerstone was laid, Cunningham deserves credit for starting the process that led to the creation of the Santa Fe Scottish Rite Temple. The crypt also contains the remains of Martin Ferguson, a Scottish Rite Mason who was indigent and buried by the order as an act of charity. When the City of Santa Fe intended to enlarge the street in front of the Scottish Rite Temple, enforcing eminent domain to have the stairs removed, the presence of human remains under the stairs prevented that desecration of the building.

The upper lobby and administrative offices of the Scottish Rite Temple have changed little over the past century (top, *1950;* bottom, *2016*).

Entrance to the theater balcony in the upper lobby. The bronze portrait of Albert Pike (1809–91), considered a modern founder of the Scottish Rite in the United States, was a gift of the Governor Charles Bent Class, initiated May 1924.

Upper Lobby and Offices

At the top of the stairs is a doorway framed by a multifoil horseshoe arch framed by an alfiz—all elements found at the Alhambra and elsewhere in Islamic architecture. Beyond is a reception room, with stained-glass windows dedicated to Solomon Spitz and Richard Henry Hanna, early-twentieth-century leaders of the Santa Fe Scottish Rite. Spitz (1852–1927) owned a jewelry store on the Santa Fe Plaza and installed the large clock that still stands at the corner of Lincoln and Palace Avenues, in front of the New Mexico Museum of Art. Hanna (1878–1946) was instrumental in superintending the construction of the Scottish Rite Temple. He served as Deputy of the Supreme Council in New Mexico from 1911 to 1924, served on the first New Mexico Supreme Court after statehood (1912–19), and was a key figure in the passage of federal legislation relating to Native American lands, especially the Pueblo Lands Act of 1924. In 1899 Hanna formed a law firm with Francis Cushman Wilson, another Scottish Rite member, who later served as attorney for the Pueblo Indians of New Mexico.[51]

The offices of the Santa Fe Scottish Rite's four constituent bodies are located on this level. From this space a door leads to the balcony of the theater and a staircase gives access to one of the dormitory spaces, the library, and the tower. Another staircase leads down to the lower lobby and the banquet hall. Two pictorial Navajo rugs, dating to the early twentieth century, hang over the landing.

While one depicts the Scottish Rite Temple and is dated 1911, the other is an altar cloth with symbols of different Masonic groups, including the Symbolic Lodge, the York Rite, the Shriners, the Order of the Eastern Star, and the four Scottish Rite Bodies. Many Masonic groups require that a book of sacred scripture be displayed on an altar when the lodge is in session. Whether the book is the King James Bible, the Quran, the Hebrew Torah, or another text depends upon the religion of those present at the meeting. While altar cloths are commonly used in Masonic ritual, they are not usually of Navajo manufacture, a fact that speaks to Santa Fe's location in the southwestern United States. The temple also counts among its collections another Navajo rug altar cloth, which was given by Brother E. R. Vaughn of Guam, New Mexico, a member of the Cunningham Class (April 1911). Guam was located in McKinley County, in western New Mexico.[52] Next door to the Scottish Rite Temple, Montezuma Lodge No. 1 has a Navajo rug with Masonic symbols hanging in its lodge room.

The main entrance to the theater is in the lower lobby. Installed in 1916, the lobby is decorated with a floor mosaic of the double-headed eagle, a Scottish Rite symbol, and a statue of George Washington, US president and Mason.

The upper lobby stairwell is decorated with Navajo Indian pictorial rugs with Masonic themes. On top is a small rug, dated 1911, with an image of the Scottish Rite Temple. On the bottom is an early-twentieth-century rug that was used as an altar cloth. It displays symbols of the four Scottish Rite Bodies, as well as symbols of other Masonic orders, including the York Rite, the Symbolic Lodge, the Order of the Eastern Star, and the Shrine.

Early-twentieth-century Scottish Rite Masons living near Navajo Indians gave traditional rugs as gifts to their Masonic lodges, including Santa Fe's Montezuma Lodge No. 1 (left)*. Handwoven rugs, such as one that now hangs in the Scottish Rite Temple development office* (right)*, were also used as Masonic altar cloths.*

The Cody Class, initiated in March 1918, included 175 soldiers from Camp Cody, New Mexico, who were training for deployment during World War I. Collection of the Scottish Rite Temple, Santa Fe.

A PLACE FOR SCOTTISH RITE REUNIONS Santa Fe's Scottish Rite Masons use the building for many functions, from the fraternal to the charitable. The temple has also been used by outside organizations for social events, including high school graduations, art fairs, operatic performances, and even Hollywood film productions. While the constituent bodies of the Santa Fe Scottish Rite meet monthly to conduct routine business, degrees are either communicated or conferred to candidates twice per year at special meetings called reunions, at present held in May and October.[53] These gatherings are called reunions because they offer Scottish Rite Masons from the Northern New Mexico district, called the Valley of Santa Fe, an opportunity to meet and renew bonds of fellowship in the context of a three-day affair, where candidates participate in and witness the Fourth through Thirty-second Degrees. Candidates and members spend hours together, using spaces at the temple that were designed for various reunion-related activities, from degree presentations to meals and banquets, study and instruction, and even overnight stays, all discussed below. During the 2016 May reunion, 346 Masons participated. Of this number, approximately 109 individuals—almost one-third of the attendees—filled specific roles during the event, in the areas of registration (5), dining room (5), kitchen (7), store (3), class directions (7), tiling (15), degree communications (7), direction of degree work (4), music (16), stage (10), sound and light (3), small properties (6), wardrobe (13), makeup (3), and publications (5). This is a far cry from 1936, when 150 members were solely involved with the degree productions during each reunion.

The Valley of Santa Fe assigns a number to each reunion, from the first, held in 1909.[54] A name is given to each group of candidates to identify their class. Some of the names honor historical figures or notable Masons, while others refer to significant events, like the Statehood Class, so named because it was the first to be initiated after the Territory of New Mexico became the forty-seventh US state in 1912. Scottish Rite Masons initiated in the First Reunion, held on April 26–28, 1909, were named the Aleph Class. Among the forty candidates was Edgar Lee Hewett, who suggested the temple's Moorish revival style a year later. His classmates included Masons from all over New Mexico—from Albuquerque, Cerrillos, Chama, Clayton, Clovis, Datil, Dawson, Lake Valley, Las Vegas, Mountainair, Raton, Rincon, Roswell, Van Houten, Watrous, and Willard. For a time before each reunion, the Santa Fe Railway advertised special rates in the *Santa Fe New Mexican* for Masons traveling to the capital from the state's farthest reaches. Three years later, the sixty members of the Dedication Class were so called because they were the first to be initiated in November 1912 in the newly completed temple.

The 1912 Dedication Class at the Santa Fe Scottish Rite gifted this Moorish revival altar as a memorial. It is still used during contemporary reunions.

Most of the two hundred initiates at the Twenty-Seventh Reunion, held March 18–20, 1918, and called the Cody Class, were soldiers training for World War I who had traveled to Santa Fe from Camp Cody, located near Deming in southern New Mexico. The Cody Class was one of the largest in the history of the Valley of Santa Fe and was even more notable in that it was held just a month after the Twenty-Sixth Reunion to initiate as many candidates as possible before they left for the war in Europe.[55] During World War I, bulletins of the Valley of Santa Fe were filled with rosters of Scottish Rite Masons from New Mexico serving in the military, as well as letters from Europe and notices that members were well received at the offices of the Orient of France, headquarters of French Freemasonry. Inevitably, there were also obituaries of those Brethren who died in the war. During World War II, the Eighty-Ninth Reunion, held in November 1944, was organized solely to initiate US servicemen.[56] The 105th Reunion, held May 7–10, 1951, was one of the largest, with 175 initiates. That reunion coincided with completion of a significant expansion of the temple, including enclosure of the courtyard and the dormitory wing.[57]

GIFTS BY SCOTTISH RITE CLASSES Many Scottish Rite classes made gifts to the temple after their initiation. The Dedication Class (November 1912) commissioned a Moorish revival altar to be used as a prop for several of the degrees.[58]

Corner Stone
August 21-22-23-24 1911

Opposite: *Stained-glass windows in the theater were gifts from different Scottish Rite Mason reunion classes. These are from the Cornerstone Statehood Class, 1911* (left); *the Alhambra Class, 1913* (center)*; and the Kit Carson Class, 1925* (right).

Other classes donated stained-glass windows for the theater, including one with an image of a five-pointed star, a common Masonic and Scottish Rite symbol, donated by the Cornerstone Statehood Class (1911); a window given by the Rose Croix Class (1915);[59] another donated by the Service Class (1918);[60] one with the Scottish Rite symbol of the double-headed eagle, donated by the Kit Carson Class (1925); a window with a kneeling man praying, from the V-E Day Class (1945); and one with the Masonic square and compasses, from the Louis C. Crockett Class (1944). Stained-glass windows without dedications show George Washington dressed as the Master of his lodge; a Seal of Solomon, or six-pointed star; the scales, symbols of justice; and an image of the Alhambra.

While some reunion class gifts were directed toward improving the temple, others were directed toward charity. Scottish Rite members, like all Freemasons, believe in a higher power. Charity, along with Faith and Hope, represents one of the three pillars of the organization. Santa Fe Scottish Rite Bodies have more than a century of history of charitable activities in the community. We read in the *Santa Fe Scottish Rite Bulletin* in November 1918 that the Service Class (February 1918) contributed $288 to the Almoner's Fund, equivalent to almost $5,000 in 2017 dollars.[61] Each Scottish Rite Valley has an Almoner, who reviews requests for financial assistance, which are kept confidential. In 1989 the New Mexico Scottish Rite Masons founded the Rite Care program, assisting dyslexic children. Scottish Rite Masons from both Valleys of the Orient of New Mexico participate in the program.[62] The Santa Fe Scottish Rite also gave back to the community by contributing about $93,000 in discounts to nonprofits that organized events in the building in 2016.

The Santa Fe Scottish Rite Bodies also have a long history of supporting education outside the Fraternity. In 1916 the New Mexico Education Association held its annual session in the new building, where Scottish Rite Mason Frank H. H. Roberts of East Las Vegas was elected president of the association. The retiring New Mexico Education Association secretary, J. H. Wagnerhad, who was also a Mason, had been elected the state superintendent of schools at the state election the previous month.[63] The Scottish Rite encourages members to study and expand their knowledge about other peoples, times, and places. The order teaches that education is the foundation for productive citizens who can positively affect society. In 1927 the *Santa Fe Scottish Rite Bulletin* published the following statement: "We are all intensely interested in the development of our state materially, intellectually, educationally and in the tone and character of its citizenship. Did it ever occur to you that there is not a greater force acting within the bodies of social life in New Mexico, looking toward the building up of a sober, industrious, capable, reliable, tolerant and enlightened citizenship than the Scottish Rite."[64]

The Fraternity has supported the instruction of not only its members but also the next generation to shape the future. In the 1960s, the Santa Fe Scottish Rite began to sponsor academic scholarships, helping students attend George Washington University in Washington, DC, and the University of New Mexico School of Medicine.[65] The Scottish Rite also contributes an additional $150 toward every educational scholarship awarded by Symbolic Lodges throughout New Mexico.

The library at the Santa Fe Scottish Rite Temple contains many rare books on Masonic and esoteric subjects.

The Library

The significance of education is nowhere as apparent as in the libraries of many Masonic buildings, whether in Symbolic Lodges or Scottish Rite Temples. Especially for Scottish Rite Masonry, further study is essential for greater understanding of many degrees. In 1917 Frank Staplin was appointed the official librarian of the Valley of Santa Fe and immediately began raising funds and securing books. Two years later, he started a drive to purchase much needed bookcases for volumes that were already on hand and a number of books and other publications that were badly needed: "[for] reference and study, particularly by members whose privilege it is to be where they have an opportunity of exemplifying the greater part of the 'work.'"[66] Then as now few public libraries owned books about Freemasonry or the Scottish Rite. Access to highly specialized or esoteric publications remained limited. Many Scottish Rite libraries are thus collections of rare and hard-to-find books, such as encyclopedias of world religions, histories of Freemasonry, dictionaries of symbols, and compendiums of rituals.

The bulletins of the Santa Fe Scottish Rite are peppered with references to the library and notices of valuable donations. The June 1915 bulletin noted that for some time the New Mexico Scottish Rite Bodies had been accumulating books and publications for the temple library and that if any Brother had a Masonic work of any kind and wished to donate it, it would be accepted.[67] In 1941 Edgar Lee Hewett donated several books, including the seven-volume *History of Freemasonry* (1898–1905) by Albert G. Mackey and W. R. Singleton and a two-volume *Encyclopedia of Freemasonry* by Mackey and Charles T. McClenachan.[68] The library also houses rare editions of historical works, such as David Roberts's illustrated *The Holy Land* and Owen Jones's *Grammar of Ornament*. Furthermore, wives often donated their husbands' collection as memorials; the widow of Louis C. Rocket presented the library with a six-volume set of Mackey's *Revised History of Freemasonry*.[69]

The library was originally located in a spacious room on the third floor of the tower, which also served as a reception and waiting room. That space underwent various changes over the years, including its partial conversion into a dormitory and

The reception room and library, above the upper lobby, were converted into a dormitory during the early 1950s due to record numbers of candidates traveling from all over New Mexico to receive degrees. The keyhole-shaped windows are hallmarks of the Moorish revival style.

installation of washroom facilities in 1959. In 2015 the library was moved to a secure area on the same floor, near the head of the stairs, when the crew for the Paramount Pictures film *Whiskey Tango Foxtrot* turned the space into a set featuring the front desk of the Kabul Hotel. The library still houses many important publications about Freemasonry and the Scottish Rite. It also contains painted portraits of Santa Fe Scottish Rite members Thomas B. Catron and Will Shuster.

In 2015 the dormitory was made to look like the Kabul Hotel lobby as a film set for the Paramount Pictures movie Whiskey Tango Foxtrot. *Photograph by Frank Masi, © Paramount Pictures 2016.*

The Classroom

Classrooms and other teaching spaces are found in many Scottish Rite buildings because instruction, discussion, and continuing education are essential aspects of Freemasonry in general and the Scottish Rite in particular. The classroom at the Santa Fe Scottish Rite Temple is located across the lobby from the main entrance to the theater. The space is used during reunions for degrees that are communicated rather than staged. Depending on the will of the leadership, the classroom is sometimes also used for the monthly business meetings of the Scottish Rite constituent bodies and for meetings of the Building Committee.

In 1952 the classroom was enlarged to accommodate up to 170, the largest number of candidates who could sit in the theater seats that were also upgraded at the time.[70] A restroom was installed in the rear of the classroom. In 1967 a considerable sum was spent to remodel the classroom space, which is why this room does not match the rest of the building's style.

On the classroom walls are photographs of every deceased Thirty-third Degree Scottish Rite Mason from the Valley of Santa Fe. The Thirty-third Degree is an honor bestowed on Scottish Rite Masons. The photos are a regular who's who of twentieth-century New Mexico history. Thomas B. Catron (discussed in chapter 2) is there, as is Clinton P. Anderson, who served in both houses of the US Congress, with more than twenty years in the Senate (1949–73). Anderson divided his time between New Mexico and Washington, DC, and was known at the Santa Fe Scottish Rite for playing the role of the Satrap in the Fifteenth Degree.

Photographs of living Thirty-third Degree honorees hang in the theater lobby outside the classroom. The classroom is frequently used as a dressing room for brides being married in the theater and as a cloakroom when the building is buzzing with large events.

The Banquet Hall

One of the largest spaces at the Scottish Rite Temple is the banquet hall, which is used for both fraternal and community events. The hall features custom Moorish revival wooden chairs and chandeliers once thought to have been made by Louis Comfort Tiffany. The minutes of the Board of Directors show that the light fixtures were furnished by the Mandel Brothers department store in Chicago, with brackets supplied by Santa Fe's Seligman Brothers and the glass globes by Frank Hill.[71] The chandeliers were designed for fraternal use, since they feature the Shrine crescent symbol. The banquet hall originally ended where a row of Moorish revival columns divides the space. It was enlarged in the 1950s. The rear third of the hall was the original kitchen. The banquet hall is used during reunions for meals and as a place to socialize. Each year the Scottish Rite constituent bodies hold four ceremonial banquets, including a feast of remembrance for deceased brothers.

Many community organizations also use the banquet hall. Even before the Scottish Rite Temple officially opened, dances were held in the banquet hall. The *Santa Fe New Mexican* reported on December 3, 1912, about the continuing progress of construction and noted that the question on the minds of non-Masons was "How about another dance in that fine hall?" The vignette is recorded in the *Santa Fe Scottish Rite Bulletin*, suggesting that the banquet hall was the first space to be completed

View of the Scottish Rite Temple from Bishop's Lodge Road, showing the dining hall and the 1950s addition at right, 2017.

The banquet hall was the first space of the Santa Fe Scottish Rite Temple to be completed. It includes Arts and Crafts–style chandeliers and custom Moorish revival–style chairs. The banquet hall is used not only for reunions and Masonic ceremonials but also for community events.

and that dances may have been held there to raise funds for the continuing construction.[72] In 2016 and 2017, the Keshi Foundation held the Zuni Show in the banquet hall, with more than one hundred Native artists selling arts and crafts to the public. The hall has hosted art auctions, wedding receptions, flamenco performances, and a Bollywood dance party. Santa Fe's Museum of International Folk Art held a chocolate tasting in the banquet hall, related to an exhibition on New World cuisines. Santa Fe High School held dances in the banquet hall until the 1950s, when loud music and vibrations caused one of the roof tiles to fall. Dances were then banned, until the 1990s.[73]

Recently, the Santa Fe arts collective Meow Wolf used the hall for a party to celebrate the burning of Zozobra, a Santa Fe tradition started by artist and Scottish Rite member Will Shuster. For more than fifty years, Shuster's fellow Mason Harold Gans groaned as the voice of Zozobra—Old Man Gloom—as he burned in the Fiesta tradition. As Shuster aged, Gans was instrumental in getting the Kiwanis Club to take over the event, which has become a scholarship fund-raiser.

Annually, an effigy called Zozobra burns during the Santa Fe Fiesta. Scottish Rite Mason and artist Will Shuster designed and built the first Zozobra in 1924. For decades, fellow Scottish Rite Mason Harold Gans was the voice of Zozobra. Palace of the Governors Photo Archives (NMHM/DCA 047328).

The Kitchen

At the far end of the banquet hall and running along one side of the courtyard is the industrial kitchen and serving room. The original kitchen was located in what is now the northern end of the banquet hall. When the temple was enlarged in 1951 to relieve cramped quarters resulting from a recent growth in membership, a new kitchen was added. It was said to be the largest kitchen in New Mexico, until it was superseded by the kitchen at the state penitentiary.[74] Other additions included the

The 1951 kitchen in the new addition (left, *photograph by Martin Stupich for the HABS Collection, Library of Congress, Washington, DC), with coffee urns* (right, *photograph by Jo Whaley). Feeding hundreds of Masons during reunions requires a large kitchen. Throughout much of the twentieth century, the Santa Fe Scottish Rite Temple kitchen was one of the largest in New Mexico.*

"dormitories for degree workers, the large robing room on the first floor, spacious quarters for the choir, and the storage room and workshop."[75] The bulletins singled out two men for their key roles in the planning and construction of this additions: Scottish Rite Valley Secretary Leslie Gillett and Trent Thomas, the architect who had worked for Isaac Rapp on La Fonda hotel (1920). Thomas died just before the addition was completed.

Since its initial construction, the kitchen has fed generations of Masons during fraternal events, such as monthly business meetings, special feasts, and reunions. The stainless-steel countertops continue to feed not only area Masons but also many in the surrounding community. Caterers from throughout the region use the space to prepare thousands of meals, ranging from wedding banquets to school lunches. The kitchen has also been a set for the television show *Longmire*, where it served as a morgue.

The Courtyard and Tower

West of the banquet hall and south of the kitchen, the central courtyard evokes the outdoor spaces and terrace gardens at the Alhambra, especially the Court of the Myrtles.[76] Although the program for the Tenth Reunion of the Santa Fe Scottish Rite (1912) states that the courtyard was modeled after the Court of the Lions at

The Alhambra's Court of the Myrtles was an inspiration for the courtyard at the Santa Fe Scottish Rite Temple. Left: *photograph taken in winter by Juan Laurent in the late-nineteenth century, The Hallwyl Museum, Stockholm.* Right: *Santa Fe Scottish Rite Temple, 2016. Photograph by Martin Stupich for the HABS Collection, Library of Congress, Washington, DC.*

Opposite: *The Santa Fe Scottish Rite Temple courtyard was inspired by both the Court of the Myrtles and the Court of the Lions at the Alhambra. The courtyard was enclosed in 1951.*

The garden room of the tower is now primarily used for storage of abandoned items, like these decommissioned roof vents. Horizontal lines on the walls mark the daily pours of concrete during the building of the temple in 1911–12. All the concrete for the building was mixed by hand and moved to the site by wheelbarrow and bucket and raised by pulley.

Scottish Rite Mason and photographer Jesse Nusbaum captured this view of Santa Fe in 1912, taken from the temple's tower room, the highest room in the structure. Palace of the Governors Photo Archives (NMHM/DCA 061382).

the Alhambra, it bears only a superficial resemblance to that storied patio.[77] When the temple debuted in 1912, the courtyard was open on the north and west sides. The space was enclosed in 1951 with the aforementioned addition of a new kitchen and dormitory wing. The addition continued the Moorish revival style of the original Hunt and Burns structure, including pitched roofs of red tile. Today the courtyard is planted with grass and flowers and is used for weddings and public events, fraternal and otherwise. During the 2016 and 2017 Zuni Shows, Native dances were presented in the courtyard.

High above the courtyard, rising 71 feet above street level, looms the tower. This prominent feature of the building combines architectural attributes from both the Alhambra's Gate of Justice (1348) and the Comares Tower (early fourteenth century). Windows in the upper story command a beautiful view of Santa Fe. This space was initially intended as an enclosed garden terrace. Unfortunately, the room immediately attracted birds and has remained closed for most of the building's history. It is now home to many abandoned artifacts.

The Dormitories

Large Scottish Rite temples built in the United States prior to 1950 often included dormitories, because reunions required members to travel long distances to Masonic spaces for stated degree work. Some members stayed in hotels, and in the 1910s the

Santa Fe New Mexican identified many who traveled to the capital for Scottish Rite reunions on the society page or in lists of out-of-towners and their hotels. But staying at the Scottish Rite Temple itself encouraged social ties among men from all over the state. In 2016, candidates for Scottish Rite degrees were expected to be seated in the theater no later than 7:30 a.m., and the last degrees often finished after 11:00 p.m., making for very long days.

A dormitory wing was added to the Scottish Rite Temple when the west side of the courtyard was built in 1951. The third floor of the tower was converted into a dormitory in 1959–60 with the addition of metal bunk beds and a washroom, which was later renovated to include showers.[78] Above the kitchen on the north side of the temple are rooms that were originally a lounge for female family members of Masons attending meetings and reunions. Reunions always include women's programs, such as lectures and sightseeing. That space is now used as an overflow dormitory and the development office. While bulletins mention that additional space for candidates to sleep was once sorely needed, at present, classes of initiates are smaller and dormitory spaces are primarily used by Brothers who travel to Santa Fe to assist with the reunion.

The Auditorium

Much of the reunion activity focuses on degree productions, which take place in the theater. The interior of the theater was described in a 1916 issue of the *Santa Fe Scottish Rite Bulletin* as a "symphony of rich brown, the walls, tapestry and carpets being different shades of brown and gold."[79] It was this dark background that allowed the metallic gold painting on much of the architectural ornamentation to dance with life. Deep gold is the hue of the painted wooden screens in the southwest and northwest corners, the latter concealing the organ and the choir loft. The columns, walls, and proscenium are also painted gold or golden brown, with complex painted designs that echo the Islamic art in Owen Jones's *Grammar of Ornament*. As depicted in the illustrations, brilliant jewel tones dot the recesses of the gold decor, such as in the proscenium opening to the stage. The proscenium is flanked by gold-colored stucco in the geometric and star patterns common at the Alhambra, also adapted from Jones.

The ceiling of the theater is elaborately painted as the vault of the sky and is used to suggest nighttime skies for some of the degree work. Many believe that the thirty-two stars lit by electric lightbulbs signify the First through Thirty-second Degrees of Freemasonry. The selected constellations suggest Masonic instruction for

When the Santa Fe Scottish Rite Temple opened in November 1912, many details of the theater were incomplete. These images show an early reunion class in the theater, with the proscenium, organ, and choir loft screens still incomplete (top), *and a 1915 view of the theater after completion, showing the mural above the proscenium* (bottom). *Photographs by Jesse Nusbaum, Palace of the Governors Photo Archives (NMHM/DCA 061383 and 023100).*

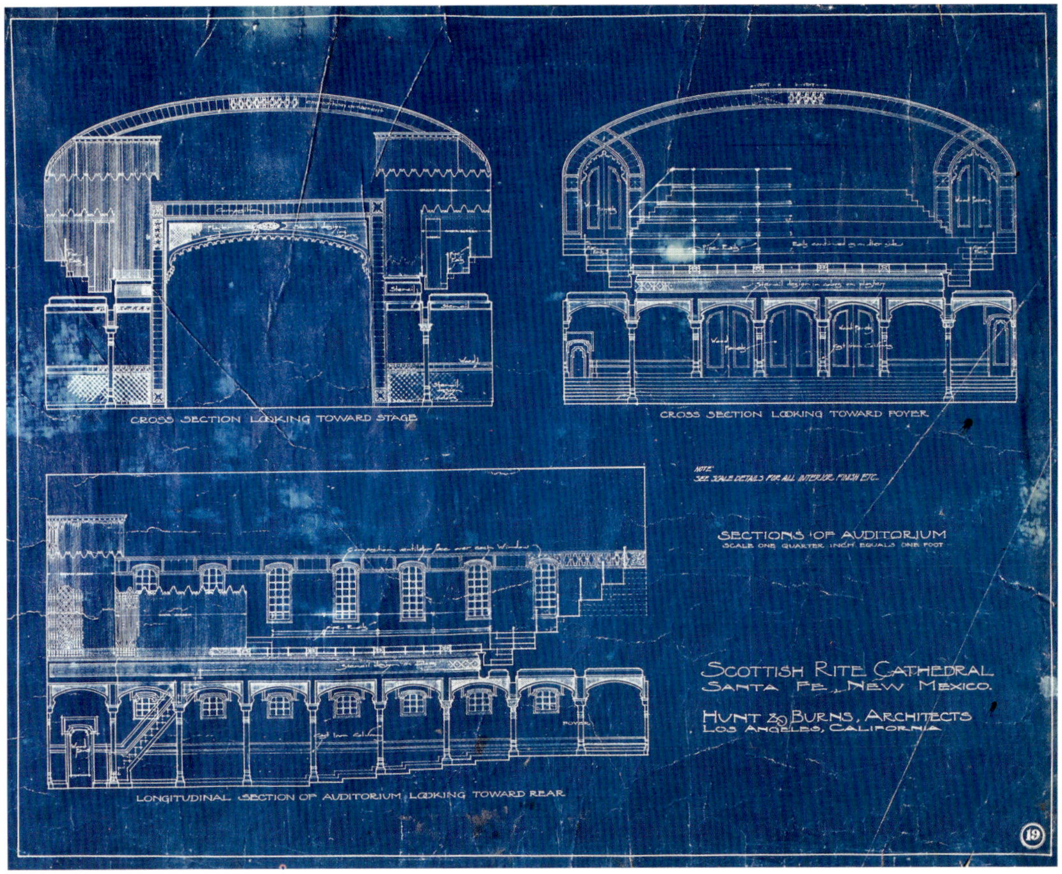

Above, left: *Original blueprint depicting a sectional view of the Santa Fe Scottish Rite auditorium by architects Hunt and Burns of Los Angeles. Photograph by Martin Stupich for the HABS Collection, Library of Congress, Washington, DC.*

Above, right: *Geometric designs on the theater curtain and the proscenium were adapted from Owen Jones's drawings of the Alhambra, published in his* Grammar of Ornament, *1856. Scenic artists also referenced Jones's book when painting backdrops, such as the Santa Fe Scottish Rite front curtain. Collection of the Scottish Rite Temple.*

the Second Degree of the Scottish Rite, which is seldom performed.[80] The interior decoration was incomplete when the Dedication Class took its degrees in November 1912. Two years later, after the contract for the decoration was put out to bid and assigned, it was described as having "an elaborate color scheme with tinting and fresco," but there is no mention of the designer.[81] The interior decorations were not completed until February 1915.[82]

The Scottish Rite Temple theater today with the Forest *scene. The circular medallion with the Hebrew letter* yod *mounted on the left screen was brought from the former Scottish Rite Masonic meeting rooms on Water Street in Santa Fe.*

Left: *The ceiling of the Scottish Rite Temple is painted to show the sky with thirty-two stars arranged in constellations. It is used in some of the degrees that are set at night.*

THE VYSEKEL PAINTING The interior decorations were not completed until February 1915 with the installation of J. G. Vysekel's painting above the proscenium arch.[83] Vysekel was a commercial artist for Mandel Brothers of Chicago, hired to paint the mural to be installed above the proscenium. A front-page article in the *Santa Fe New Mexican* on January 9, 1915, noted that the Santa Fe firm of Seligman Brothers directed the work and that Vysekel's painting, in six sections, had arrived from Chicago and was stretched out on the floor of the Scottish Rite dining hall for all to admire. The painting shows the capitulation of Boabdil, or Muhammad XII, to the Spanish monarchs Ferdinand and Isabella. The episode marked the end of seven hundred years of Islamic control of large regions of the Iberian Peninsula and was likely selected to highlight how Santa Fe's history, culture, and architecture were entwined with aspects of both Christian and Islamic Spain. The painting is related to, but not an exact copy of, *La Rendición de Granada* by Francisco Pradilla y Ortiz (1882), in the collection of the Senado de España, which itself is modeled on Diego Velázquez's *La Rendición de* Breda (1634–35).[84]

SEATING When the building opened in 1912, there were 96 swivel seats on the orchestra level of the theater and another 117 seats in the balcony upstairs; wire frames under the seats were designed to hold the large cowboy hats common to the Southwest. With two hundred initiates, the Cody Class of 1918 nearly exhausted the theater's seating capacity, leaving just thirteen seats for visitors or Brothers who were not involved in the degree teams. The theater seating was reimagined in 1953, when the orchestra level was redeveloped as a ramp and the seats were more closely spaced, resulting in 164 large opera seats without expansion of the footprint. This change coincided with enlargement of the seating capacity of the classroom to equal the number of class chairs in the auditorium. Since 1953 the theater has accommodated 331 patrons.[85]

THE ORGAN Instrumental and choral music has always played an essential role in the presentation of Santa Fe Scottish Rite degrees. The theater was designed to include a pipe organ, which is concealed behind a gold-painted decorative screen above stage left, in the theater's northwest corner. The pipe organ was installed in November 1912, just one week before the Tenth Reunion. Manufactured by the Los Angeles firm Murray M. Harris Company, the organ consists of 1,173 pipes and cost $5,000. Organ concerts for the public were an early fixture of reunion programming and were described in the *Santa Fe Scottish Rite Bulletin* as "rapidly becoming one of the most interesting features of the reunions."[86] The Scottish Rite organist gave

Opposite: *Above the proscenium arch is J. G. Vysekel's mural of the surrender of Muhammad XII to the Spanish monarchs Isabella and Ferdinand, installed in 1915, three years after the building opened.*

PAINTED BY
MANDEL BROTHERS

View from the stage of the Santa Fe Scottish Rite Temple auditorium. The number of theater seats was greatly increased in the early 1950s.

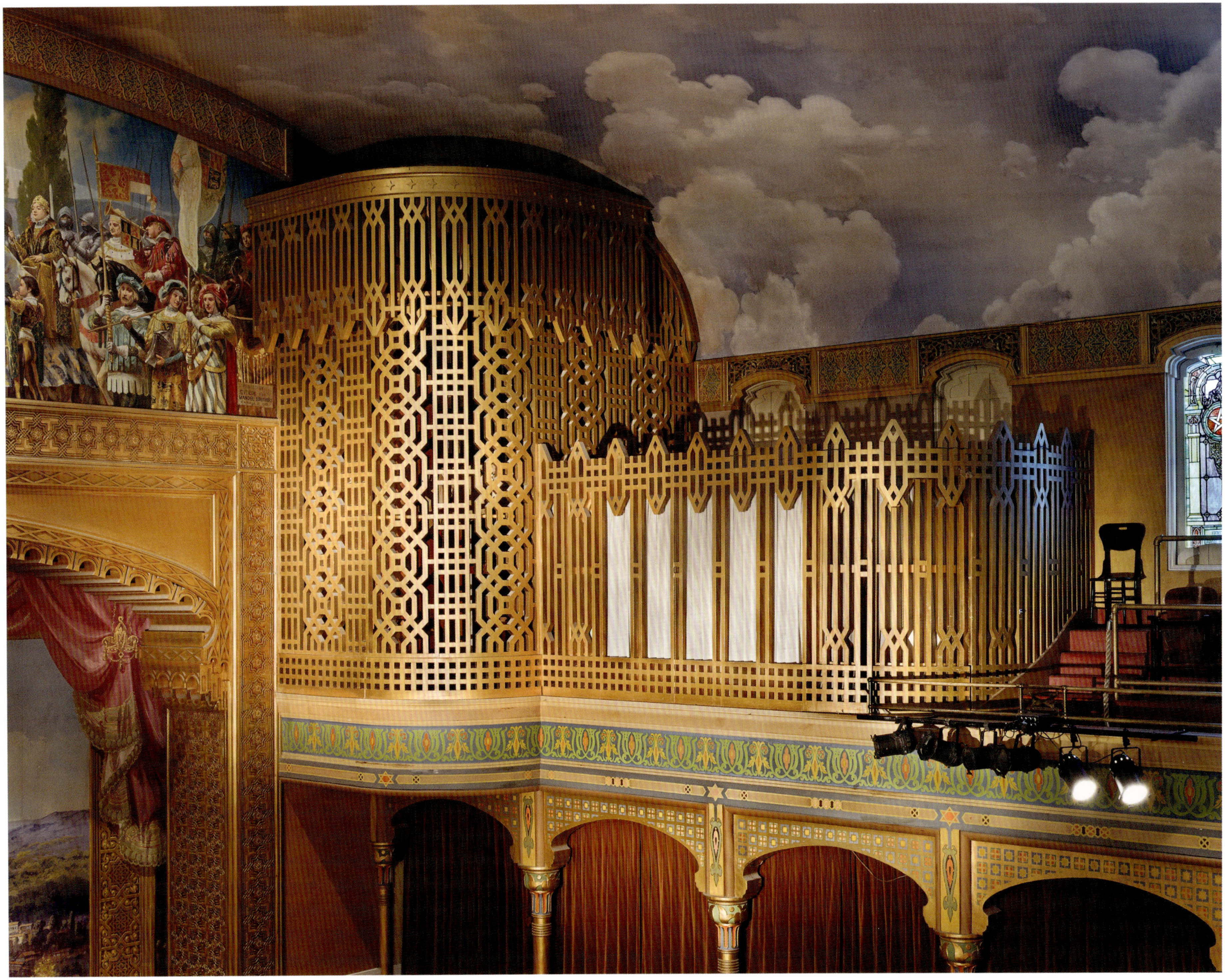

The organ and choir loft at the temple are concealed behind a golden screen. Music plays an important role in Scottish Rite degrees. The painted frieze decorations above the stained-glass windows, below the choir loft, and on the capitals of the columns are all drawn from Owen Jones's Grammar of Ornament, *1856.*

recitals during the evening before each reunion. Interestingly, during the World War I era, women were selected to both play the organ during degrees and lead the Scottish Rite choir. The organ was completely overhauled during the summer of 1958, and a second electric organ was purchased for use in some of the other degree work.

When the temple opened, the theater included a choir loft in the space next to the organ. The choir included both men and women; special curtains prevented the women from seeing actors or sets in the theater below. Observing the Scottish Rite degrees is for initiates and the initiated only, and at present, women are ineligible. In 1917 a total of nineteen singers and musicians, including the organist and a cellist, provided musical accompaniment for the degrees.[87] Today, music still plays an important role in Scottish Rite degrees. For example, the choir and organ present the aria "O Isis and Osiris" from Freemason W. A. Mozart's *The Magic Flute* in the first section of the Thirty-first Degree, which, like Mozart's opera, is set in ancient Egypt. Since 1964 the choir has been all male.[88] Above the northwest corner, the curved screen is decorated with a round emblem with a star and a *yod* within. *Yod* is a Hebrew letter and is the first letter of the name of God. This emblem is one of the only artifacts brought from the old Scottish Rite meeting space on Water Street in Santa Fe.

THE FRONT CURTAIN Perhaps the most impressive aspect of the theater is the 20-by-30-foot front drop curtain behind the 19-by-26-foot proscenium arch. The purpose of the painted front curtain was to complete the fourth wall of the auditorium space, linking three-dimensional architectural ornamentation of the auditorium with the promise of pictorial illusion that lay just behind the proscenium arch. The decorative painting around the curtain's perimeter mirrors the dimensional detail of the proscenium arch, framing a historic scene. The composition depicts the scene of Granada as viewed from the Alhambra. At the right is the Islamic city, while at left we can see the tent city headquarters of the troops of the Spanish monarchs Ferdinand and Isabella. Writing in the *Santa Fe New Mexican* on November 20, 1912, Nan O'Neill discussed the drop curtain and how it depicted the original Santa Fe, in Granada, a town connected to the Spanish discovery and conquest of the New World and eventually to Santa Fe, New Mexico. Interestingly, the central placard of the frame, which was common to most drop curtains, was left blank, leaving the painting's title a mystery. Although the artist of this work remains unknown, the individual was in the employ of the same studio that created the remainder of the scenery collection. (The origins and evolution of painted scenery for the Scottish Rite stage are presented in chapter 4 by Wendy Waszut-Barrett.)

Opposite: *The painted front curtain shows a view from one of the terraces at the Alhambra, depicting the Islamic city of Granada in 1492, during the Spanish siege. The Spanish forces' tent city is visible in the hills in the upper left.*

USE OF THE THEATER, THEN AND NOW From the beginning, many members of the Masonic family, as well as outside groups, used the Santa Fe Scottish Rite Temple theater. Santa Fe High School, founded in 1899 and originally located nearby on Lincoln Avenue, held its annual graduation ceremonies in the temple theater until the 1950s.[89] One of first fraternal groups to use the temple theater was the Order of the Eastern Star (OES), a Masonic fraternal order for Master Masons and their female relatives. The OES held its Grand Chapter meeting in the space on October 24–25, 1913, bringing women from all over the state together in Santa Fe.[90] Masonic youth groups, such as DeMolay International, Job's Daughters International, and the International Order of Rainbow for Girls, have used the theater. Until recently, the DeMolay organization used the theater, as well as the costumes and the forest set, to confer degrees for its Knighthood Priory. DeMolay also held many statewide conclaves in the theater.

The Grand Lodge of New Mexico, which oversees all the state's Symbolic Lodges, met in the theater in 1937 and 1956.[91] During the Thirtieth Reunion (June 18–20, 1919), Santa Fe's Montezuma Lodge No. 1 used the theater, sets, costumes, and props to present a staged demonstration of the Master Mason (Third Degree). Although the presentation of Symbolic Lodge degree productions had appeared sporadically throughout the country, the *Santa Fe Scottish Rite Bulletin* reported that this was the first time in the history of Masonry in New Mexico that any of the Symbolic Lodge degrees were fully staged.[92]

Hosting Masonic lodges from other jurisdictions is one of the Landmarks, or foundational principles, of Freemasonry. But Masons can visit only lodges that have been recognized by their own Grand Lodge as "regular," meaning that they are of legitimate origin, have an exclusive territorial jurisdiction, and adhere to the Ancient Landmarks—specifically requiring members to profess a belief in a higher power, having a sacred book as an indispensable part of lodge furnishings, and prohibiting discussions of religion and politics.[93] Many New Mexican Masons throughout the state's history have actively sought to promote tolerance and acceptance of others, taking a stand during times of moral uncertainty. For instance, in 1921 the Grand Master of Masons in New Mexico, Francis E. Lester, issued an edict prohibiting New Mexico Masons from joining the Ku Klux Klan or allowing that organization to use Masonic facilities, as was common elsewhere in the United States.

Once serving only a small corner of Santa Fe's diverse community, the Scottish Rite Temple theater now regularly hosts cultural events. Numerous theatrical, musical, film, and visual arts groups rent the building, utilizing this unique and atmospheric venue. Shakespeare plays, operettas, children's productions, musical concerts,

The Scottish Rite Temple theater has been used for many contemporary productions, such as Performance Santa Fe's 2017 staging of The Mikado *by Gilbert and Sullivan.*

weddings, and memorials have all been presented. Many Santa Fe nonprofits, such as the Georgia O'Keeffe Museum, use the theater for conferences and lectures. The exotic building and grounds are ideal settings for a variety of events. The anachronistic qualities of the structure are part of its appeal. It is a time capsule preserved, yet repurposed. Allowing public access to the Scottish Rite Temple directly contributes to the cultural heart of Santa Fe's vibrant arts community.

Preservation of the Scottish Rite Temple

Since the early twentieth century, the Santa Fe Scottish Rite Temple has presented many significant maintenance challenges. In the 1980s, a pipe above the kitchen burst and water flooded the basement, nearly ruining the natural gas-burning boiler and the electrical box. While the building is no longer heated with coal, the original coal chute still exists. The flood also undermined the foundation beneath the banquet hall and on the east side of the building, along Bishop's Lodge Road. In April 1989, water leaked through the roof of the theater, damaging the ceiling mural. Santa Fe Scottish Rite Mason Sean Graystone assisted art restorer Steven Prins in erecting scaffolding in the theater for the repair. But perhaps the greatest threat to the Scottish Rite Temple was when its leadership tried to sell the temple in 2013, citing declining membership and rising maintenance costs.[94] These same factors have led many American Scottish Rite and Masonic lodges to sell their buildings. In early 2017, the Zembo Shriners in Harrisburg, Pennsylvania, listed their sprawling Moorish revival–style building for sale for $950,000, citing declining membership and rising costs.[95] The year 1978 marked high tide for membership in the Scottish Rite, with 1,166,974 total members in the United States.[96] Whereas in 1968 Santa Fe's Scottish Rite Valley counted 5,836 members, in 2017 there were only 790.[97] Faced with the loss of a beloved building, since 1987 listed on the National Register of Historic Places, Santa Feans began to organize to save the Scottish Rite Temple. Many Scottish Rite Masons also wanted to save the building, and a series of meetings in fall 2014 led to a change in leadership. The temple was taken off the real estate market.[98] Since that time, the Santa Fe Scottish Rite Temple Historical Preservation Foundation and the Santa Fe Scottish Rite Building Association, both nonprofit corporations, have been working diligently to preserve the temple and to make it self-sustaining.

1. An earlier version of this chapter first appeared in the *Santa Fe New Mexican's Pasastiempo* magazine in the articles "Orientalism in Santa Fe" (September 20–26, 2013) and "More Orientalism in Santa Fe" (October 4–10, 2013).

2. For a thorough history of the development of the Spanish Pueblo revival architecture style, see Chris Wilson, *The Myth of Santa Fe: Creating a Modern Regional Tradition* (Albuquerque: University of New Mexico Press, 1997). And see below in this chapter for a discussion of how the Scottish Rite Temple relates to the question of which architectural style best represented Santa Fe's history and identity.

3. Cyril M. Harris, *American Architecture: An Illustrated Encyclopedia* (New York: W. W. Norton, 2003), 220; Hipólito Rafael Chacón, "Creating a Mythic Past: Spanish-Style Architecture in Montana," *Montana: The Magazine of Western History* 51 (2001): 48; "Survey LA: Los Angeles Historic Resources Survey," City of Los Angeles, December 2015, http://preservation.lacity.org/sites/default/files/Exotic%20Revival%2012-2-2015_0.pdf.

4. Edward Said, *Orientalism* (New York: Pantheon Books, 1978), 3.

5. Commission des Sciences et Arts d'Égypte, *Description de l'Égypte, ou recueil des observations et des recherches qui ont été faites en Égypte pendant l'expédition de l'armée française, publié par les ordres de sa majesté l'empereur Napoléon le grand*, 23 vols. (Paris: Imprimerie impériale, 1809–29).

6. "Orientalism," Oxford Islamic Studies Online, 2017, http://www.oxfordislamicstudies.com/article/opr/t276/e704 (accessed August 16, 2017).

7. "Moorish Style," Oxford Islamic Studies Online, 2017, http://www.oxfordislamicstudies.com/article/opr/t276/e624 (accessed August 16, 2017).

8. For Orientalism in the visual arts, see also Jennifer Meagher, "Orientalism in Nineteenth-Century Art," Heilbrunn Timeline of Art History, The Metropolitan Museum of Art, October 2004, http://www.metmuseum.org/toah/hd/euor/hd_euor.htm.

9. David Roberts, *Picturesque Sketches in Spain, 1832 & 1833* (London: Hodgson & Graves, 1837); John Frederick Lewis, *Lewis's Sketches of Spain and Spanish Character: Made During His Tour in That Country in the Years 1833–4* (London: F. G. Moon and John F. Lewis, 1836).

10. David Roberts, *The Holy Land, Syria, Idumea, Arabia, Egypt, & Nubia* (London: Day & Son, 1855–56). The Santa Fe Scottish Rite Temple library owns a copy of this six-volume series, donated by Deforest Lord.

11. See Jules Goury, *Plans, Elevations, Sections, and Details of the Alhambra, from Drawings Taken on the Spot in 1834 by Jules Goury, and in 1834 and 1837 by Owen Jones; with a Complete Translation of the Arabic Inscriptions, and an Historical Notice of the Kings of Granada from the Conquest of That City by the Arabs to the Expulsion of the Moors, by Pasqual de Gayangos* (London: Owen Jones, 1842–45); and Owen Jones, *The Grammar of Ornament* (London: Day and Son, 1856). The Santa Fe Scottish Rite Temple library owns a copy of the 1890 edition of Jones.

12. See John MacKenzie, *Orientalism: History, Theory and the Arts* (Manchester, UK: Manchester University Press, 1995), 71; Holly Edwards, *Noble Dreams, Wicked Pleasures: Orientalism in America, 1870–1930* (Princeton, NJ: Princeton University Press, 2000); Omar Khalidi, "Architecture of Islamic Inspiration in the United States," Archnet, n.d., https://archnet.org/system/publications/contents/4620/original/DPC1194.pdf?1384786143(2002) (accessed August 16, 2017); John E. Sweetman, *The Oriental Obsession: Islamic Inspiration in British and American Art and Architecture, 1500–1920* (New York: Cambridge University Press, 1988).

13. Trumbull White and William Igleheart, *The World's Columbian Exposition, Chicago, 1893* (Boston: John K. Hastings, 1893), 589–90. For the Scottish Rite at the World's Columbian Exposition, see Waszut-Barrett, chapter 4, this volume.

14. For an extended discussion of how Islam and Islamic architecture and culture were presented at nineteenth-century world's fairs, see Zeynep Çelik, *Displaying the Orient: Architecture of Islam at Nineteenth-Century World's Fairs* (Berkeley: University of California Press, 1992).

15. Ivan Davidson Kalmar, "Moorish Style: Orientalism, the Jews, and Synagogue Architecture," *Jewish Social Studies*, n.s., 7, no. 3 (2001); "Moorish Style," Oxford Islamic Studies Online; Clay Lancaster, "Oriental Forms in American Architecture, 1800–1870," *Art Bulletin* 29 (1947): 190.

16. William D. Moore, *Masonic Temples: Freemasonry, Ritual Architecture, and Masculine Archetypes* (Knoxville: University of Tennessee Press, 2006), 94.

17. Ibid., 107. The temple burned in 1920 and was replaced by the extant Shrine Auditorium (1926).

18. The Oriental Hall at the Philadelphia Masonic Temple was completed in 1896. Both structures include meeting rooms decorated in other revival styles, such as Greek revival, American colonial revival, Norman revival, Egyptian revival, and Gothic revival. While the Philadelphia Masonic Temple is in the Norman revival style, the Salt Lake Masonic Temple is an Egyptian revival building.

19. *Santa Fe New Mexican*, November 16, 1912.

20. Santa Fe Lodge of Perfection, Board of Directors minutes, September 17, 1912, cited in John W. Murphey, *Scottish Rite Masonic Center, Santa Fe, New Mexico*, Historic American Buildings Survey (NM-228) (Washington, DC: National Park Service, 2015), 15.

21. *Santa Fe Scottish Rite Bulletin* 31, no. 5 (1950): 5; *Santa Fe Scottish Rite Bulletin* 41, no. 4 (1960): 2.

22. Robert Francaviglia, *Go East, Young Man: Imagining the American West as the Orient* (Logan: Utah State University Press, 2011), 3.

23. The term *mudéjar* refers to works of art and architecture created in Spain after the conclusion of the *reconquista* in 1492. The term acknowledged their hybrid nature, born of both Christian and Islamic antecedents. The Spanish and Portuguese brought mudéjar art and architecture to their overseas colonial empires, especially in Latin America. There is a large literature on mudéjar art and architecture in Latin America, but see Manuel Toussaint, *Arte mudéjar en América* (Mexico City: Editorial Porrúa, 1946); Diego Angulo and Helen B. Hall, "The Mudejar Style in Mexican Architecture," *Ars Islamica* 2, no. 2 (1935); and R. Brooks Jeffery, "From Azulejos to Zaguanes: The Islamic Legacy in the Built Environment of Hispano-America," *Journal of the Southwest* 45, no. 1/2 (2003): 289–327.

24. See Samuel Y. Edgerton, *Theaters of Conversion: Religious Architecture and Indian Artisans in Colonial Mexico* (Albuquerque: University of New Mexico Press, 2001), 58.

25. Francaviglia, *Go East, Young Man*, 133, 138.

26. See Wilson, *Myth of Santa Fe*; Carl Sheppard, *Creator of the Santa Fe Style: Isaac Hamilton Rapp, Architect* (Albuquerque: University of New Mexico Press, 1988); Bainbridge Bunting, *John Gaw Meem: Southwestern Architect* (Albuquerque: University of New Mexico Press, 1983).

27. Wilson, *Myth of Santa Fe*, 91.

28. Ibid., 90.

29. Ibid., 91; Sheppard, *Creator of the Santa Fe Style*, 46–47.

30. See timeline, this volume.

31. The main branch of the Santa Fe Public Library now occupies the plot. The site was abandoned because it was discovered that the water table was just a foot below the surface. *Santa Fe Scottish Rite Bulletin* 15, no. 2 (October–November–December 1933): 6; John Murphey, "Scottish Rite Temple, History Section," draft submittal to Historical American Buildings Survey, New Mexico Section, National Park Service, Washington, DC, unpublished manuscript in author's possession, 2015, 1–2.

32. Santa Fe Lodge of Perfection, Board of Directors minutes, December 26, 1910, cited in Murphey, "Scottish Rite Masonic Center," 6.

33. Beatrice Chauvenet, *Hewett and Friends: A Biography of Santa Fe's Vibrant Era* (Santa Fe: Museum of New Mexico Press, 1983), 38.

34. Hewett, Rapp, Nusbaum, and Morley were all members of both Montezuma Lodge No. 1 and the Santa Fe Scottish Rite. While Meem was a member of Montezuma Lodge and even contributed a design for a new lodge building, he never joined the Scottish Rite.

35. Santa Fe Lodge of Perfection, Board of Directors minutes, January 25, 1911, cited in Murphey, "Scottish Rite Masonic Center," 7.

36. Sumner Hunt to Jesse Nusbaum, February 1, 1911, General Correspondence, 1911, AC105 Box 1, Folder 14, Edgar L. Hewett Collection, 1891–1960, Fray Angélico Chávez History Library, New Mexico History Museum, Santa Fe.

37. Sumner Hunt to Edgar L. Hewett, February 17, 1911, General Correspondence, 1911, AC105 Box 1, Folder 14, Edgar L. Hewett Collection, 1891–1960, Fray Angélico Chávez History Library, New Mexico History Museum, Santa Fe. Later Scottish Rite records also give Hewett credit for suggesting the Moorish revival style for the Santa Fe Scottish Rite Temple. See *Santa Fe Scottish Rite Bulletin* 28, no. 2 (1946): 1.

38. Karen J. Weitze, "Sumner Hunt," in *Toward a Simpler Way of Life: The Arts and Crafts Architects of California*, ed. Robert Winter (Berkeley: University of California Press, 1997), 184.

39. *Los Angeles Herald*, March 11, 1911, 10. For more on Cunningham, see Waszut-Barrett, chapter 4, this volume.

40. *Albuquerque Journal*, August 25, 1911, 5.

41. Santa Fe Lodge of Perfection, Board of Directors minutes, September 27, 1912, cited in Murphey, "Scottish Rite Masonic Center," 16.

42. *Santa Fe New Mexican*, October 31, 1912.

43. "Statement: Total Cost of Building, and Total Receipts, from November 17, 1908, to July 31, 1915," Santa Fe Lodge of Perfection, Board of Directors minutes, 1915, cited in Murphey, "Scottish Rite Masonic Center," 18.

44. See Wilson, *Myth of Santa Fe*, 110–25.

45. Morley, "Santa Fe Architecture," 278–301.

46. Wilson, *Myth of Santa Fe*, 99.

47. Francaviglia, *Go East, Young Man*, 138.

48. Twitchell, "Old World City in the New," cited in Francaviglia, *Go East, Young Man*, 138.

49. Sheppard, *Creator of the Santa Fe Style*, 73–100.

50. In most parts of the United States, Scottish Rite Bodies confer only the Fourth through the Thirty-second Degrees, leaving the first three degrees—the Entered Apprentice, Fellow Craft, and Master Mason—to other Masonic lodges in the Blue Lodge system. In Santa Fe, the first three degrees are conferred by the city's two Masonic lodges, Montezuma Lodge No. 1 (founded 1851) and Cerrillos Lodge No. 19 (founded 1890). The Santa Fe Scottish Rite Bodies confer the degrees up to the Thirty-second. They are as follows: Lodge of Perfection degrees: Fourth to Fourteenth; Chapter of the Rose Croix degrees: Fifteenth to Eighteenth; Council of Kadosh degrees: Nineteenth to Thirtieth; Consistory degrees: Thirty-first and Thirty-second. The degrees are short morality plays, each lasting from forty-five minutes to two hours. Certain degrees (Fourth, Fourteenth, Eighteenth, Thirtieth, and Thirty-second) must be performed for the candidates, while others can be summarized in a classroom. Performing all twenty-nine degrees, Fourth through Thirty-second, is both time-consuming and labor-intensive, as each requires extensive memorization, costume changes, sets, and props. In 2017 the Valley of Santa Fe presented about three-fourths of the degrees as fully staged affairs, and the process required almost three full days, from sunup to midnight. When the Scottish Rite Temple opened in 1912, the degrees were presented on four successive days, and fewer degrees were fully staged.

51. Twitchell, *Old Santa Fe: The Story of New Mexico's Ancient Capital* (Santa Fe: Santa Fe New Mexican Publishing Company, 1925), 480.

52. *Santa Fe Scottish Rite Bulletin* 1, no. 12 (December 1914): 1.

53. The Constituent Bodies of the Santa Fe Scottish Rite are the Santa Fe Lodge of Perfection No. 1, Aztlan Chapter of the Rose Croix No. 1, Coronado Council of Kadosh No. 1, and New Mexico Consistory No. 1. Each of these groups manages and confers a group of Scottish Rite degrees. See note 50 (above) for a list of the Scottish Rite Constituent Bodies and the degrees for which each is responsible.

54. Reunions are not to be confused with the regular meetings of the Scottish Rite constituent bodies. Although Scottish Rite Masons who had been initiated elsewhere founded the Lodge of Perfection No. 1 in Santa Fe in 1882 and they subsequently admitted new members, the current system of numbered reunions and named classes began in 1909, soon after the Valley of Santa Fe was incorporated.

55. *Santa Fe Scottish Rite Bulletin* 4, no. 3 (March 1917): 4; *Santa Fe Scottish Rite Bulletin* 5, no. 4 (April 1918): 1.

56. *Santa Fe Scottish Rite Bulletin* 26, no. 6 (November–December 1944): 2.

57. *Santa Fe Scottish Rite Bulletin* 32, no. 3 (1951): 1.

58. According to *Santa Fe Scottish Rite Bulletin* 1, no. 3 (August 1913): 4, members of the Dedication Class decided upon an altar as a class memorial; it was probably to be in place by the next reunion. The altar is still used and bears a plaque with the dedication from the November 1912 class.

59. According to *Santa Fe Scottish Rite Bulletin* 6, no. 1 (January 1919): 2, the Rose Croix Class, which received degrees in June 1915, after purchasing a window for the theater, turned over the rest of its class fund of $102.96 to the Scottish Rite Board of Directors, to be used at its discretion for whatever the temple needed. The bulletin noted further that the north side of the auditorium was then replete with windows.

60. *Santa Fe Scottish Rite Bulletin* 5, no. 11 (November 1918): 3.

61. Ibid.

62. Scottish Rite Freemasonry in New Mexico is currently divided into two organizations, the Valley of Santa Fe and the Valley of Las Cruces. Both are part of the statewide Orient of New Mexico.

63. *Santa Fe Scottish Rite Bulletin* 3, no. 12 (December 1916): 2.

64. *Santa Fe Scottish Rite Bulletin* 14, no. 7 (July 1927): 4.

65. *Santa Fe Scottish Rite Bulletin* 50, no. 4 (1969): 6; *Santa Fe Scottish Rite Bulletin* 53, no. 6 (1972): 4.

66. *Santa Fe Scottish Rite Bulletin* 6, no. 3 (March 1919): 6.

67. *Santa Fe Scottish Rite Bulletin* 2, no. 6 (June 1915): 2.

68. *Santa Fe Scottish Rite Bulletin* 23, no. 3 (May–June 1941): 1.

69. *Santa Fe Scottish Rite Bulletin* 40, no. 4 (July–August 1959): 1.

70. *Santa Fe Scottish Rite Bulletin* 34, no. 3 (1953): 8.

71. Santa Fe Lodge of Perfection, Board of Directors minutes, May 17, 1915, cited in Murphey, "Scottish Rite Masonic Center," 18. The Seligman brothers were Scottish Rite members.

72. *Santa Fe Scottish Rite Bulletin* 42, no. 6 (November–December 1961): 8.

73. Dan Irick and Sean Greystone, personal communication, 2017.

74. Dan Irick, personal communication, 2017.

75. *Santa Fe Scottish Rite Bulletin* 32, no. 3 (1951): 1.

76. Murphey, "Scottish Rite Masonic Center," 10.

77. *Ancient and Accepted Scottish Rite, Valley of Santa Fe, Orient of New Mexico, Dedication Reunion, November 17, 18, 19, 20, 1912*, Tenth Reunion program (Santa Fe: Lodge of Perfection, 1912), 5. The program actually states that *when completed*, the courtyard would be a reproduction of the Court of the Lions, since for decades the court had an L-shaped form and was not entirely enclosed until 1950.

78. *Santa Fe Scottish Rite Bulletin* 40, no. 4 (July–August 1959): 1; *Santa Fe Scottish Rite Bulletin* 41, no. 1 (January–February 1960): 1.

79. *Santa Fe Scottish Rite Bulletin* 3, no. 4 (April 1916): 5.

80. In almost every US Scottish Rite jurisdiction, conferral of the first three degrees is left to the Symbolic Lodge. Most US Symbolic Lodges confer these degrees based upon the York Rite of Anglo-American Freemasonry. The first three degrees of the Scottish Rite are of French origin and are rarely conferred.

81. *Santa Fe Scottish Rite Bulletin* 1, no. 10 (October 1914): 2.

82. *Santa Fe Scottish Rite Bulletin* 2, no. 2 (February 1915): 2.

83. Ibid.

84. Wilson connects the scene to José Moreno Carbonero's 1879–82 painting of the same scene: *Surrender of Granada, Capilla Real, Granada, Spain*. See Wilson, *Scottish Rite Cathedral*, National Register of Historic Places inventory (Washington, DC: United States Department of the Interior, National Park Service, 1987), 2.

85. *Santa Fe Scottish Rite Bulletin* 34, no. 3 (May–June 1953): 8.

86. *Santa Fe Scottish Rite Bulletin* 4, no. 1 (January 1917): 1.

87. *Santa Fe Scottish Rite Bulletin* 4, no. 3 (March 1917): 2–3.

88. *Santa Fe Scottish Rite Bulletin* 45, no. 4 (July–August 1964): 3.

89. Dan Irick, personal communication, 2017.

90. *Santa Fe Scottish Rite Bulletin* 1, no. 10 (October 1914): 6.

91. *Santa Fe Scottish Rite Bulletin* 24, no. 1 (January–February 1937): 2; *Santa Fe Scottish Rite Bulletin* 37, no. 3 (May–June 1956): 2.

92. *Santa Fe Scottish Rite Bulletin* 7, no. 7 (July 1919): 1.

93. See 2017 Commission Report, The Commission on Information for Recognition, The Conference of Grand Masters of Masons of North America, 2004–2017, http://www.recognitioncommission.org, for the criteria of recognition for Grand Lodges.

94. Grimm, Julie Ann, "Scottish Rite Center Could Be Put Up for Sale," *Santa Fe New Mexican*, March 4, 2013; Kathaleen Roberts, "Scottish Rite Center on Sale for $8.4M," *Albuquerque Journal*, April 12, 2013.

95. Lawrance Binda, "History for Sale: Harrisburg's Zembo Shrine Put on the Market," *Burg News*, February 3, 2017.

96. The Scottish Rite total is for both Northern and Southern Jurisdictions. Brent Morris, personal communication, 2017. For the sake of comparison, the Shrine reached its highest membership in 1978, with a total of 941,799 members, according to the *Shrine International Book of Reports*. The Santa Fe Scottish Rite counted 529 members in 1914, 1,763 in 1924, 2,100 in 1944, and 5,838 in 1967. *Santa Fe Scottish Rite Bulletin* 1, no. 8 (August 1914): 3; *Santa Fe Scottish Rite Bulletin* 12, no. 1 (January 1925): 3; *Santa Fe Scottish Rite Bulletin* 27, no. 1 (January–February 1945): 3; *Santa Fe Scottish Rite Bulletin* 49, no. 1 (January–February 1968): 7.

97. Dan Irick, personal communication, 2017.

98. Ann Constable, "Historic Scottish Rite Temple Removed from the Real Estate Market," *Santa Fe New Mexican*, October 7, 2014.

4
Staging the Santa Fe Scottish Rite

WENDY WASZUT-BARRETT

Opposite: *The Egyptian House of the Dead expands on the continued theme of justice for the Thirty-first Degree, illustrating the path toward final judgment and immortality.*

Anticipation filled the Scottish Rite theatre as men waited for the lights to dim. Slowly, the front curtain rose to reveal an exotic setting—Egypt!

THERE IS A MAGICAL MOMENT when audience members enter the world of the play. For centuries, a willing suspension of disbelief allowed countless spectators to journey far beyond their own regions. In the early twentieth century, degree productions provided numerous opportunities for Ancient and Accepted Scottish Rite Freemasons to explore distant lands. During a time when many individuals stayed within the confines of their own state, the Fraternal stage transported generations of men to exotic locales. Exoticism in elaborate productions especially appealed to those living in areas where visual spectacle and staged entertainment were limited. The theatrical interpretation of degree work became an incentive to join Freemasonry. It was the inclusion of staged spectacle that propelled a once fledgling organization to the forefront of American fraternalism. This chapter examines the popular appeal, design, and mass production of painted scenery for Scottish Rite theaters, exploring an era when both the Fraternity and the general public eagerly sought the same material culture.

Scottish Rite degree productions fascinated members when portions of their degree work moved from the lodge room floor to the elevated stage. Before degree productions, most Scottish Rite activities were performed within the confines of a lodge room. Traditionally rectangular in shape, the lodge room had seating on all four sides with an altar in the center, such as at the current Cerrillos Lodge No. 19 in Santa Fe, New Mexico.

Masonic officers were placed in the symbolic East, South, and West of a lodge room, while members sat in the North and South. Many fraternal meetings took place in multipurpose rooms, often decorated with fabric wall hangings that merely suggested a location. Larger Masonic buildings contained multiple rooms permanently

Grand Portico of the Temple of Philæ — Nubia.

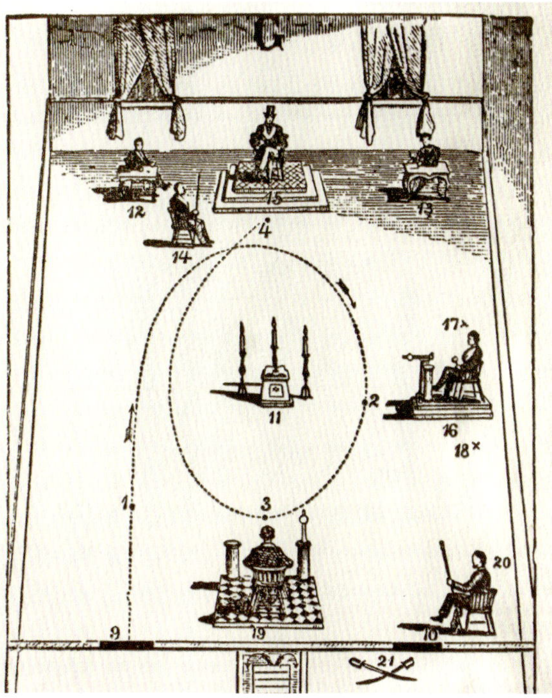

Above, left: *The initiation scene for a Master Mason from* Duncan's Masonic Ritual and Monitor*, 1866. Courtesy of Wendy Waszut-Barrett.*

Above, right: *This scene from Santa Fe's Cerrillos Lodge No. 19 is replicated in thousands of Masonic temples across the country.*

Opposite: The Temple of Isis, or Grand Portico of the Temple of Philæ*, by David Roberts, 1838. This exact composition repeatedly appears on Scottish Rite stages for Thirty-first-Degree productions. Collection of the Scottish Rite Temple, Santa Fe.*

prepared with specific themes. Members could move from one room to another during degrees to suggest a shift in locale.

Prior to the advent of Scottish Rite theaters, degrees were either communicated or conferred to a candidate, as described by Rick Hendricks in chapter 1. *Communicated degrees* involved a candidate receiving the necessary information, signs, and obligations without passing through an elaborate ceremony. *Conferred degrees* involved multiple lodge officers reciting the ritual from memory and enacting historical events in prescribed locations. The use of characters and dialogue in conferrals was an early predecessor to degree productions, placing greater emphasis on the lodge room decor, paraphernalia, and character placement. A third type of presentational format emerged when degrees became *conferred in full form*. By the late nineteenth century, the theatrical staging of degrees would involve Subordinate Bodies purchasing proper paraphernalia, or working paraphernalia, for the exemplification of the work. This staging included raised platforms, painted flats or drops, lighting effects, and costumed participants. To accommodate the increase in visual aids for the rituals, small alcoves appeared in the symbolic East, West, or North of many lodge rooms. Murals, small dioramas, and scenic tableaux were all incorporated in these early stages, establishing settings that didn't always function as active performance spaces.

Scenic spectacle associated with nineteenth-century panoramas and cycloramas was quickly incorporated into a variety of Fraternal stage spaces. The commercial theater and the Fraternity had a shared material culture; each used popularized environments that depicted geographical regions, historic figures, and significant events. Scenic tableaux were intended to educate lodge members on certain subjects. Scottish Rite stages adopted atmospheric effects and illusions to further depict the legendary occurrences as presented in Masonic degrees. The candidate, an exemplar for his Scottish Rite class, eventually entered the production as a costumed character. During this experimental period with degree productions, Masonic organizations altered existing lodge rooms for this new form of degree work. Eventually, new facilities were designed and built to accommodate degree productions, departing from the previous practice of using shared spaces. Many Scottish Rite Valleys built new facilities with performance venues to accommodate theatrically staged degree work.

The western region of the United States supported the construction of ornate Masonic theaters for degree productions, especially in areas where theatrical entertainment was scarce. Staged degrees appealed to many Masons as a source of continued brotherhood, social interaction, and local entertainment. Before members entered the Scottish Rite, the Symbolic Lodge provided them with a basic introduction to this speculative craft and an understanding of Masonic symbolism through an allegorical tale depicting the construction of King Solomon's Temple and assassination of its master architect, Hiram. Expanding on this Masonic legend, the Scottish Rite continued to stage a variety of events surrounding the reign of King Solomon. In addition to this biblical tale, the group delved into other exotic legends, notable characters, and remarkable events.

Never intended to be factual depictions of historic events, Scottish Rite degree work incorporated popular legend into the instruction, offering twenty-nine avenues for the philosophical exploration and staging of degrees from the fourth through the thirty-second. Similar to a series of morality plays, the lessons for each degree could be expanded to include additional scenes with different geographical locations and

The back wall of the auditorium features a neon sign used during degree productions.

Opposite: *Looking at the auditorium through the bobbinet center of the* Ascension *cut drop.*

LOUDER

subplots. Every degree functioned as a single play, with the duration determined by a director. A degree could contain multiple acts with numerous scenes, each production taking approximately one to four hours. Fully costumed members, performing as amateur actors on professionally outfitted stages, enacted the same stories that were once orally recounted in a fixed and neutral environment. What was once intimately revealed to individual candidates in dimly lit rooms was now performed under the glare of stage lights for several hundred members.

Masonic degrees continued to evolve throughout the nineteenth century, incorporating myths, legends, and mystic rites. Ritual revisions and Masonic legislation supported the theatrical interpretation of degree work and the introduction of new subject matter to its ceremonies. Many fraternities formed committees to rewrite the rituals, attempting to unify the degree system, identify settings, and mandate specific decor. New settings provided additional information about each degree, often including architectural descriptions, atmospheric environments, and character motivation. Most degree settings were easily adapted to the stage, providing opportunities to include scenic spectacle and adopt content from a variety of popular entertainments.

Degree productions used a standard format associated with nineteenth-century Victorian American theatre. Three specific elements characterized this type of theatrical setting: backdrops, cut drops, and leg drops. As demonstrated by the Santa Fe Scottish Rite woods scene, the backdrop provided the background of the composition and established the subject matter. It was placed farthest from the audience, with other painted drops in front of it to create a stage picture. Cut drops and leg drops formed the middle ground and foreground, respectively, in a series of pictorial planes. The opaque center section of a cut drop was removed and replaced with a transparent material, such as one-inch netting or open weave mesh. All three scenic elements worked together to create an illusion of depth on stage. Since the seventeenth century, scenic artists had successfully utilized a system of forced perspective for the theater, suggesting great depth on a relatively shallow stage. This painted illusion consistently enthralled audiences throughout the centuries, regardless of the theatrical format, painted substrate, or lighting source. Furthermore, there were theatrical conventions for metamorphosis on the stage, combining painted illusion with stage machinery. Transformation scenes created vivid sunsets, starlit skies, erupting volcanoes, and turbulent seas. Secret messages, hidden objects, and ghostly apparitions were also revealed on stage, such as in the Thirtieth-degree *Catacomb* setting, where a man is transformed into a skeleton.

The scenic illusion "Pepper's Ghost" uses a piece of plate glass to reflect a concealed image, such as in the Thirtieth Degree, where a man transforms into a skeleton. (See page 197 for full scene.)

Opposite: *View of* Forest *leg drops and backstage area. (See page 155 for full setting.)*

Ritual Revision and the Theatrical Interpretation of Degree Work

Staged spectacle beckoned to members of the Fraternity, prompting innovation in their degree work during the mid-nineteenth century. Degree productions offered endless possibilities for Masonic instruction. Early experimentation with theatrical interpretations of degree work began in the Northern Jurisdiction of the Scottish Rite, a territory that included all areas east of the Mississippi and north of the Ohio River. The Northern Jurisdiction included the theatrical centers of New York City, Philadelphia, Boston, Indianapolis, Cincinnati, and Chicago. The Southern Jurisdiction controlled the remainder of the United States and its territories south of the Ohio and west of the Mississippi. The creation and propagation of two distinct and geographically defined authorities furthered the diversity and innovation in degree work, allowing degree productions to flourish, especially in metropolitan areas.

Scottish Rite degree presentations took on the regional characteristics of the organization's membership. This was especially apparent in the western cities of Indianapolis, Cincinnati, and Chicago during the mid-nineteenth century.[1] Continued membership growth and increased funding allowed the larger Scottish Rite Bodies to construct massive Masonic complexes with elaborate rooms for their ceremonials. Furthermore, competitive governing bodies in the Northern Jurisdiction encouraged degree discrepancies to flourish under rival Supreme Council leaders.[2] Such was the case with the adoption and promotion of theatrically interpreted degrees. Northern Masonic Jurisdiction Scottish Rites marketed degree productions to Symbolic Lodges as a superior ritual experience and incentive to join.[3] They not only attracted Master Masons, but also lured existing Scottish Rite members away from competing Supreme Councils. While degree productions thrived throughout the Northern Jurisdiction, they remained relatively stagnant in the Southern Jurisdiction under the leadership of a single individual who controlled Fraternal activities for more than three decades, from 1859 to 1891.

Grand Commander Albert Pike (1809–91) suppressed the melodramatic interpretation of degrees throughout the Southern Jurisdiction. Prior to becoming Grand Commander, Pike had revised the Scottish Rite ritual.[4] His text not only unified the degree system but also had a transformative effect on all future degree work in the United States, especially in the Northern Jurisdiction. Pike provided detailed information for various degree settings, labeling them as "apartments." The Northern Jurisdiction immediately revised its own ritual to closely mirror Pike's format and content but added a series of detailed illustrations.[5] Northern Jurisdiction Scottish Rite Valleys began to stage portions of their degrees. The earliest documented degree productions included moving panoramas with fantastic sea voyages past Malta,

Albert Pike, photograph by Mathew Brady, 1877. Library of Congress Prints and Photographs Division, Washington, DC (LC-BH832-30276<P&P>).

Rhodes, Cyprus, and Joppa, causing an excitement to sweep throughout the Scottish Rite membership.[6] The immediate popularity and success of staged spectacle fueled the demand for degree productions, resulting in even grander stages throughout the Northern Jurisdiction.

Despite Pike's personal opinions on the matter and attempts at regulation, degree productions continued to gain support throughout the Southern Jurisdiction. In 1882, the widening gulf between the degree works in each jurisdiction was noted in Pike's allocution, in which he stated, "The Rite in this Jurisdiction is a Rite of instruction, and not of scenic pomp and stage-show."[7] Pike then lashed out against the use of elaborate degree productions, declaring, "I cannot conceive of a more useless occupation than the arranging and performing of degrees, neither the effect nor the purpose of which is to make men wiser or better, but which are acted as melodramas, to gratify an aesthetic taste and please the imagination, like the pageantry of cardinals and orioles."[8] Regardless of Pike's staunch dismissal of degree productions, theatrical stages began to appear in the Southern Jurisdiction too.

Early experimentation with Southern Jurisdiction degree productions initially appeared in existing theaters and altered spaces, similar to what had occurred in the Northern Jurisdiction more than a decade earlier. One of the earliest documented examples appeared in Minnesota. This was a region where both the Northern and Southern Jurisdictions competed for Masonic membership, since the state straddled the western demarcation for jurisdictional division. In the city of Winona during the 1880s, the Scottish Rite met in a lodge hall on the third floor of the post office building. This Masonic hall included a small stage on the north wall of the room, with a proscenium opening that measured 19 feet wide by 10 feet high. A painted front curtain with blue draperies and Masonic emblems concealed "four sets of scenery, all Masonic designs," behind the proscenium opening.[9]

The Scottish Rite stages the story surrounding the construction of King Solomon's Temple and the murder of its chief architect, Hiram.

Degree Productions for the Southern Jurisdiction

International exposure to Scottish Rite degree productions and the manufacturers of Fraternal scenery didn't take place until 1893. Masons traveled to Chicago from all around the world to attend a variety of Fraternal activities scheduled to coincide with the world's fair, including a gathering of the International Masonic Congress. In 1891 the Grand Lodge of Illinois had decided to hold a Masonic Congress: "for the interchange of fraternal sentiments concerning the general interest of Masonry throughout the world, and especially looking to a greater uniformity in the modes of recognitions, and the fundamental features which characterize our system the world over."[10] From August 14 to 17, 1893, delegates from forty-five states, the District of Columbia, and several countries gathered at the Oriental Consistory's theater in the newly constructed Masonic temple on Randolph Street. In this Scottish Rite space, some of the most eminent Masons from every jurisdiction were gathered under one roof.[11]

Many of the theatre scenes produced for the Oriental Consistory and the numerous Columbian Exposition attractions were manufactured by Chicago-based Masons who owned theatrical, lighting, regalia, paraphernalia, and publishing companies. Furthermore, the passing of Pike meant that there was no longer a Grand Commander suppressing degree productions throughout the Southern Jurisdiction. There was an increased fervor to purchase new and correct paraphernalia for the proper rendition of degree work. The planning of Southern Jurisdiction Scottish Rite theaters immediately commenced throughout the western region, resulting in impressive stages for degree productions. Arguments ensued in the Supreme Council, as some criticized Scottish Rites that adopted "northern work." In 1894 the Inspector General for Arkansas, James Austin Henry, explained a sudden increase in membership as a result of his granting special dispensations for classes numbering eleven or more at Arkansas Consistory No. 1 starting in 1892. This positive outcome followed an investment of more than $1,000 in 1891 for the purchase of proper paraphernalia for the exemplification of degree work. In 1895, Henry further reported to the Supreme Council that the Scottish Rite Bodies were securing and furnishing a permanent home with working paraphernalia. This meant using painted backdrops to stage their degree work. In 1896, Scottish Rite theaters appeared in Little Rock, Arkansas, and Oakland, California. Throughout the 1890s, theatrical trappings were purchased and implemented in retrofitted lodge rooms throughout the Southern Jurisdiction, their success documented over the years in transactions from Supreme Council meetings.

During this first phase of Southern Jurisdiction construction, many Scottish Rite Valleys contracted with photographers to document their buildings and scenery. These images were included in both reunion programs and Masonic journals. This was a significant moment in Fraternal history, as the interiors of many Scottish Rite spaces were recorded for the first time. When the Southern Jurisdiction first published its official journal, *The New Age Magazine,* in 1904, scenery from the Little Rock Scottish Rite stage was pictured in a full-page collage and extensive article on the new building.[12] The new structures were praised for their impressive theaters and scenery. In 1912 professional photographer and Mason Jesse Nusbaum carefully documented the Santa Fe Scottish Rite Temple's architecture, interior decoration,

Opposite: Lantern slides by Jesse Nusbaum *(1921) depict* (clockwise from upper left) *the Eighteenth Degree* Constellation *(see pages 122 and 191), the Eighteenth Degree* Peristyle *(see page 185), the Fourteenth Degree* Secret Vault *(see pages 123 and 178), and the Thirty-second Degree* Cathedral *(see pages 124 and 196). Scottish Rite Temple Collection, Palace of the Governors Photo Archives (NMHM/DCA HP.2016.53.014, HP.2016.53.003, HP.2016.53.001, HP.2016.53.002).*

FAITH

INFINITY
NATURE
REASON
IMMORTALITY

AUM

This Constellation *setting incorporates translucenct sections in the backdrop to illuminate the starlit words* Faith, Hope, *and* Charity *during the Eighteenth Degree. (See page 191 for the revelation of stars.)*

The central section of the Secret Vault *backdrop is theatrical gauze. When backlit, this section reveals hidden artifacts or painted objects to the audience.*

theater, and painted scenery. The incorporation of staged degrees and scenic illusions was advertised and promoted nationwide, highlighting the recent successes and overall prosperity of many Scottish Rite Valleys.

Change was rapidly sweeping throughout the Fraternity as degree productions appeared in the Southern Jurisdiction. By 1908 a second wave of new construction necessitated the replacement of original scenery collections as membership continued to surge. Many Scottish Rite Valleys outgrew their initial facilities. Such was the case for the Scottish Rite Valleys in McAlester and Guthrie, Oklahoma. Harper S. Cunningham, appointed in 1890, was instrumental in propagating degree productions throughout the western region. Cunningham's understanding of the region's membership and demographics placed him at the forefront of the Fraternal theater movement, first in Oklahoma and later in New Mexico. He understood the need to purchase paraphernalia to do the degree work properly and to actively promote degree productions for both the Symbolic Lodge and Scottish Rite.

When Cunningham first arrived in Santa Fe, it was to meet with local architects and advise Scottish Rite Masons on the construction of a new building. He immediately appointed a committee on paraphernalia to purchase and transport a set of used scenery from McAlester, Oklahoma.[13] An explosive increase in McAlester's membership necessitated construction of a larger theater, requiring new equipment. This was the second Scottish Rite stage planned and constructed under Cunningham's direction. When Cunningham took charge in Santa Fe, he implemented a plan to create a demand for a new theater and degree productions. In 1909 the secondhand scenery was shipped and immediately installed in the Masonic Hall on Water Street (see page 66). This familiarized Santa Fe Masons with the theatrical interpretation of degrees on an introductory level, preparing them for later performances on the new stage. The scenery was used at the Masonic Hall until the group moved into their new building in the fall of 1912.

The immediate success of degree productions allowed the youngest Scottish Rite Valleys to outshine their eastern predecessors, quickly surpassing them in membership. The western regions of the Southern Jurisdiction had the perfect combination of incentive, land, and resources. Money poured into Supreme Council headquarters as a direct result of continued growth, with Grand Commander James D. Richardson expressing his surprise and delight at this newfound economic resource. Submitting to the Supreme Council a membership chart that tracked the degree work of 3,972 members entering the Scottish Rite between July 1899 and June 1901, he showed that 3,275 members successfully proceeded through all twenty-nine degrees.[14] Up to this point, the Southern Jurisdiction had continued to

Raising the backdrop in the Cathedral *scene. Painted wood panels blend with three-dimensional wood furniture.*

struggle financially; only 4,794 members in the entire jurisdiction had achieved the Thirty-second Degree by 1896.[15] In only two years, this number almost doubled as marked growth appeared throughout the western region.

A variety of manufacturers and suppliers were waiting in the wings, as scores of salesmen marketed Fraternal products for this new venue. The design and marketing of Fraternal products for Scottish Rite theaters were coordinated to promote a series of purchases. The initial purchase of rigging systems, lights, scenery collections, and costumes evolved into the continued expansion of these inventories, necessitating additional orders. One purchase led to another, especially when Scottish Rite Valleys expanded the number of degree productions performed during a reunion.

Costumes and Props

Scottish Rite degree productions in Santa Fe provided participants with endless opportunities to wear lavish stage costumes. Distinguishing a high priest from a lowly shepherd necessitated obtaining the appropriate costumes, available from various fraternal supply companies, such as M. C. Lilley & Co., Inc. A well-established fraternal supply and regalia house in Columbus, Ohio, the company staffed individual departments—including the Masonic Department, Odd Fellows Department, Knights of Pythias Department, Military Department, and Trade Department—for its primary clientele.[16] A 1914 company flyer sent to potential clients urged them, "To see all the degrees of Masonry exemplified by officers and team properly costumed, according to their stations. The worth of such effort is, to YOU in the pleasure of witnessing such spectacle . . . to the CANDIDATE in the impression it leaves upon his mind."[17] Like other regalia companies, M. C. Lilley offered historically appropriate and accurate garb for every character, basing prices on the quality of fabrics, the elaborate trimming, and the embroidery. Costumes were offered in various grades, but quality came at a price. The 1914 M. C. Lilley flyer cautioned organizations to avoid inferior materials: "Just remember that PRICE is soon forgotten, while QUALITY (be it high or low) is with you so long as the Costume lasts."[18] Ordinary individuals were transformed into kings, soldiers, priests, and knights by costumes that could rival those of any Broadway star. Velvet capes, plumed hats, and sword belts elaborately outfitted amateur actors in degree productions, transporting them to foreign lands.

Costume collections were substantial investments, necessitating many Scottish Rite buildings to include large wardrobe rooms in their construction plans. Dressing areas and extensive costume storage systems were prominent features in most

High priest costume manufactured by M. C. Lilley & Co. in 1912.

Rose Croix---Sixteenth Degree

Costumes

Robe 421 Ephod 6462 Mitre 422

Robe 1069 Mitre 1070

Robe 417 Ephod 6461 Mitre 418

High Priest robe, full lined, with under-sleeves, lining of large flowing outer sleeves and band around bottom of contrasting color, artistically embroidered in silk. Ephod handsomely silk embroidered. Mitre with curtain, nicely trimmed and "Holiness to the Lord" embossed on front. A highly effective costume offered in following materials.

Robe—421

421P1 Robe of Poplin ....$.....
421V3 Robe of S. F. Velvet...... .....
421S9 Robe of Silk Serge ....
421S4 Robe of Satin ....
421P7 Robe of Silk Plush ....

Ephod—6462

6462S9 Ephod of Silk Serge ...$.....
6462S4 Ephod of Satin ....

Mitre —422

422P1 Mitre of Poplin ....$.....
422V3 Mitre of S. F. Velvet ....
422S9 Mitre of Silk Serge ....
422S4 Mitre of Satin ....
422P7 Mitre of Silk Plush ....

A distinctively designed High Priest costume that is very authentic. Robe, attachment and surplice ornamented with silk embroidery, surplice edged with fringe. Mitre as illustrated, curtained, edged with heavy fringe and tassels, has "Holinessto theLord" embossed on front.

Robe—1069

1069P1 Robe of Poplin ....$.....
1069S9 Robe of Silk Serge ....
1069S4 Robe of Satin ....
1069S4A Robe of Skinner's Satin.. .....

Mitre—1070

1070S4 Mitre of Satin ....$.....
1070S4A Mitre of Skinners' Satin . .....
1070P1 Mitre of Poplin ....
1070S9 Mitre of Silk Serge ....

One of our most pleasing High Priest's costumes. Robe is full lined, with under-sleeves, lining of large flowing outer sleeves and band around bottom of contrasting color, artistically embroidered in silk and elaborately trimmed with jewel sets. Ephod and mitre are elaborately trimmed in keeping with the robe.

Robe—417

417V3 Robe of S. F. Velvet......$.....
417S9 Robe of Silk Serge ....
417S4 Robe of Satin ....
417P7 Robe of Silk Plush ....

Ephod—6461

6461S9 Ephod of Silk Serge ......$.....
6461S4 Ephod of Satin ....

Mitre—418

418V3 Mitre of S. F. Velvet .....$.....
418S9 Mitre of Silk Serge ....
418S4 Mitre of Satin........... .....
418P7 Mitre of Silk Plush ....

FOR PRICES, CONSULT PRICE BOOKLET INSIDE BACK COVER.

Beards and Wigs

Make Characterizations Complete

Beard 134858

Wig 134859 Beard 134860

Wig 134863 Beard 134864

Wig 135614

130421

Wig 130417 Beard 130437

JEWISH TYPE WIGS AND BEARDS

134858 **Beard,** with moustache, made of real hair, grey colored, carefully combed and curled. This beard is a true Jewish type, and is especially suitable for officers such as Secretary, Treasurer, Almoner, etc., of the 14°; **each** ....$.....

134859 **Wig,** made of long, select white hair on gauze, carefully combed and curled, to match Beard 134860; **each**.............................. .....

134860 **Beard,** with moustache, finely made of long, select, straight white hair; **each**.............. .....

Wig and Beard described above are for characters who are to have the appearance of great age, such as the Venerable Master of the 14°.

134863 **Wig,** made medium length of fine brown hair, on gauze, combed and curled, to match Beard 134864; **each**.............................. .....

134864 **Beard,** with moustache, made of medium length, select brown hair, full and bushy, to match Wig 134863; **each** ....

Beard and Wig, 134863-54 are recommended for the Sr. and Jr. Warden of the 14°.

JUDICIAL STYLE WIG

135614 **Wig,** Judicial Style, made on a net of fine, white (real) hair, carefully combed and curled, full length, comes down well on the shoulders; **each** .$.....

PERSIAN TYPE WIGS AND BEARDS

130421 **Wig,** made of select hair, medium length, combed and curled, choice of colors, black, brown, grey or white; **each**...........................$.....

130417 **Wig,** made of fine, black hair, on net, combed and curled, to match Beard 130437; **each**...... .....

130437 **Beard,** with Moustache, made of fine, black hair on net, to match Wig 130417—true Persian style; **each** ....

COLONIAL WIG

134891 **Colonial Wig,** made of fine, white hair, very realistic, carefully combed, tie at back; **each**.......$.....

In order to maintain uniformity in color and to secure best results in characterizations, we suggest that you order the combined wigs and beards as they are illustrated on pages 76 and 77.

FOR PRICES, CONSULT PRICE BOOKLET INSIDE BACK COVER.

A C. E. Ward Company catalog for the Southern Jurisdiction of the Scottish Rite advertising historically accurate costumes and accessories for every character in degree productions. Great Western Stage Equipment Company Collection (PA44), Performing Arts Archives, University of Minnesota Libraries, Minneapolis.

Scottish Rite facilities, signifying the organization's reverence for, and continued investment in, degree costumes. In 1952 the wardrobe department at the Santa Fe Scottish Rite received a donation of costume cabinets from Everett P. Moore and G. Cleve Moore. Scottish Rite Masons and owners of Moore's Men Store on the Santa Fe Plaza, they donated top-of-the-line cabinets, each complete with a sliding rack and locking glass door.[19] In addition to costume storage, the wigs, shoes, spats, hose, collars, gloves, and belts all had special storage compartments with corresponding labels for each character and degree. Every crown, turban, biretta, and helmet was carefully stacked and available in another set of supplementary cabinets. Costume bibles recorded the outfit and accessory locations for each degree, allowing entire outfits to be assembled within minutes.

A myriad of members worked behind the scenes not only to dress the actors but also to set the stage. In addition to regalia, numerous fraternal supply companies manufactured and sold paraphernalia for degree productions. Each degree demanded a series of unique artifacts, such as the Ark of the Covenant, the Scales of Justice, the Delta of Enoch, golden vessels, candelabras, skeletons, caskets, silken banners, and even stuffed sheep. As with costumes, items for each degree were meticulously labeled and safely stored in the properties room. And as with costumes, the items' materials and craftsmanship varied, as supply companies sought to accommodate any budget. Whether the actor wore it, carried it, sat on it, or simply stood in front of it, each element was part of a cohesive stage picture.

Banners, set pieces, and hand props are carefully stored in a properties room near the stage area.

Scenic Spectacle for the Stage

Exotic scenes popularized in nineteenth-century print and on the commercial stage were replicated for other theatrical venues, such as Scottish Rite degree productions. Visual depictions of foreign settings were eagerly sought after, appearing in print, on glass slides, and on stereoscopic cards. The art of stereoscopy brought the individual to foreign lands; the viewer intimately experienced the exotic in his or her own home. The Scottish Rite stage provided a similar journey, but for Masonic audiences. Avid collectors fervently sought images depicting travel to Egypt and the Holy Land. Ancient cities and sumptuous palaces uncovered in archaeological digs appeared in various art forms. Sand dunes with distant pyramids, caravans with cameleers, oasis palm trees, and veiled figures under Egyptian porticoes all suggested an exotic essence from the East. Visual spectacle permeated many nineteenth-century entertainment venues, including commercial theaters, operas, public pageantry, tableaux vivant, cycloramas, moving panoramas, circus spectacles, and midway amusements.

Massive costume collections necessitated extensive dressing areas and storage systems.

Scenic artists marketed their skills to a variety of clientele, capturing geographic characteristics, atmospheric conditions, and ornamental details. Identified in chapter 3, artist David Roberts (1796–1864) traveled to the Middle East and captured images of the exotic. Roberts also worked as a scenic artist in Scotland and England, enlarging many of these subjects for the theatrical stage. His artwork provided source material for fellow scenic artists well into the twentieth century. The 1912 Egyptian scene for the Thirty-first Degree in Santa Fe replicates Roberts's 1838 composition *The Temple of Isis, or Grand Portico of the Temple of Philæ*, reproducing the exact same hieroglyphic characters on the foremost columns (see pages 110 and 112). Similarly, the picturesque landscapes and medieval relics from Europe were also a popular subject, with alpine castles, dungeons, catacombs, and armories all conjuring up the romantic visions of knights and noble quests. The ruins of Gothic cathedrals and ornate mausoleums remained shrouded in mist, while secret vaults and treasure chambers lay hidden underground, each silently awaiting discovery. But it was the metamorphic change on stage that dominated popular culture.

Visual spectacle was especially popular for world's fair midways, such as the electric theater spectacle titled "A Day in the Alps" for the 1893 Columbian Exposition. For this production, the darkness of parting night gave way to the first rays of sunlight, transitioning into shining splendor at noon. Shepherds appeared with their herds, entering the stage to the music of the Alps. Then clouds gathered and an approaching storm with lighting and thunder shadowed the valley. Sunlight returned after the storm passed, soon to be replaced by the dim glow of twilight. Finally, darkness enveloped the stage to reveal twinkling stars. This scenic spectacle utilized 250 electric incandescent lamps, which were operated in full view of the audience with thirty-six switches controlling red, white, and blue lights.[20] "A Day in the Alps" became so popular that two electric theaters with similar scenic effects were created for the Masonic Temple Roof Theatre the following year, located at the northeast corner of State and Randolph Streets.[21] Each electric theater accommodated seventy-five individuals. One replicated the popular Alpine setting and the other depicted the Court of Honor at the Columbian Exposition. Both used electric light to change the painted compositions from morning to evening scenes.

Many scenic illusions featured during the world's fair reappeared on Scottish Rite stages in the ensuing decades. One example was the tropical setting at the Javanese theater, a unique landscape that would later appear in many Eighteenth-degree *Peristyle* settings. Divided by a rambling river, the composition separated palm trees from deciduous trees before rocky peaks. It would become a standard composition for Eighteenth-degree productions throughout the Southern Jurisdiction, with palm trees facing either deciduous or coniferous trees on either side of a river. The same scenic

Native Javanese perform in front of a backdrop painted by Thomas G. Moses for the midway at the 1893 Columbian Exposition in Chicago. Courtesy of Wendy Waszut-Barrett.

Opposite: *Backdrop painted by Thomas G. Moses for the Eighteenth-degree* Peristyle *scene. (See page 185 for full scene with cut drop.)*

Prompt

artist who created the 1893 Javanese drop would later paint the 1912 scene for the Santa Fe stage, as well as for many other Scottish Rite stages across the country.[22]

Scenic artists painted numerous scenes for midway amusements and other spectacles that would later appear on Scottish Rite stages, including scenes of Bethlehem, the Jordan River, Mount Hermon, Damascus, and Bayreuth as depicted in the Turkish Pavilion. The Egyptian exhibit included painted scenes from the Temple of Luxor as a background for replicas of mummified remains, monolithic obelisks, colossal statues, and sphinxes. An attraction depicting the Hawaiian Islands incorporated a cyclorama measuring 54 feet high and 400 feet long, using scenic illusion and skillful pyrotechnic displays to show molten lava flowing down volcanic slopes. Contrasted with this fiery landscape was the tranquil glitter of moonlight on the Pacific Ocean, while nearby midway amusements showcased fiery eruptions, rainstorms, starlit skies, and brilliant sunsets. Scenic studios systematically designed and marketed such stage illusions for the Scottish Rite based on tried-and-true formulas.

Mandating the Theatrical Interpretation of Degree Work

The complete and successful staging of Scottish Rite degree work was a revolutionary break from early-nineteenth-century ritual in dark and nondescript spaces. It was legislation mandating a theatrical interpretation of degree work that laid the foundation for later degree productions. By the mid-nineteenth century, Scottish Rite legislation in both Northern and Southern Jurisdictions required the dramatic presentation of five degrees, referred to as the Indispensable, or Obligatory, Degrees.[23] This meant that Masonic legislation mandated the inclusion of both scenic elements and costumes for the Fourth, Fourteenth, Eighteenth, Thirtieth, and Thirty-second Degrees. The initial settings ranged from the inner sanctum of King Solomon's Temple (see page 168) and secret underground chambers (see page 123) to military camp scenes (see page 203). The five Indispensable Degrees were expanded to fourteen Indispensable Degrees by 1892. Later statutes included the Fifth, Ninth, Thirteenth, Sixteenth, Twenty-second, Twenty-fifth, Twenty-seventh, Twenty-ninth, and Thirty-first Degrees. In addition to these mandated theatrical interpretations, Masons were eager to stage degrees that included impressive settings depicting medieval cathedrals, Egyptian temples, and ancient forests.

Degree productions became a focal point at Scottish Rite Reunions and other Masonic events. Many Scottish Rite Valleys presented their Obligatory Degrees twice each year, every spring and fall. These performances afforded opportunities for both the individual Mason and his Masonic community to shine in a regional

Stereoscope cards were popular sources for images of ancient ruins and foreign cultures in the nineteenth and early twentieth century. Detail, The Forum of Pompeii and Vesuvius, *1894. Courtesy of Wendy Waszut-Barrett.*

Classical Interior *for the Thirty-first Degree with bobbinet in cut drop opening.*

spotlight. Groups of Masons from neighboring areas formed dramatic teams to participate in a single degree production. Practicing each scene for months prior to a reunion, this was the first time when most men would appear in front of an audience. For many, there was a sense of terror, stage fright, and forgotten lines. There was both excitement and hesitation as amateur actors stepped under the stage lights. The stage crew and audience waited in anticipation, wondering whether the newcomer would remember all his lines and staging. Degree directors hovered in the balcony, hoping for success. A neon sign on the back wall of the Santa Fe auditorium would tell actors if they needed to speak "louder" and "slower" (see page 114).

Working as a director, performer, stagehand, costumer, or lighting technician was a special experience. Many delighted in sharing the unique camaraderie of the Masonic degree production team. Joining a degree team was an additional opportunity to nurture fellowship, promote fraternalism, and socially interact with other Masons. It was this individual investment in a Scottish Rite Reunion that brought members from outlying lodges together to be part of the greater Masonic community. Everyone had a responsibility during a reunion, whether it was setting up for the degree, cooking meals, delivering class lectures, or selling Masonic memorabilia. Those on stage and behind the scenes, however, were Masonic stewards who continued a long tradition that had lasted for more than a century. Degree productions provided an anticipated format, presenting moments from a shared past to preserve history for the future. In many ways, Scottish Rite theaters became time capsules for both Masonic history and theatre history. Information and staging techniques were passed from generation to generation, locking the tradition into an early-twentieth-century Victorian American format.

Stagehands and performers, abuzz with activity, attend to last-minute details during a scene change.

The Significance of Scottish Rite Scenery

Degree productions that were once representative of technological innovation now represent a remote heritage. Many drops are no longer used by the membership and have been hidden above the stage for years. Yet these collections provide invaluable information about both Fraternal and theatrical history. Nineteenth-century degree productions, staging practices, painting techniques, and color palettes serve as primary resources for modern historians, scholars, theatre practitioners, and art enthusiasts. Many drops are large-scale artworks produced by nationally recognized artists. These artworks represent a stylistic shift that occurred both on the popular stage and in the world of fine art. Many turn-of-the-twentieth-century scenic artists yearned to exhibit in galleries and to leave the hard work of the scenic studio behind. However, it was in the studio that many young artists gained experience. All started as "potboys"

Raising the Constellation *backdrop reveals painted flats stored against the back wall.*

and assistants to the older artists—apprentices during the day and art students in the evening. Constantly exploring the splendors of color, many learned how to combine paints or dyes harmoniously, to the delight of theatre audiences. Scenic artists explored the same subject matter, compositional layouts, and color palettes of fine art.

Unlike fine art, painting for a theater was never intended as a permanent installation. It was ephemeral, disappearing at a production's close. The backdrops and flats were frequently repainted or repurposed for another production. Unfortunately, this has left us primarily with secondary source material, such as theatre programs, newspaper reviews, technical journals, trade magazines, and personal manuscripts. These are often the only sources of information about the composition and coloration of painted stage settings. Most Scottish Rite scenery in use today originated between 1900 and 1929. Scottish Rite Masons have inadvertently become the stewards of American theatre history. Unfortunately, the collections are slowly deteriorating, and many are in desperate need of restoration. Scottish Rite theaters across the country currently house thousands of painted scenes depicting an important aesthetic shift in the field of American scenic art and stage design.

These collections also identify theatre manufacturers and suppliers of the early twentieth century. As the demand for Scottish Rite degree productions increased, business alliances formed, linking the largest fraternal supply houses with smaller regalia, paraphernalia, and theatre manufacturers. The Santa Fe Scottish Rite contracted with M. C. Lilley & Co., Inc., for all its theatre needs. Mitchell C. Lilley (1819–82) began his business as a publisher, later expanding to supply regalia and paraphernalia for both military and fraternal organizations, as well as Masonic stages. M. C. Lilley contracted entire projects for many Scottish Rite Valleys and then subcontracted individual portions to various manufacturers and suppliers. In March 1913, the *Consistory Bulletin* for the Ancient and Accepted Scottish Rite in New Mexico informed members that $13,000 had been designated for the purchase of all necessary scenery, stage fixtures, and costumes.[24] The scenery installation included seventy-two painted drops, masking draperies, and six border lights spread out over ninety-seven line sets. Other necessary items included painted flats, set pieces, props, and lighting equipment. By the Fall Reunion of that year, fifteen degrees had been staged as theatrical productions.[25] At that same time, approximately twenty-three other Scottish Rite theaters across the country were in the planning or construction stage. As with quality scenery collections, state-of-the-art lighting systems were incorporated into these early-twentieth-century theaters.

Wooden arbors are part of the Santa Fe Scottish Rite counterweight system, allowing stagehands to effortlessly raise and lower scenes for each degree.

Seventy-two drops are suspended above the Santa Fe Scottish Rite stage.

Lowering the backdrop for King Solomon's Throne Room.

Movable floor lights with blue, red, green, and white lamps illuminate the lower sections of painted scenes.

Scottish Rite Stage Lighting

Nineteenth-century oil and gas lighting afforded limited control over hue, intensity, and light distribution. Early electrical fixtures for the stage imitated their predecessors, but the overall intensity and saturation of color were greatly improved. Scottish Rite theaters used either three-color or four-color lighting systems. Each system provided a wide range of colors and possibilities for painted illusion and transformation scenes. A three-color system of red, blue, and white lamps successfully transformed many scenes from daytime to nighttime. Raising the intensity of one light color would dramatically change the appearance of the painted drop or object.

Scottish Rites with greater funding installed four-color systems of red, blue, green, and white lamps. The combination of red, blue, and green light resulted in amber. Additional white light simply increased the overall intensity of light on the stage. In some cases, Scottish Rite Valleys used red, green, and white lighting. This became problematic, as blue was crucial to depict the cool glow of moonlight for nighttime scenes. Over time, many Scottish Rite theaters with the original red, green, and white systems introduced blue lamps into their border lights, ground row lights, and sidelights.

The M. C. Lilley contract with Santa Fe specified a three-color light system for the new stage. Six rows of border lights were hung between painted scenes to provide down light on the scenery and actors. Similarly, six portable ground rows of three-color light strips were placed throughout the stage, illuminating the lower portions of each scene. Two vertical strip lights, installed on either side of the proscenium opening, and two portable bunch lights provided the necessary sidelight for scenery (see page 117). For the balcony, M. C. Lilley included a spotlight to highlight any area on the stage that was not adequately lit or needed special emphasis. A switchboard and a dimmer plant controlled the lighting fixtures on the stage and in the auditorium.[26]

Frank Adam Electric Company of Saint Louis designed and manufactured the lighting controls. Slow or quick lighting changes could be achieved with a single individual working only a few levers. The switches on the main board, a remote unit installed in the basement, were handled from the stage and ensured that the lighting operator was not exposed to electricity from the heavy feed lines. For the dimmer plant, nameplates denoted lighting instrument areas and colors used throughout the space. The system used thirty-four dimmers and other effects, including a manual flasher for lightning and a gong. Frank Adam Electric worked in conjunction with the Major Corporation, which furnished additional lighting equipment and lamps for many Scottish Rite theater installations across the country.

A Frank Adam Electric Company dimmer plant (left) *with a corresponding switchboard in the basement* (right). *The system controls the stage and auditorium lighting.*

The development of electric lighting and modern lighting theory for the theater used light to set the mood and atmosphere of the play. Lighting catalogs advertised, "Modern lighting, in various buildings and theatres, paints with glorious effects the whole range of human emotions, and is accomplished only by engineering."[27] Lighting equipment manufacturers even used small model theaters to test new products for their clients.[28] This coincided with a movement to replace two-dimensional scenes with three-dimensional settings. Traditionally, scenic artists were responsible for painting both the perspective and the atmospheric lighting effects for the setting. The demand for painted scenes began to diminish on the commercial stage, but not on the Scottish Rite stage. It is possible that the design and manufacture of Masonic scenery were still controlled by scenic artists. Two-dimensional scenery for twenty-nine degrees remained easier to store than dimensional settings for the same number.

Early-twentieth-century color combinations and historical lighting systems still create vibrant settings for contemporary degree productions. One example of a paint color combination repeatedly used on scenery is the mixture of ultramarine blue and French mineral orange, producing lavender. This color combination created deep shadows that reflected both warm and cool lights and was prominent throughout painted landscapes, woodland paths, and architectural structures. As the twentieth century progressed, subtle color combinations gave way to brighter versions where a single hue dominated the painted shadows, such as those depicted in the Santa Fe *Quarry* scene. Ultramarine blue or purple lake began to characterize the shadows of the 1920s, allowing cool colors to glow under blue lights for nighttime scenes.

At this same time, some scenic artists employed the practice of placing complementary colors next to each other for visual contrast on the stage. Yellow petals jumped out from purple shadows, orange reflective lights sparkled in blue depths, and bright red curtains framed green marble columns. Scottish Rite scenery collections depict these shifts in the scenic artist's color palette over the course of decades. Theatre artists wrote about current trends in stage design, often demanding the harmonization of scenic painting with improved lighting and color saturation. In 1918 the summer issue of *Theatre Arts Magazine* included an article titled "The Newest Art." It commanded the modern scenic artist to add the "glow" and "science of the Impressionists," using the paintings of Monet, Gauguin, Van Gogh, and Cezanne as examples.[29]

Scenery for the Scottish Rite stage continued to incorporate a turn-of-the-twentieth-century painted aesthetic. Identical compositions were reproduced and repeated by scenic studios for several decades. Although painted years apart, extant Scottish Rite scenery collections provide an opportunity to examine the evolution of drop construction, color palettes, and painting techniques. The mass production of

Painted details from the Hiram's Tomb *backdrop* (left) *and the* Peristyle *backdrop* (right) *demonstrate the subtle shadow colors used in early-twentieth-century scenery. (For the complete scenes see pages 170 and 185.)*

Opposite: *Stagehand with a quarry scene. The predominantly blue shadows signify a shifting aesthetic in the world of twentieth-century scenic art for the stage.*

Masonic scenery codified the Scottish Rite stage settings, despite the ever-evolving aesthetic on most commercial stages. Many Scottish Rite stages have become time capsules. The collections are still as they were when they were originally installed decades ago. Only recently have some Scottish Rite Valleys abandoned these painted scenes for digital projections and video productions.

The Mass Production of Masonic Scenery by Studios

Prior to the rise of the scenic studio system, regional or traveling artists produced much of the mid- to late-nineteenth-century scenery for the theatre. Itinerant artists journeyed from site to site, painting settings for a variety of performance venues, including paraphernalia and early set pieces for Masonic lodges. It was a versatile artist who could design and paint theatrical scenery, murals, signs, and decorative ornaments for theaters, opera houses, cathedrals, public buildings, and private residences. This versatility was common for artists during the early years of the scenic studio system. A significant change occurred when scenery was manufactured in a studio and shipped to distant locations. Building a paint studio near a transportation hub was essential. Chicago became an ideal location. Its massive transportation network facilitated the manufacturing and selling of painted scenery, along with other theatrical goods, to Scottish Rite theaters across the country.

Scenic studios took advantage of this transportation network in another way. They employed traveling salesmen to present various Masonic scenery designs in model stages. In the convenience of a client's office, the salesman assembled custom installations for any Scottish Rite theater. Masonic model designs ranged from 9 inches high by 19 inches wide to 17 inches high by 24 inches wide. Back at the studio, immense filing cabinets stored sets of duplicate designs, as well as other model pieces depicting drops, flats, and profiles for a variety of venues. Each design was organized by scenery type and composition, receiving a unique identification label for immediate retrieval from the studio's complex filing system when a salesman placed an order. Upon securing the contract, the sales representative would wire the specifications back to the studio, and the fabric department would begin.

The mass production of stock scenery for the Fraternity increased overall profitability at many studios. Both Northern and Southern Jurisdictions had their own versions of stock designs for Scottish Rite degree work. Like commercial theatre, Masonic stages used a standard set of scenes that depicted specific compositions. Many were generic enough to suggest a variety of settings for their use in multiple

Details of marble and drapery painting techniques employed during creation of King Solomon's Throne Room. *(See page 175.) Scenic studios employed artists who specialized in specific genres, such as palatial interiors.*

degrees. Mass-producing identical compositions not only economized the process but also indirectly constructed an industry standard. Studios also replicated popular designs of their competitors, marketing them as their own. Furthermore, when scenic artists left one studio, they sometimes took their sketches along to another. Studio stamps and other markings on the back side of a design record its journey; names of previous ownerships are crossed out or replaced with other studio labels. Over time, studios created new designs to replace existing ones in an effort to market additional scenery, hoping that each Scottish Rite would purchase the "new and improved" versions.

Sosman & Landis Studio designed the earliest set of stock scenery for Scottish Rite degree productions. The studio had designed and manufactured installations for more than thirty Scottish Rite theaters by 1912, including the 1893 Oriental Consistory scenery in Chicago. Chapter 5 depicts examples of stock designs by Sosman & Landis for the Santa Fe scenery collection. These same designs were replicated for other Scottish Rite theaters throughout the country.

Sosman & Landis

The Sosman & Landis Studio specialized in the design, construction, painting, and installation of stage scenery and rigging systems. Established in 1877, the studio was well-known for its quality painted scenery, especially that created for Masonic theaters. As with many scenic studios, one of its founders was a scenic artist. Born in Chillicothe, Ohio, Joseph Sanek Sosman (1845–1915) moved to Macomb, Illinois, after serving in the Union army during the Civil War. Advertising as a sign painter in the local directory, Sosman began painting theatrical scenery too. He became an assistant to Chicago-based artist T. B. Harrison in 1872. Four years later, Sosman moved to Chicago, where he and Harrison painted for a variety of entertainment venues. By 1877, Sosman met his eventual business partner, Abraham "Perry" Landis (1848–1905) and they rented their first studio.[30]

Landis was born into a theatrical family and moved to Chicago at age twelve. Although Landis wasn't an artist, he traveled extensively throughout the southwestern United States and Mexico before entering the scenic studio business with Sosman. Landis worked primarily as a traveling salesman, crossing the country by rail and securing orders for scenery painted by Sosman and his crew. Sosman & Landis built a new studio on Clinton Street in 1886. The company remained in the building until 1923, when a new tenant, Chicago Studios, rented the space.

View of the main studio at Sosman & Landis in an advertising catalog, ca. 1910. Courtesy of Lance Brockman.

A Sosman & Landis Masonic design for Hiram's Tomb. *These small paintings provided clients with various options for Scottish Rite degree productions. Holak Collection (PA049), Performing Arts Archives, University of Minnesota Libraries, Minneapolis. Photograph by Wendy Waszut-Barrett.*

The earliest designs for Masonic scenery at Sosman & Landis were attributed to the studio's top scenic artist, David Austin Strong (1820–1911). Strong was also a Freemason, having entered the Fraternity in 1852 while living in New Haven, Connecticut. He joined the Scottish Rite after moving to Chicago in 1876.[31] Chicago's Oriental Consistory gave Strong an honorary Thirty-third Degree after his extensive role in creating its scenery.[32] Credited as "the Daddy of Masonic design," Strong's understanding of degree work, stage machinery, and his ability to paint for a variety of artistic genres made him a perfect fit to design and paint some of the earliest Fraternal scenery installations.[33] Prior to Chicago, Strong enjoyed a successful career in New York City, creating visual spectacle for a variety of stages. It was a well-known and experienced scenic artist, like Strong, who became the key to a studio's success.

The studio continued to expand as the demand for Fraternal scenery increased, with Masonic production peaking at Sosman & Landis in 1913. Sosman passed away the following year. Sosman's absence necessitated another artist, Thomas Gibbs Moses (1856–1934), to supervise all studio production. Like Sosman, Moses started his career as a scenic artist at an early age. His desire to become an artist lured him from the small town of Sterling, Illinois, to the bustling city in 1873 at the age of seventeen. In Chicago, Moses found work at Jevne & Almini's fresco studio, as assistant to head artist C. Louis "Lou" Malmsha (1847–1882), who had been an employee there since 1863. Malmsha was also the lead scenic artist at McVicker's Theatre. He introduced Moses to scenic art in 1874. Eventually, Moses secured work at the newly founded Sosman & Landis Studio. His quick completion of studio projects prompted him to accept additional painting work after hours. Sosman & Landis initially supported these freelance projects, advising Moses to forge ahead and gain some experience.[34]

Thomas G. Moses works on a theater model in 1906. Harry Ransom Center, University of Texas at Austin (John R. Rothgeb, Box 6, Moses T.G. Photographs folder).

This was a common occurrence, but one that enticed many artists to establish their own companies. Scenic artists constantly struggled between the desire for freedom and the desire for a steady income. Moses had a basic desire to control the painted outcome, accept independent projects, and travel. Freedom from supervision and the ability to control his own schedule were more appealing than the security of a reliable studio income. Sosman desperately sought to keep Moses on staff, providing him with a furnished studio and all painting supplies. Additionally, Moses was promised all subcontracted work. In spite of these generous terms, he continued to leave the studio for extended periods, particularly during 1894–96 and 1900–04.

Moses's absence was acutely felt at the studio when business dramatically increased and Landis left the company due to health reasons in 1902. Sosman had to assume many of Landis's administrative duties, so he needed Moses to return to the company as head artist on the studio floor. In 1904 Moses returned to the Sosman &

The paint sweater and cap of Thomas G. Moses were hidden above the Scottish Rite stage in Fort Scott, Kansas, until their discovery by Wendy Waszut-Barrett in 2015. Photograph by Wendy Waszut-Barrett.

Landis Studio. The sharp increase in Masonic business prompted the studio to open an annex space. By 1909 the company retained a staff of forty-eight at its main studio and a staff of twelve at the annex. The studio's largest and most lucrative projects were Scottish Rite theaters. A Masonic installation typically averaged eighty drops, a substantial contract when compared with commercial theater installations that only numbered ten to forty. Scottish Rite scenery installations were massive endeavors that yielded significant profits.

Business continued to boom, and by 1912 the main studio increased its staff to sixty full-time employees. Between 1912 and 1915, Moses was personally responsible for eleven Scottish Rite scenery installations: Santa Fe, New Mexico; Portland, Maine; Austin, Texas; Milwaukee, Wisconsin; Ashville, North Carolina; Grand Forks, North Dakota; Tucson, Arizona; Pittsburg, Pennsylvania; Omaha, Nebraska; Helena, Montana; and Los Angeles, California. At the same time, the company began to change course. Sosman had started to slowly withdraw from the running of the business, taking extended family vacations and sending postcards from distant locations. Moses now worked as a combined salesman, studio supervisor, and lead scenic artist.

When Sosman passed away in 1915, stockholders elected Moses president, Sosman's son Arthur vice president, and Abraham Perry's son Perry "Lester" Landis secretary and treasurer. Unfortunately, none of these men had the business intuition or connections of the original studio founders. Moses continued to lead the design and painting at the studio but struggled with the administrative duties, expenses, and difficult clients. All the while, he battled with the shareholders, whose primary concern was profitability.

The Studio System

The scenic art career of Thomas G. Moses coincided with the rise of the scenic studio system. Unlike their itinerant predecessors, studio artists specialized in a particular genre. New artists were expected to be well versed in a specific subject matter, whether it was draperies, interiors, exteriors, or human figures. They utilized specific painting techniques for each specialty. This division of artistic labor enforced the economical and quick application of paint by well-trained individuals. Studios hired scenic artists not only for their artistic strengths, but also their speed. Recalling his success as a painter, Moses wrote, "The others were able to draw more, because they were better in the artistic end, but I had it over them when it came to speed."[35] It was this speed that returned the greatest profits to shareholders. The entire painting staff needed to produce scenery as quickly as possible. As soon as one drop was finished on the paint frame, it would be immediately removed and another would take its place.

This quick turnaround of painted scenery production demanded a unique type of building with special equipment and scenic art tools. The Sosman & Landis studios were designed and built for the sole purpose of painting theatrical scenery, with special frames, painting bridges, and skylights. Suspended on lines operated by a windlass or counterweight system, mechanized paint frames were raised and lowered into slots that were constructed in the paint studio floor. This system allowed the scenic artist to remain stationary throughout the entire painting process and to easily access all areas of the drop, thus greatly reducing the overall time required to paint a composition. The photograph of the main Sosman & Landis studio on page 146 depicts the complexity of rigging for movable paint frames. The annex studio was located in the spacious old Waverly Theater, rented by Sosman & Landis for Moses in 1882. It measured 210 feet in length and 93 feet in breadth with walls that were 40 feet in height.[36] The studio included four paint frames that provided ample floor space for all kinds of scenery work and construction.

A scenic artist's case with a pounce wheel used to punch small holes in paper for the transfer of patterns onto backdrops (top). *The original marks left from a pounce pattern are still visible on the* Cathedral *backdrop* (bottom). *Courtesy of Wendy Waszut-Barrett.*

Backdrops, cut drops, and leg drops were called "soft goods," beginning their lives in the fabric room of a studio. They were constructed from a tightly woven fabric such as strong unbleached muslin of cambric or Russian linen. Prior to the mass production and shipping of scenery, many drops were constructed with wide pieces of fabric and horizontal seams. This process used bolts measuring two yards in width, or six feet. Only moving panoramas necessitated perpendicular seaming, as these long drops scrolled from one vertical cylinder to another. The studio system's transportation of painted scenery altered its practice of constructing drops. The studio drops were now vertically rolled onto tubes for transportation, as was the case with moving panoramas. Sosman & Landis used 36-inch widths of fabric to create backdrops, thus reducing the overall cost of materials. After construction, the drop was attached to a paint frame and secured with 2-inch clout nails. Placed approximately 4 inches apart, these nails were driven in only halfway, since they needed to be taken out again when the painting was completed. Now the drop was ready for sizing, priming, and painting.

The adhesive medium for sizing, priming, and painting occurred in a natural process when rendering animal hides. Gelatinous hide glue was reduced to a solid dry form and sold by weight to a variety of artisans as a binding medium for both painting and building. Dry glue was soaked overnight in water and cooked in a double boiler. Once melted, the thick syrup was diluted with an equal amount of water to form the "strong size." Applying strong size would tighten and seal the fabric's surface. Sizing a drop prepared the surface for painting with aniline dye, the medium used to produce translucent stage effects when portions of a drop were backlit. Many vaudeville acts required dye drops that could be folded and placed with others in a steamer trunk for safe and easy transport. This need resulted in the creation of scenery painted solely with aniline dye. Most other scenery for permanent installation in a theater was painted with dry pigment, not dye.

Opaque paint needed a prime coat prior to any color application. The traditional formula for primer was strong size mixed with whiting, a fine powder primarily consisting of silica, zinc, lead, or a mixture thereof. Whiting powder was soaked in a galvanized tub of water overnight, ensuring that it was thoroughly dissolved and free from lumps. It was then slaked before use, a process that separated the gritty substance from the chalk. The gritty residue settled to the bottom, while the remaining paste was placed in priming buckets. The white paste was then mixed with a little touch of color to make a contrast when it was applied to near-white fabric. Strong size was added to this mixture and evenly worked into the fabric, providing a clean and uniform base on which to draw the composition.

Once the drop was sized and primed, the artist used charcoal to draw both a horizontal line and a perpendicular line to lay out the composition. These two lines were reference points from which all other lines would be measured; artists thus constructed a grid to enlarge the small-scale design. One-foot increments were marked along the perimeter of the fabric, allowing scenic artists to successfully transfer the drop composition without having to step back from the canvas. As multiple paint frames were closely spaced in the Sosman & Landis studios, artists had only a narrow platform to work along. This confined space prevented artists from stepping back to examine their entire subject from a distance. After the composition was drawn out, the drop was ready to paint.

Dry Pigment Painting

The success of dry pigment painting depended on several factors during the preparation of both binder and paint. The quality of materials, as well as the preparation, was crucial to the overall success and longevity of the painted scene. Careful attention to detail throughout the entire process was the key to success. Many Scottish Rite installations have long outlasted the average life expectancy of a painted drop

Dry pigment colors, dry hide glue, and scenic art brushes. Courtesy of Wendy Waszut-Barrett

Charcoal sticks used to draw compositions (bottom)*, such as in the detail of the* Forest *scene* (top). *Courtesy of Wendy Waszut-Barrett.*

due to their expert creators. These scenery collections were never intended to be permanent art installations. Regardless, many Fraternal collections have survived for well over a century.

Scenic artists created working size for the application of color by adding four parts water to one part strong size. The exact amount of water depended upon the quality of the glue, and the final strength of working size could vary considerably, even from the same manufacturer. When the working size set, it became a firm jelly, especially in a cold environment. A common practice for scenic artists to test the strength of size involved dipping their fingers into the size water and pressing them together for a few minutes, allowing them to dry. If their fingers separated freely, the size was too thin. If their fingers stuck together too quickly and firmly, the mixture was too strong. Scenic artists avoided weak size, as the colors would soon wear off the surface, thus destroying the painted illusion. Artists also avoided strong size, as the final result would have a shiny appearance. The sheen from strong size reflected lights and destroyed the effect of painted illusion. Additionally, over time, strong size would crack and flake off the fabric surface.

Dry pigment was sold as either a solid block or ground powder. Large amounts of color were shipped in wooden boxes from pigment suppliers such as Chicago's Western Dry Color Company, Wadsworth-Howland Company, and Alston-Lucas Paint Company. Some pigments were transported as consolidated blocks, requiring a color mill to grind the pigment into the necessary powder. This powder was then plunged in water to soften it into a thick paste without bringing it to a completely liquid state. The paste was placed either directly into bowls on the palette or in earthenware containers for storage. For most painting, dry pigment colors were left in their pure state. Mixing straight colors on a palette was economical for the studio and greatly reduced waste. Every evening, the soft mounds of paste hardened on the palette. In the morning, these mounds were crushed into a fine powder again and moistened with water to reconstitute the necessary paste. Once again, the pigment was ready to be mixed with size water for application to the painting. Malachite green, magenta, and certain other colors were sold pre-dampened in a pulpy state. If these pigments dried out, the water would simply sit on the surface without being absorbed into the color. A solvent, such as denatured alcohol, was then necessary to moisten the pigment so that it would accept the water.

The duties surrounding the time-consuming endeavor of dry pigment preparation and priming fell primarily to young boys, often aspiring artists. Earning approximately one-fifth of the standard scenic artist salary, they were completely at the disposal of the older staff and not always guaranteed the advancement of an apprenticeship program. These young workers were responsible for a myriad of tasks, including much of the heavy lifting at the studio. They prepared size, filled paint bowls, cleaned palettes, shifted scenery, primed drops, cut and shellacked stencils, netted drops, swept the floor, loaded transportation wagons, ran errands, and picked pounces. A pounce pattern is an artistic technique used to transfer any pattern to a backdrop. A pounce wheel creates holes in the pattern and powdered charcoal or chalk is rubbed through the pounce holes (see page 150).

The title "pot boy" referred to the task of filling earthenware paint pots, but really identified cheap labor.[37] The young workers dutifully cleaned and filled palettes with the available colors. Dry pigment colors kept at Sosman & Landis included zinc white, lemon yellow, medium yellow, orange chrome, orange mineral, Turkey red, burnt sienna, Venetian red, rose lake, ultramarine blue, cobalt blue, celestial blue, Italian blue (also called alpine blue), yellow ochre, raw sienna, Dutch pink, chrome green light, chrome green dark, raw umber, burnt umber, Van Dyke brown, malachite green, black, and magenta.[38] Scenic artists selected their colors to fit the needs of each composition. When an artist wanted his palette cleaned, he called for a "swipe up," which included having the palette washed with a sponge, his brushes cleaned, and the old working size replaced with new working size.[39]

Certain drops required aniline dye instead of opaque pigment. Unlike opaque dry pigment, dyes allowed light to shine through the fabric. Backlighting dyed areas allowed translucent sections to glow, such as in the Santa Fe *Woods* scene. Stained-glass cathedral windows and starlit skies incorporated dyed sections within their opaque compositions. For staging the Eighteenth Degree, *Faith*, *Hope*, and *Charity* were revealed as starlit constellations to the candidate on cue, as depicted on page 191. Although light boxes placed on the back of translucent sections localized the light, back painting was often necessary to prevent light from spilling through the surrounding fabric areas.

The dry pigment painting system continued as an affordable alternative to premixed paint throughout the twentieth century. During the peak of Scottish Rite scenery production, there was no cost-effective method to produce painted scenery with premixed paints either in the studio or on site. In addition, it was easier to ship and store the necessary colors separately, extending the shelf life for each. Once dry pigment and size water were combined, the resulting paint had a fairly short shelf life before turning rancid. Although premixed paints were increasingly available to artists, they had yet to be fully integrated into any theatrical painting system.[40] Scenic artists for the theater continued to mix their product by hand, purchasing dry pigments and water-based binding medium separately.

The front of a transparent section painted with aniline dye (top) *and a back view of the same section* (bottom).

Opposite: Forest *scene. The use of aniline dye on raw fabric creates translucent sections, allowing the light to shine through when backlit. Translucencies provide an opportunity to depict picturesque sunsets in forest scenes.*

It was not until the mid-twentieth century that casein became a practical and useful alternative to hide glue. Advancements in the paint industry discouraged the imperfect mixing of paint with hand paddles; this scenic art skill was no longer required, and knowledge of dry pigment paint systems slowly began to vanish. New machinery was developed to grind, mix, and tint thousands of gallons in a few minutes, providing an easy-to-use product for professionals and amateurs alike. Products and painting techniques for scenic art continued to adjust in an ever-changing industry, forever altering the dynamic of the early-twentieth-century scenic art trade. Yet, on the Scottish Rite stage, theatrical traditions stood still.

Cut Drops

Many painted illusions for Scottish Rite scenes incorporated cut centers, supported with theatrical gauze, bobbinet, or netting. Theatrical gauze functioned as a predecessor to contemporary sharkstooth scrim. In a transformation scene, theatrical gauze allowed the painted surface to "dissolve" and become transparent on stage if lit from behind. Made from cotton or flax, open weave fabric worked with stage lights to reveal hidden objects placed behind a backdrop. Front lighting allowed the painted surface to appear solid and uniform with the composition. Backlighting revealed objects placed behind the drop, such as the Ark of the Covenant in the *Treasure Chamber*.

Opera netting and open weave netting were also used for cut drops when the background needed to remain visible. Open weave netting was especially effective for cloud scenes or heavenly compositions, as it provided an atmospheric haze, placing individuals, scenes, and objects in a mystical netherworld that was softened when viewed through the netting (see page 133). One-inch netting glued on cut drops allowed the audience to permanently view whatever was behind the cut opening, creating a dimensional plane and visual depth for the stage picture. Attaching 1-inch netting between tree trunks in a woods scene provided the necessary view of the backdrop (see page 158). Cut sections were identified and marked with an *X* for removal. Complex compositions often demanded a massive amount of labor; pot boys traditionally did this time-consuming task. A cut drop was flipped facedown, and charcoal lines were snapped to identify the area where netting would be attached to the fabric. The netting was placed parallel to the drop's edges, stretched, and tacked to the floor for the gluing process. With a long-haired brush, dots of glue were placed on each knotted intersection of netting to secure it to the fabric. For theatrical gauze or bobbinet, the entire cut edge of the opening received a thin coat of glue.

A section of theatrical gauze lit from the front (top) *and the back* (bottom) *to reveal the Ark of the Covenant in the* Treasure Chamber *scene (for full scene, see page 184).*

Foil strips were attached to a painted backdrop to reflect stage lights, such as in the Fiery Torments *scene. (See page 190 for the full scene.)*

Scottish Rite scenery also incorporated a variety of decorative accessories applied to the painted surface and attached with a mixture of pitch, turpentine, resin, beeswax, and tallow. This mixture was used in a hot and liquid state to attach foil strips or Dutch metal. These small metallic areas on the drop reflected stage lights.[41] For Scottish Rite scenery, foils accentuated the fires of the underworld and created sizzling reflections suggesting the heated atmosphere. Red, blue, green, gold, and silver foils were attached to the edges of tormented souls, strange creatures, and rocky outcrops. The slightest air current would move the drop, allowing the foils to catch the light. Similar techniques were used to simulate the glitter of golden vessels in treasure chambers or to depict twinkling stars. For stars, silver spangles of various sizes were either glued to the painted surface or hung from long, dark blue cotton strings to reflect stage lights throughout the scene, such as in the Constellation setting on page 191.

Masonic Scenery Installations

Masonic installations at Sosman & Landis made up approximately 30 percent of all incoming orders by 1910.[42] Moses documents his direct involvement with more than one hundred Masonic scenery collections between 1891 and 1929. During this time, half of all recorded installations were produced from 1905 to 1915. This

Detail of the netted section in the Forest *scene cut drop from front* (left) *and back* (right). *(See page 155 for complete scene.)*

Glue pot, glue brush, and 1920s netting. Courtesy of Wendy Waszut-Barrett.

massive amount of fraternal scenery necessitated the implementation of a new labeling system. Prior to this time, drops were labeled solely with in-house identification, all written in charcoal. Sosman & Landis drops created before 1905 seldom include any specific identification denoting either degree or subject matter—only size and location. With the simultaneous creation of many Scottish Rite collections, scenery handlers needed an effective system to identify drops as they made their way from the studio to a final location. The fabric department initially labeled drops on the top left of the back side, using charcoal to denote the size and location. This facilitated the drop's placement on the correct paint frame. For the Santa Fe Scottish Rite, the standard drop size was 24 × 36 feet. Occasionally, a descriptor would be included nearby. However, the charcoal labels were hidden once the drop was rolled for transport and were of no use to scenery installers.

Sosman & Landis implemented a secondary labeling system when Masonic scenery production dramatically increased and multiple installations were simultaneously produced in the same studio. After 1908, individual drops for large Scottish Rite installations included a stencil denoting the degree, subject matter, and destination location. The information was placed on the top stage-left side and bottom stage-right side of each drop, always parallel to the side of the drop. The stencil on the stage-right side was for identification from the stage floor so that the stagehand could easily identify the scene. The stage-left stencil near the top batten was for shipping identification. As each drop was rolled vertically for shipping, the placement of the label further instructed the installation crew how to unroll each drop. Even if a pot boy had rolled a drop incorrectly at the studio, the installers knew how to unroll the drop and correctly orient it for hanging.

The drops were rolled and shipped from the studio to each Scottish Rite theater by rail as either full or half-carload lots.[43] On location, the drops were prepared for hanging by attaching wooden sandwich battens to the top and bottom of each scene. The painted fabric was "sandwiched" between top battens measuring 1 × 4 inches and directly attached to the counterweight system. Bottom battens, measuring 1 × 3 inches, provided the necessary weight and tension to ensure a wrinkle-free surface once a drop was hanging. First, the top sandwich batten was clout-nailed into the stage floor to form a straight line and hold it securely in place. With 0.25-inch upholstery tacks spaced every 4 inches, the top of the drop was then attached to the secured wooden batten. Another wooden batten sandwiched this fabric and was attached with slotted screws. Once a complete unit, the top batten was pried up from the stage floor, and the clout nails were hammered into the back of the batten.

Typically, three 0.5-inch holes were drilled into top wooden battens, creating pick points to accept wire rope made of Plow Steel. At the Santa Fe Scottish Rite stage, pick points connected the top of each drop to a counterweight rigging system that M. C. Lilley & Co. referred to as "Brown's special counter weighted style of installation" (see page 136).[44] Offstage counterweights in wooden arbors allowed Masonic stagehands to effortlessly raise and lower the drops. For decades, most drops have hung from the same cables and hardware that were attached during installation.

Volunteers prepare to lower Peristyle *backdrop for restoration in 2005. Courtesy of Wendy Waszut-Barrett.*

Restoring the Past

The scenery at the Santa Fe Scottish Rite Theater hung undisturbed for ninety years—from installation in 1912 until 2002. It was the gentle handling of generations of Masonic stagehands that ultimately preserved this remarkable collection. In addition to necessary building maintenance to prevent roof leaks, a dry temperate climate contributed to the overall longevity of the historic stage paintings. Members have lovingly looked after their treasured scenery for decades. Good stewardship, ideal environmental conditions, and sheer luck have preserved these painted scenes. The most common damage to Scottish Rite scenery collections has resulted from water, rental groups, and amateur repairs. Of all the factors that affect the overall condition and longevity of a painted backdrop, water damage and high humidity are the most treacherous. The other causes of deterioration are often easily addressed and corrected.

The Valley of Santa Fe also actively sought historical scenery experts to repair its collection. Santa Fe Masons contacted Lance Brockman at the University of Minnesota in Minneapolis in its search for someone to examine the collection and recommend a course for preservation. Brockman is a leading expert in both historical scene painting and Scottish Rite scenery; for almost two decades, he traveled with two other theatre professors, Larry Hill and Rhett Bryson, to document scenery collections across the country. For more than three decades, Brockman instructed undergraduate and graduate students in historical scene painting techniques, the dry pigment painting system, and early-twentieth-century scenery design.

When Brockman received the call from Santa Fe in 2001, I was a doctoral candidate in the University of Minnesota Department of Theater Arts and Dance. I had been trained in the dry pigment paint system under Brockman's tutelage as an undergraduate, and my primary focus was early-twentieth-century scene painting techniques and the origin of Scottish Rite scenery. I spent most of my undergraduate years replicating historic scenery, studying fraternal stage design, and placing it within the context of both art history and theatre technology. As an undergraduate,

I processed two Masonic scenery design collections and replicated many subjects as both small-scale watercolor paintings and large-scale dry pigment drops.

I traveled south to evaluate the Santa Fe scenery collection in 2002, proposing a phased plan to restore the entire collection. The restoration project utilized a combination of Masonic volunteers and local hires from the Santa Fe area. The crew included Scottish Rite Masons, their families, and local artists—a combination of both retirees and those still active in the workforce. Local hires were selected through both newspaper advertisements and word of mouth. Many area artists joined the force, bringing a variety of fine art skills and conservation techniques. Each day of work involved between five and fifteen individuals, depending on the task.

Each assisted with the cleaning, repair, and stabilization of every drop. During the summers of 2002 and 2005, more than half of the drops were carefully removed from their cables, stripped of all stage hardware, and loosely rolled for transport to the banquet room for cleaning, stabilization, and repair. We worked on six drops simultaneously. The cut drops with netted centers required immediate attention and took the greatest amount of time to repair. Although much of the netting was still intact, some was starting to fail and affect the painted surround. New netting and bobbinet replaced older damaged versions. The crusty remnants of old glue dots were removed, with each knotted intersection receiving an individual dot of new glue. Dozens of workers spent weeks on the floor carefully attaching new netting to the historic cut drops.

Wendy Waszut-Barrett (center) *and two local artists glue new netting onto a leg drop in 2005. Courtesy of Wendy Waszut-Barrett.*

The removal of old battens, hardware, and deteriorated fabric provided an opportunity to discover lost remnants of history and early-twentieth-century scenic studio practices. Long-forgotten information about materials, standard processes, and studios that had manufactured the drops was slowly revealed during each restoration. Every discovery was documented in detail. This information would be compared with other collections from the same era. From 2002 to 2005, I was also restoring a Sosman & Landis Scottish Rite scenery collection in Saint Paul, Minnesota. Created in 1910, it was much larger, and it included scenes for both the Symbolic Lodge and the York Rite of Freemasonry. The compositions from the two collections were almost identical, with many of the original designs contained in the scenery collection database at the University of Minnesota Libraries Performing Arts Archives.

I had first encountered these scenery designs as an undergraduate student. Between 1989 and 1991, I received two grants from the Undergraduate Research Opportunities Program to process two Masonic scenery design collections. My duties included the unpacking, organizing, and processing of the Great Western Stage Equipment Company Collection and the Holak Collection. It was the Holak Collection that contained the majority of the Sosman & Landis designs for Scottish

Rite theaters throughout the Northern and Southern Jurisdictions, including the Valleys of Santa Fe and Saint Paul. The Holak Collection contained 174 color renderings and 8 pencil sketches of stage designs for fraternal organizations. The majority of these designs represented the original compositions designed by Sosman & Landis. They were salvaged from an abandoned studio in New York City during the late 1980s by a former New York Studio employee.

New York Studio was founded and managed by former Sosman & Landis employee David Hunt. In 1910, Hunt moved to New York and became the eastern affiliate for Sosman & Landis, sharing contracts and artists for more than a decade. Hunt also used the Sosman & Landis scenic studio as his "Chicago Studio" branch. At this time, many studios established regional offices; studio affiliations were common during times of plenty to handle the increased workload.

Looking toward the Future

The Santa Fe Scottish Rite scenery collection is a unique example of early-twentieth-century scenic art and stage design. Remarkably, the Valley of Santa Fe did not replace its scenery during the two later periods of Masonic theater growth. Many Masonic organizations renovated their spaces and enlarged or replaced their scenery collections during the decades after World War I and World War II. Their original collections were removed and refurbished for the use of new Scottish Rite Valleys emerging across the country. The Valley of Santa Fe continued to use its scenery as intended, without shifting the original order of backdrops. The members did not drastically alter their collection during the decades that ensued to accommodate new degree presentations.

Creating an exact replica of any historic drop from the Santa Fe Scottish Rite scenery collection is impossible. There is a dearth of scenic artists well versed in historic painting techniques and the dry pigment paint system used in the United States. Any contemporary replicas of historical compositions will fail to capture the original depth of color, as many dyes and dry pigments used to create the 1912 scenery are no longer available. Furthermore, the brushstrokes of a contemporary artist will never show the same fluidity of motion or technique used in historical compositions. Modern artists lack the technical knowledge gained over decades of work in an early-twentieth-century scenic studio. Their scenic art predecessors worked six days a week, ten to twelve hours each day, producing hundreds, if not thousands, of dry pigment backdrops. Their expertise remains unequaled. Although a close approximation of a composition can be produced with certain accuracy, the overall

Historical backdrops from King Solomon's Apartments *were used during the Afghani wedding scene in the film* Whiskey Tango Foxtrot. *© Paramount Pictures 2016, photograph by Frank Masi.*

economy in paint application and the simplicity of brushstroke remain absent from contemporary replicas.

Scottish Rite scenery and regalia collections are rapidly disappearing across the United States. The maintenance and repair of these beautiful artifacts are often perceived as optional. Tattered remnants of once lavish settings continue to deteriorate high above Masonic stages. Many Masons fail to understand the significance of their holdings as a material culture shared between the American public and the Fraternity. These are holdings of regional, national, and international significance. As long as the backdrops can be lowered and costumed characters appear on cue, much needed repairs are often deferred in lieu of other expenditures. The inability to utilize a drop during a Scottish Rite Reunion is often the only instigator to repair a scene or examine its rigging. Most Valleys are unable to finance the repair and restoration of their damaged scenes, so they are often retired or discarded. A few Scottish Rite Valleys have replaced their theatrical settings with digital productions. The justification for this is that removal is cheaper than restoration. As the Fraternity continues to witness decreased membership, some Scottish Rite Valleys auction off their beloved artifacts and sell their buildings, moving to smaller facilities. Masonic membership has ebbed and flowed throughout the group's history and is currently in a period of decline. The Valley of Santa Fe has remained in its home and kept Masonic traditions alive for itself and for members of the community. Successfully responding to the changing times, it has opened its doors to the public, maintained its building, and restored its scenery collection.

Just as degree productions transported early-twentieth-century members to distant landscapes, contemporary filmmakers now use the Scottish Rite space to transport millions of moviegoers to foreign locales. In 2015 the stage and other areas of the building were transformed for various foreign settings, including a twenty-first-century hotel in Afghanistan. The magical moment when the audience entered the early-twentieth-century world of the play continues. The Santa Fe Scottish Rite is a perfect example of a how a Masonic organization blends Fraternal history with current events, preserving the past for future generations.

NOTES

1. For information on the first appearance of degree productions in the western region of the Northern Jurisdiction, see Wendy Waszut-Barrett, "Scenic Shifts upon the Scottish Rite Stage: Designing for Masonic Theatre, 1859–1928" (PhD diss., University of Minnesota, Minneapolis, 2009), University of Minnesota Digital Conservancy, http://hdl.handle.net/11299/52606.

2. Ibid., 57–70.

3. The name Symbolic Lodge refers to the first three degrees. This is the entry point for speculative Freemasonry and necessary for further entrance into Masonic organizations by Master Masons and their families.

4. Pike was a member of a ritual revision committee, self-publishing and personally distributing the first printing of his *Magnum Opus,* or *Great Work.*

5. Charles Thompson McClenachan, *The Book of the Ancient and Accepted Scottish Rite of Freemasonry Containing Instructions in All the Degrees from the Third to the Thirty-Third and Last Degree of the Rite* (New York: Macoy Publishing and Masonic Supply), 1913.

6. Jack P. A. De Vise, *Magnificent Heritage: 150 Years of Scottish Rite Freemasonry in the Valley of Cincinnati* (Cincinnati, OH: Scottish Rite, 2003), 152.

7. Supreme Council for the Southern Jurisdiction, *Transactions of the Supreme Council of the 33rd Degree for the Southern Jurisdiction of the United States of America, October 1882* (Washington, DC: Joseph L. Pearson, 1882), 12.

8. Ibid., 12.

9. "Winona, Minnesota," *Masonic Chronicle* 8, no. 7 (April 1889): 75.

10. Grand Lodge of Illinois, *Proceedings of the Grand Lodge of Illinois* (Chicago: Grand Lodge of Illinois, 1892), 121.

11. Grand Lodge of Illinois, *Proceedings of the Grand Lodge of Illinois* (Chicago: Grand Lodge of Illinois, 1894), 205.

12. Charles E. Rosenbaum, "Albert Pike Consistory, Little Rock, Arkansas," *The New Age Magazine* (1904): 286.

13. *Santa Fe Scottish Rite Bulletin* 15, no. 2 (October–November–December 1933): 6.

14. James D. Carter, *History of the Supreme Council, 33rd (Mother Supreme Council of the World) Ancient and Accepted Scottish Rite of Freemasonry, Southern Jurisdiction, U.S.A., 1891–1921* (Washington, DC: Supreme Council 33rd, 1971), 146.

15. Ibid.

16. Harriet W. McBride, "Business and the Brethren: The Influence of Regalia Houses on Fraternalism," *Heredom* 12 (2004): 188.

17. M. C. Lilley & Co. brochure, *It Takes You Back* (Columbus, OH: M. C. Lilley& Co., January 16, 1914), 1.

18. Ibid.

19. *Santa Fe Scottish Rite Bulletin* 33, no. 2 (1952): 6.

20. "Electric Scenic Theatre," Chicagology, January 3, 2016, https://chicagology.com/2016/01/03/electric-scenic-theater/.

21. Ibid.

22. *Gems of the World's Fair.* This drop and the landscape for the Eighteenth-degree Peristyle was the work of Thomas Gibbs Moses, whose world's fair work included the Javanese Theater, the Chinese Theater, "A Day in the Swiss Alps," "South Sea Islanders," "Kansas State Exhibit," "Fabio Romano," "The Black Crook," and "Columbus"—and outside shows for the Trocodevs, Empire Theatre, and Isabelle Theatre. He additionally completed a dozen big floats for the fair, including "Lady of Venice" for William F. Cody (Buffalo Bill).

23. The Obligatory, or Indispensable, Degrees were the Fourth, Fourteenth, Eighteenth, Thirtieth, and Thirty-second.

24. *Consistory Bulletin* (Santa Fe) 15, no. 2 (December 1933): 6.

25. Ibid.

26. Bestor G. Brown, Kansas City, Missouri, to Wm. G. Bell, Austin, Texas, January 7, 1913, John R. Rothgeb Collection, Box 11, Harry Ransom Center, University of Texas at Austin.

27. Major Equipment Company, *Lighting Equipment by Major: General Catalogue Number 17* (Chicago: Schmidt Printing, 1931), 2.

28. Ibid., 3.

29. Rollo Peters, "The Newest Art," *Theatre Arts Magazine* (Summer 1918): 124.

30. The first Sosman & Landis scenic studio was located at 277–279 Clark Street in Chicago.

31. David Strong became a member of Hiram Lodge No. 1 AF & AM in New Haven, Connecticut.

32. Stanley F. Maxwell, Lexington, Massachusetts, to John R. Rothgeb, John R. Rothgeb Collection, Box 11, Harry Ransom Center, University of Texas at Austin.

33. Thomas Gibbs Moses, *My Diary and Scrapbook*, unpublished manuscript, Theatre Arts Collection, Harry Ransom Center, University of Texas at Austin, 55.

34. Ibid., 20.

35. Ibid.

36. Ibid., 33.

37. John Hanny, Chicago, Illinois, to John R. Rothgeb, Austin, Texas, October 8, 1979, John R. Rothgeb Collection, Box 2, Harry Ransom Center, University of Texas at Austin.

38. Ibid.

39. Ibid.

40. Industries using solvent-based paint on wood, cement, and other nonporous surfaces readily incorporated premixed colors into their painting processes. Fine artists also sought out premixed oil paints in tubes for convenience in the studio and for plein air painting.

41. Dutch metal was a form of brass sold in thin sheets, cut and applied as a reflective element to backdrops and other stage props.

42. Hanny, Chicago, Illinois, to Rothgeb, Austin, Texas, April 22, 1980, John R. Rothgeb Collection, Box 2, Harry Ransom Center, University of Texas at Austin.

43. Bestor G. Brown, Kansas City, Missouri, to Wm. G. Bell, Austin, Texas, July 11, 1912, John R. Rothgeb Collection, Box 11, Austin, Texas, Harry Ransom Center, University of Texas at Austin.

44. Ibid.

Z

5
Scenic Symbolism: Degree Productions for the Scottish Rite

PHOTOGRAPHY BY JO WHALEY
AND TEXT BY WENDY WASZUT-BARRETT

SCOTTISH RITE MEMBERS WILLINGLY TRAVELED GREAT DISTANCES to enjoy degree productions during a reunion. The process of incorporating theatrical scenery and visual spectacle into Scottish Rite degrees represents a shared material culture between Freemasonry and the American theatre. It constitutes a unique lineage that documents a significant moment in the early twentieth century. During the fall of 2016, Jo Whaley and Wendy Waszut-Barrett staged scenes from degree productions that a Masonic audience would have witnessed in 1912. Not indicative of current degree presentations, this chapter provides a unique and colorful look into Santa Fe's dramatic past.

SCENIC ILLUSION
BEHIND THE SCENES DURING THE FOURTH DEGREE
This aerial view is from the fly rail, where stagehands work lines to deftly raise and lower drops for degree productions. From this perspective, three-dimensional props stand out from their two-dimensional backings, and painted floor cloths cover linoleum squares.

4° SECRET MASTER

HOLY OF HOLIES, SETTING FOR THE FIRST SCENE

5° PERFECT MASTER
VEIL OF TEARS, SETTING FOR THE FIRST SCENE

5° PERFECT MASTER

HIRAM'S TOMB, SETTING FOR THE SECOND SCENE

6° INTIMATE SECRETARY
KING SOLOMON'S PRIVATE APARTMENTS, SETTING FOR THE FIRST SCENE

9° ELU OF NINE

CAVE SET, SETTING FOR THE FIRST SCENE

9° ELU OF NINE

KING SOLOMON'S AUDIENCE CHAMBER OR *THRONE ROOM*, SETTING FOR THE SECOND SCENE

10° ELU OF FIFTEEN

QUARRY, SETTING FOR THE FIRST SCENE

12° MASTER ARCHITECT
CLASSICAL LANDSCAPE, SETTING FOR THE FIRST SCENE

14° PERFECT ELU
SECRET VAULT, SETTING FOR THE FIRST SCENE

15° KNIGHTS OF THE SWORD, OF THE EAST, OR OF THE EAGLE
SOLOMON'S RUINS, SETTING FOR THE FIRST SCENE

15° KNIGHTS OF THE SWORD, OF THE EAST, OR OF THE EAGLE
TOWER OF CYRUS, SETTING FOR THE SECOND SCENE

15° KNIGHTS OF THE SWORD, OF THE EAST, OR OF THE EAGLE
KING CYRUS'S COURTYARD, SETTING FOR THE THIRD AND FIFTH SCENES

15° KNIGHTS OF THE SWORD, OF THE EAST, OR OF THE EAGLE
TREASURE CHAMBER, SETTING FOR THE FOURTH SCENE

18° KNIGHT ROSE CROIX
PERISTYLE, SETTING FOR THE FIFTH SCENE

18° KNIGHT ROSE CROIX
CRUCIFIXION, SETTING FOR THE THIRD SCENE

18° KNIGHT ROSE CROIX
ASCENSION, SETTING FOR THE FOURTH SCENE

18° KNIGHT ROSE CROIX

FIERY TORMENTS, SETTING FOR THE SIXTH SCENE

18° KNIGHT ROSE CROIX

CONSTELLATION, SETTING FOR THE SECOND AND FINAL SCENE

21° NOACHITE, OR PRUSSIAN KNIGHT
WOODS, SETTING FOR THE FIRST SCENE

27° KNIGHT COMMANDER OF THE TEMPLE
GOTHIC INTERIOR, SETTING FOR THE FIRST SCENE

27° KNIGHT COMMANDER OF THE TEMPLE
CATHEDRAL, SETTING FOR THE SECOND SCENE

30° KNIGHT KADOSH, OR KNIGHT OF THE BLACK AND WHITE EAGLE
CATACOMBS, SETTING FOR THE FIRST SCENE

30° KNIGHT KADOSH, OR KNIGHT OF THE BLACK AND WHITE EAGLE
MAUSOLEUM, SETTING FOR THE THIRD SCENE

30° KNIGHT KADOSH, OR KNIGHT OF THE BLACK AND WHITE EAGLE
CLASSICAL INTERIOR, SETTING FOR THE SECOND SCENE

MINOS
CONFUCIUS

NUMA
AL
MOSES
HERMES

31° INSPECTOR INQUISITOR

HALL OF EQUITY, SETTING FOR THE THIRD SCENE

32° MASTER OF THE ROYAL SECRET
GRAND ENCAMPMENT, SETTING FOR THE FIRST SCENE

Notes on the Degree Productions

4° SECRET MASTER
HOLY OF HOLIES, SETTING FOR THE FIRST SCENE

King Hiram of Tyre sent his Master Architect, Hiram, to work on King Solomon's Temple. During his stay, Hiram prayed daily in a lodge room adjacent to the Temple's Holy of Holies, or Sanctum Sanctorum. This stage setting depicts this inner sanctum, initially staged in the east end of a lodge room. The auditorium floor mirrored the traditional lodge room setting, with the proscenium opening often designating the symbolic East. (p. 168)

5° PERFECT MASTER
VEIL OF TEARS, SETTING FOR THE FIRST SCENE

The Lodge is in sorrow, mourning the loss of Master Architect Hiram. Black draperies with silver tears denote the continued state of grief surrounding his murder. King Solomon orders the construction of an elaborate tomb to hold Hiram's remains. (p. 169)

5° PERFECT MASTER
HIRAM'S TOMB, SETTING FOR THE SECOND SCENE

Each year on the anniversary of Master Architect Hiram's death, a ceremonial tribute reenacts the burial of their Perfect Master. The scenery depicts his tomb, marking the discovery of his murdered remains. Constructed of black and white marble, a great urn pierced with a sword was to hold Hiram's heart. (p. 170)

6° INTIMATE SECRETARY
KING SOLOMON'S PRIVATE APARTMENTS, SETTING FOR THE FIRST SCENE

King Hiram of Tyre visits King Solomon in his private apartments, lodging a complaint concerning the promised remuneration for labor and materials provided during the Temple's construction. This setting is often labeled Solomon's Audience Chamber *or* Solomon's Apartments. *It depicts an elaborate interior space nestled within an exotic landscape. (p. 171)*

9° ELU OF NINE
CAVE SET, SETTING FOR THE FIRST SCENE

In the mountains east of Yapū, a shepherd named Pharos searches for a stray sheep. He discovers the slain animal's carcass near a cave in the mountain. Pharos decides to hide among the rocks and wait for the perpetrators. At nightfall, three ruffians return to the cave while discussing their murder of King Solomon's Master Architect, Hiram. (p. 174)

9° ELU OF NINE
KING SOLOMON'S AUDIENCE CHAMBER OR *THRONE ROOM*, SETTING FOR THE SECOND SCENE

King Solomon calls an assembly to determine the best means to discover and apprehend the assassins of Master Architect Hiram. Deliberations are halted when a shepherd from Joppa enters the room, reporting his discovery of three ruffians and their discussion of murder. King Solomon instantly chooses a group of men to return these assassins for trial and judgment. (p. 175)

10° ELU OF FIFTEEN
QUARRY, SETTING FOR THE FIRST SCENE

Two of Master Architect Hiram's assassins conceal their identities by posing as quarry workers near the city of Gath. King Solomon sends a group of fifteen to apprehend the criminals. The candidate and two others represent three of the fifteen. They capture the men alive and return them to King Solomon for justice. (p. 176)

12° MASTER ARCHITECT
CLASSICAL LANDSCAPE, SETTING FOR THE FIRST SCENE

A white classical interior and serene landscape are the setting for multiple degrees. In this degree production, the Mason's everlasting quest for knowledge is presented through the symbolic interpretation of a master architect's tools. In the Twenty-eighth Degree, the Council of the Knights of the Sun meets near an open landscape, reinforcing the power and wisdom found in nature. (p. 177)

14° PERFECT ELU

SECRET VAULT, SETTING FOR THE FIRST SCENE

A series of underground chambers runs beneath King Solomon's Temple. In the innermost chamber, under the Holy of Holies, King Solomon hid a sacred cube bearing the Ineffable Name of the Deity. In this Secret Vault, the lost word is recovered and pronounced for the candidate, thus completing the quest. (p. 123 and p. 178)

15° KNIGHTS OF THE SWORD, OF THE EAST, OR OF THE EAGLE

SOLOMON'S RUINS, SETTING FOR THE FIRST SCENE

Zerubbabel travels from Babylon to inspect the Temple ruins in Jerusalem on behalf of King Cyrus of Persia. An impoverished people camp amidst the rubble of broken columns and scattered stones. They ask Zerubbabel to remind King Cyrus of his promise to restore the captives' freedom, allowing the Hebrews to return to Jerusalem and rebuild the Temple of the Lord. (p. 179)

15° KNIGHTS OF THE SWORD, OF THE EAST, OR OF THE EAGLE

TOWER OF CYRUS, SETTING FOR THE SECOND SCENE

Zerubbabel arrives at the outer door of King Cyrus's palace in Babylon. He has returned from Judea, where he inspected the Temple ruins. As promised, he appeals to King Cyrus's sense of justice and good faith, reminding the king of his promise to release the Hebrews and rebuild King Solomon's Temple. (p. 180)

15° KNIGHTS OF THE SWORD, OF THE EAST, OR OF THE EAGLE

KING CYRUS'S COURTYARD, SETTING FOR THE THIRD AND FIFTH SCENES

The palace courtyard provides the setting for various scenes, including the interpretation of King Cyrus's dream. There the prophet Daniel interprets the dream as a possible fate if King Cyrus does not keep his promise to free the Hebrew captives and rebuild King Solomon's Temple. (p. 181)

15° KNIGHTS OF THE SWORD, OF THE EAST, OR OF THE EAGLE

TREASURE CHAMBER, SETTING FOR THE FOURTH SCENE

The lost treasure from the first Temple remains hidden in an underground chamber beneath King Cyrus's palace at Babylon. There, the king tempts Zerubbabel with untold riches as a test. (p. 184)

18° KNIGHT ROSE CROIX

CONSTELLATION, SETTING FOR THE SECOND AND FINAL SCENE

Broken columns and crumbling ruins represent a world in chaos during the search for the lost word. To prepare the candidate for this difficult task, three constellations magically appear in the night sky, depicting the virtues of Faith, Hope, and Charity. They will guide the candidate throughout his quest. (p. 191)

18° KNIGHT ROSE CROIX

CRUCIFIXION, SETTING FOR THE THIRD SCENE

Staged as the first half of a scenic tableau, this transformation scene initially appeared as small paintings in the symbolic East of a lodge room during degree work. The candidate is presented with the idea of a spiritual redeemer on his symbolic journey. This degree production does not promote Christianity. (p. 186)

18° KNIGHT ROSE CROIX

ASCENSION, SETTING FOR THE FOURTH SCENE

This degree shows that every religion has a spiritual redeemer, whether individuals acknowledge the redeemer's arrival or are still waiting for the redeemer's appearance. In this scene, Jesus is presented as the central figure of a cut drop, slowly ascending into the heavens. (p. 187)

18° KNIGHT ROSE CROIX

PERISTYLE, SETTING FOR THE FIFTH SCENE

The candidate continues on his quest for truth and light during a time of grave darkness. Symbolic objects are revealed throughout this painted composition. They include translucencies promoting Infinity, Nature, Reason, and Immortality of man. More so than any other Masonic design, this classical colonnade was uniquely identified as Masonic and labeled the Peristyle. *(p. 185)*

18° KNIGHT ROSE CROIX

FIERY TORMENTS, SETTING FOR THE SIXTH SCENE

This scene depicts the terror that awaits those who succumb to temptation and vice, choosing to follow the wrong path. It is only with Faith, Hope, and Charity that an individual may overcome these evils, thus avoiding the punishments and tortures described in the writings of Dante Alighieri and John Milton. This degree reminds the audience that a Freemason's life should remain ruled by Faith, Hope, and Charity. (p. 190)

21° NOACHITE, OR PRUSSIAN KNIGHT
WOODS, SETTING FOR THE FIRST SCENE

In each lunar month on the night of a full moon, knights gather to ensure justice during dark times. They seek justice at a time when wrongdoing remains unchallenged and the people are in need of aid. (p. 192)

27° KNIGHT COMMANDER OF THE TEMPLE
GOTHIC INTERIOR, SETTING FOR THE FIRST SCENE

Constans seeks to attain the title Knight Commander of the Temple. Prior to any admittance to the Chapter of Commanders, Constans must complete several tasks. As he prepares for this great honor, the Chapter of Commanders meet in the main room of a medieval castle where they determine the fate of those who seek entrance to the order. (p. 193)

27° KNIGHT COMMANDER OF THE TEMPLE
CATHEDRAL, SETTING FOR THE SECOND SCENE

To attain the title Knight Commander of the Temple, Constans must stand vigil at the altar until dawn. To leave for any reason would cause him to forfeit his knighthood. He withstands many temptations but ultimately leaves the castle's chapel to battle brutal invaders. Although he is initially chastised, his selfless and noble actions to save the town surpass his own desires and ambitions. This degree harkens back to chivalric times, when a knight's honor developed out of his constant practice of humility, temperance, and generosity. (p. 196)

30° KNIGHT KADOSH, OR KNIGHT OF THE BLACK AND WHITE EAGLE
CATACOMBS, SETTING FOR THE FIRST SCENE

Death is inevitable and signifies the moment when all rank and privilege disappear. This degree production reinforces the need for an individual's faith in God, the love of all mankind, and the necessity for personal sacrifice. The three skulls symbolize the tragedy that often befalls those driven by power, greed, and self-interest. The candidate vows to honor and revere the immortal martyrs of faith and freedom, ultimately choosing death over dishonor. (p. 197)

30° KNIGHT KADOSH, OR KNIGHT OF THE BLACK AND WHITE EAGLE
CLASSICAL INTERIOR, SETTING FOR THE SECOND SCENE

The message that accompanies this setting concerns the continued fight against corruption, bigotry, and intolerance. This is part of the battle against those who represent modern personifications of Hiram's assassins. The candidate vows to protect the innocent and oppressed, bringing to justice criminals who threaten humanity. In a pristine classical setting, Supreme Judges offer warning to those who break their vows. They admit only honorable postulants of great integrity, whose faith and honor lift them above the mass of mankind, thus deeming them worthy. (p. 199)

30° KNIGHT KADOSH, OR KNIGHT OF THE BLACK AND WHITE EAGLE
MAUSOLEUM, SETTING FOR THE THIRD SCENE

This scene honors those who were victims of tyrannical rule, fanaticism, and ignorant brutality. The story describing the unjust murder of Jacques DeMolay, Grand Master of the Knights Templar during the Crusades, is presented within the setting of his mausoleum. (p. 198)

31° INSPECTOR INQUISITOR
HALL OF JUSTICE, SETTING FOR THE SECOND SCENE

The Egyptian House of the Dead expands on the continued theme of Justice for the Thirty-first Degree, illustrating the path toward final judgment and immortality. (See p. 110 for the scene.)

31° INSPECTOR INQUISITOR
HALL OF EQUITY, SETTING FOR THE THIRD SCENE

In a classical setting, ancient sages offer instructions for judgment, starting with an introspection of their own actions. They seek out their own guilt and faults before those of others. (p. 202)

32° MASTER OF THE ROYAL SECRET
GRAND ENCAMPMENT, SETTING FOR THE FIRST SCENE

This degree encapsulates all the lessons and duties of previous degrees. The setting incorporates the symbolic nonagon, with camps represented by flags, symbolic objects, and other alphabetical designations. Each corresponds to the placement of specific individuals from the first through thirty-first degrees. Here the candidate affirms his commitment to the continuation of learning and education throughout the remainder of his life. (p. 203)

Masonic procession for the dedication of the Scottish Rite Temple, Santa Fe, New Mexico. The building was dedicated at a special meeting of the Coordinate Bodies on November 17, 1912, Deputy Richard H. Hanna presiding and Alphonso C. Steward, Grand Inspector General for Missouri, delivering the dedication address. Photograph by Jesse Nusbaum. Scottish Rite Temple Collection, Palace of the Governors Photo Archives (NMHM/DCA HP.2016.53.006).

Timeline

Events Surrounding the Rise of Scottish Rite Freemasonry in New Mexico

1801: The Supreme Council of the United States of America is established in Charleston, South Carolina, with nine Inspectors General governing development of the Ancient and Accepted Scottish Rite of Freemasonry.

1813: Emmanuel de la Motta, an original officer from the Charleston Supreme Council, organizes the second Supreme Council for the United States in New York.

1826: William Morgan is abducted in Batavia, New York. Masons are suspected, as he was preparing to publish and publically distribute the ritual. A period of anti-Masonic sentiment ensues, and memberships in many fraternal organizations plummet, causing some closures.

1832: Albert Pike (1809–1891) accompanies a trading group from Missouri to Santa Fe.

1845: Supreme Council of the Northern Jurisdiction moves headquarters to Boston.

1850: Albert Pike is raised as a Master Mason at Western Star Lodge No. 2 in Little Rock, Arkansas.

1851: The Grand Lodge of Missouri issues a charter for Montezuma Lodge No. 1 in Santa Fe on May 8. This is the first and only nonmilitary lodge in the territory at the time.

1852: Albert Pike represents the Creek (Muscogee) Nation of Indian Territory in a claim for ceded land. Two years later the Choctaw and Chickasaw Nations hire Pike to pursue a similar case. He wins all three cases against the US government.

1859: A year after being elected as an active member of the Supreme Council, Albert Pike becomes Grand Commander.

1860: The Supreme Council for the Southern Jurisdiction meets in Washington, DC, for the first time; Charles Laffon de Ladebat establishes the Scottish Rite in Veracruz, Mexico, and General Ignacio Comonfort is appointed Sovereign Grand Commander of Mexico.

1885: On October 8, records indicate that the Fourth through Ninth Degrees are conferred in the hall of Montezuma Lodge No. 1.

1891: Santa Fe Lodge of Perfection membership numbers thirty-eight individuals.

1892: James Cunningham Batchelor (1818–93) becomes the new Grand Commander and Albert Pike's successor.

1893: Thomas G. Casewell becomes the new Grand Commander after the unexpected death of James Batchelor. Mandated delays between receiving the Fourth through Thirty-second Degrees are removed in a new set of statutes for Scottish Rite legislation (Section 19 of Article XII).

1895: Max E. Frost reports to the Supreme Council that he has communicated the Fourth through Thirty-second Degrees on thirteen Masons, noting favorable prospects for growth despite the geographical distance between lodges and despite a full two-thirds of the population professing a Roman Catholic faith.

1899: Harper S. Cunningham is appointed an active member of the Supreme Council. He becomes Sovereign Grand Inspector General Cunningham of Oklahoma.

1900: James D. Richardson becomes the new Grand Commander and successor to Thomas Casewell.

1901: Centennial anniversary of the organization of the Supreme Council. Both the Santa Fe Scottish Rite and the York Rite meet in Montezuma Lodge No. 1, using the rooms and banquet hall in this building on the south side of the Plaza.

1903: There are seven thousand Master Masons in Oklahoma Territory and Indian Territory.

The Cornerstone Statehood Class on the steps of the territorial capitol, 1911. Photograph by Jesse Nusbaum. Scottish Rite Temple Collection, Palace of the Governors Photo Archives (NMHM/DCA HP.2016.53.008).

1905: Grand Commander James D. Richardson retires from the US Congress to devote his entire time and energies to the Scottish Rite.

1907: The First International Conference of Supreme Councils is held in Brussels, Belgium. The next one is planned for North America.

1908: Harper Cunningham makes a special request to the Grand Commander of the Supreme Council for the Southern Jurisdiction for the Scottish Rite to segregate him from the jurisdiction of Oklahoma as Inspector General and assign him to New Mexico. New Mexico's Lodge of Perfection membership, for those receiving the Fourteenth Degree, is 193.

1909: Seventy-eight new members achieve the Thirty-second Degree, bringing the total membership of the Consistory to 134. On February 3, an order is issued to transfer the jurisdiction of the Territory of New Mexico to Inspector General Harper S. Cunningham.

1911: Grand Commander James Richardson elevates Richard H. Hanna to the position of Deputy of the Supreme Council, as he is best acquainted with the plans and ideals of Cunningham and best able to carry them to completion. The cornerstone is laid on August 24 under the auspices of the Most Worshipful Grand Master Edward L. Medler, assisted by Past Grand Masters John J. Kelly, John W. Poe, and William S. Harroun and Grand Secretary A. A. Keen.

1912: The Santa Fe Scottish Rite's Statehood Class is so named because it is the first to be initiated after the Territory of New Mexico becomes the forty-seventh US state on January 6. Souvenir medallion badges for the Scottish Rite dedication are made of government bronze, with a handsome reproduction of the temple; the Second International Conference of Supreme Councils is held in Washington, DC. Bestor G. Brown, western sales representative for M. C. Lilley & Co., travels to meet with Santa Fe Scottish Rite Bodies for the first time to configure a new scenery installation.

1913: The two Scottish Rite jurisdictions under the American flag have more than 150,000 members. Thomas R. Marshall, vice president of the United State and active Scottish Rite Mason in the Northern Jurisdiction, meets with Masonic members of Santa Fe. Two stained-glass windows are installed as memorials for the Cunningham Class (April 1911) and the Cornerstone Statehood Class (August 1912).

1914: In October, the Scottish Rite Board of Directors selects an elaborate color scheme, with tinting and fresco work, for interior decorations. A painted mural above the proscenium arch of the auditorium is commissioned as a memorial to the late Harper S. Cunningham, Thirty-third Degree, late Sovereign Grand Inspector General in New Mexico, with work to be completed by the February 1915 reunion.

1915: Scottish Rite membership in New Mexico numbers 722. In June, the Honorable Manuel Bonilla, Thirty-third Degree, Sovereign Grand Commander of Mexico, visits the Scottish Rite Temple.

1916: The Santa Fe Scottish Rite building is featured as the frontispiece in the October issue of *The Gavel,* published in Portland, Oregon.

1917: Bicentenary anniversary of the organization of the United Grand Lodge of England on June 24, 1717. In July, Grand Commander Harry C. Moore visits the Santa Fe Scottish Rite.

1918: In January, the *Consistory Bulletin* announces that Montezuma Lodge No. 1 has a beautiful service flag, onto which stars are being attached for each member in any branch of military service. Masonic brethren in France find a generous and kindly welcome at the Masonic temple at 16 Rue Cadet in Paris. A letter from the Grand Orient of France says: "We, therefore, ask you to kindly inform Masons and their relatives that in applying to us they will always find us ready to be of use to them and happy to render them any service within the measure of our means and capabilities." The *Consistory Bulletin* notes, "At a Masonic gathering held recently 'Somewhere in France' there were present 100 American members of the Craft, representing 27 States. The meeting was the first of its kind to be held in France, and was marked by the close fellowship of men far from home under war conditions." In June the *Bulletin* notes: "The fee for the Degrees will be raised to $150.00 beginning January 1, 1919. The new rate is lower than in Colorado or Arizona, jurisdictions adjoining New Mexico." In September, the name Acoma is selected for the Scottish Rite Class, which means century in the language of the Acoma Pueblo Indians. Class member James Bryan Garcia is from Acoma Pueblo; New Mexico Consistory No. 1 endorses the amendment for national prohibition during the war. On October 5, the Grand Lodge of New Mexico sends out a letter to all Masons in the state, warning against the recent solicitation of members by the Ku Klux Klan.

1919: In March, Frank Staplin, appointed librarian in the fall of 1917, resumes efforts to provide a suitable library for the Rite and announces a drive to raise funds to buy bookcases for existing volumes and to purchase numerous publications "which are badly needed for reference and study." The Third Degree for Montezuma Lodge No. 1 is conferred at the Scottish Rite Temple, marking the first time the Sublime Degree is conferred by a team in the history of Freemasonry in New Mexico. The *Consistory Bulletin* notes that the new production uses the extensive scenery, robes, and paraphernalia of the Scottish Rite.

1920: Fees for Scottish Rite degrees are $160, with not less than $25 to accompany a petition to join. A Special Reunion is held at Silver City on May 12–13 to accommodate sixty-three Brethren at Fort Bayard who cannot secure military leave to attend a Santa Fe Reunion and receive degrees in the usual way. The membership of the Masonic Fraternity in the United States totals 2,246,724 by the end of December 1920.

1921: The *Consistory Bulletin* advertises that Scottish Rite Masons attending the Santa Fe Fiesta, Banker's Convention, and Knights of Pythias Conclave can secure lodging in the Scottish Rite Temple. Grand Secretary John Whicher delivers a lecture on Freemasonry by "wireless telephone" on September 3. The transmitting instrument is located on the top of the Fairmont Hotel in San Francisco, and the broadcast reaches many locations, including New Mexico. In October the *Consistory Bulletin* describes the appearance of the Ku Klux Klan: "Information is at hand that Goblins or agents of the malodorous Ku Klux Klan have invaded New Mexico, and that they are trying to organize locals in this State." The article ends by stating, "This Ku Klux Klan is to be avoided as one would a pestilence."

1922: The Santa Fe and other railroads offer a special half-price round-trip fare for the meeting of the Grand Bodies at Albuquerque if attendance exceeds 150. The *Fellowship Forum* lists the names of 56 members of the US Senate and 276 members of the House of Representatives who are said to be members of the Masonic fraternity. Representatives from the Grand Lodges of Texas, New Mexico, and Arizona formulate a plan to establish a sanatorium for Masons afflicted with tuberculosis. The name of Santa Fe's *Consistory Bulletin* is changed to *Gauge and Gavel.*

1925: An earthquake destroys a Masonic temple in Japan, home of the Scottish Rite Bodies in Yokohama. The Supreme Council sends $11,000 to assist area Masons and residents suffering from the catastrophe.

1926: In November the *Benedict Arnold Episode*—called the *Traitor Play* in the Northern Jurisdiction—is exemplified as an addendum to the Twentieth Degree at the past reunion. It will be performed at each subsequent reunion until being converted to a public play in the 1980s.

1927: *The Benedict Arnold Episode* is put on along with the Twentieth Degree at Albuquerque Scottish Rite Temple Lodge No. 6 in 1927; an article in the *Consistory Bulletin* examines the link between the Scottish Rite and productive citizens, noting, "We are all intensely interested in the development of our state materially, intellectually, educationally and in the tone and character of its citizenship. Did it ever occur to you that there is no greater force acting within the bodies of social life in New Mexico, looking toward the building up of a sober, industrious, capable, reliable, tolerant and enlightened citizenship than Scottish Rite." A large ventilation fan is installed over the ceiling of the auditorium and controlled from the stage area. Suction is through grill ventilators over the auditorium's stained-glass windows, with hot air exhausted through the fan and roof ventilators. In November, all the exterior woodwork is repainted with two full coats of lead in oil.

1928: Members propose to compile a history of the Scottish Rite for the Orient of New Mexico, noting that it has been under advisement for some time already. In September, one of the two Grand Lodges in Spain is closed, and approximately two hundred Masons are imprisoned for allegedly plotting against the government.

1929: In September the *Bulletin* notes that between five and twenty-five visitors daily tour the Scottish Rite during the summer. The tower and flat part of the auditorium are reroofed as part of ongoing maintenance.

1930: Grand Commander John H. Cowles of the Supreme Council travels to Mexico, visiting lodges under the Grand Lodge of the Valle de Mexico and the York Grand Lodge of México.

1932: The original indebtedness of $187,000 is greatly reduced; the only outstanding balance is $60,000 issued in bonds.

1933: The German Ministry of the Interior uses the Enabling Act (Ermächtigungsgesetz) of 1933 to order the disbandment of Freemasonry and confiscation of all Lodge property.

1936: A large reunion involves approximately 150 men, who perform the degree productions, staging thirty-seven different scenes. Continued building maintenance includes installing runways along steam, water, and sewer pipes under portions of the kitchen, dining room, and classroom for easy access in case of needed repair. The partition between the old office and the adjacent room is removed and replaced with a Moorish arch. The "heaviest battleship linoleum" is laid on the new floors for the office area.

1938: Planning for construction of the west wing commences. The space is to be used as a robing room and dormitory after a $5,000 estate gift by Charles H. Rathbone, a charter member of the Lodge of Perfection in 1883.

1940: After the victory of dictator General Francisco Franco, Freemasonry is officially outlawed in Spain on March 2. Being a Mason is punishable by a jail term of twelve years.

The Billy Mitchell Class on the steps of the Santa Fe Scottish Rite Temple in 1944. Collection of the Scottish Rite Temple, Santa Fe.

1941: The Supreme Council designates $1 million for the aid, assistance, and relief of Masonic institutions, members, and families in war zones.

1942: The Masonic War Emergency Committee is established at the meeting of the Grand Lodge of New Mexico in October. The committee is tasked with coordinating all Masonic efforts in military and civilian activities throughout New Mexico, promoting the welfare of Masons and their families.

1944: The Billy Mitchell Class includes thirty-eight officers and enlisted men in air training who wish to obtain their Scottish Rite degrees before shipping overseas. This special two-day reunion includes only servicemen.

1948: Mason Trent Thomas, a resident of Santa Fe and an architect, designs the remaining two wings of the Scottish Rite Temple, successfully enclosing the courtyard on the north and west sides of the building.

1949: The One Hundredth Reunion includes 286 members, a class of 139, and 29 visitors representing sixteen other jurisdictions. A stained-glass memorial window for the late Richard Henry Hanna is installed in the lobby. The Spanish government budgets almost $100,000 to fund a special tribunal tasked with suppressing Freemasonry.

1950: The Scottish Rite Board of Directors begins to study necessary improvements to the building, including replacing the wooden stage floor with pumice concrete and a final covering of linoleum flooring.

1951: The 105th Reunion includes a class of 175, of whom two candidates are given degrees in courtesy to other jurisdictions. A $222,979.91 expense resulting from construction of the addition is paid by the end of the year.

1952: Improvements are made to the building and include a sprinkling system for grass planted in the courtyard, along with flowers and shrubs. Spanish red tile, conforming to the tile color of the main lobby, is installed in the classroom and adjacent hallway. Past Deputy of New Mexico for the Supreme Council, Judge Edward R. Wright, donates a magnificent Oriental rug for use in the main lobby of the building.

1956: Construction of a private parking lot on the north side of the building begins. Work includes the installation of retaining walls. Concrete evidence of the original gas plant in the northwest corner of the parking lot area is uncovered during the initial excavation.

1957: Grand Commander Luther A. Smith tours Scottish Rite Valleys in the western region of the Southern Jurisdiction, visiting Santa Fe on March 18 and 19. His visit coincides with a Grand Lodge meeting.

1958: Fred H. Meunier of Denver, Colorado, overhauls the theater organ. New carpet is installed in the auditorium, with salvaged portions of the old carpet to be laid in the dormitory rooms.

1959: Work is completed on a dormitory to accommodate seventy-five candidates. Washroom facilities are installed in the library area of the third floor, which is used as a dormitory during reunions, as there is not enough space to house members at this time.

1960: The exterior repair and painting of the building costs approximately $20,000. The Santa Fe Scottish Rite raises its dues to cover the expense. The Executive Committee starts a program to replace costumes, ordering sets of costumes for the Twenty-ninth and Thirty-first Degrees and spending in excess of $4,000.

1962: Fiftieth anniversary of the Santa Fe Scottish Rite Temple, with a reunion of remaining members from the Dedication Class.

1964: Bishop Mendez Arceo of Cuernavaca, Mexico, proposes that Christians make peace with Freemasons during Vatican II. Read in the final weeks, a papal document grants (inter alia) power to confessors to absolve penitents from censure incurred for belonging to the Masonic Order or other forbidden societies.

1965: The Executive Committee purchases additional paraphernalia for the degree productions and requests that degree teams implement the use of understudies for each role. As part of a continued plan for building maintenance and improvement, the Board of Directors tiles the front steps and side landing for the October Reunion.

1966: An exterior sign reading "Scottish Rite Cathedral" is installed on the building's south facade and is illuminated with new floodlights at night.

1967: The *Traitor Play*, also known as the *Benedict Arnold Episode*, is mandated to remain as the second section of the Twentieth Degree and can no longer be separated from the conferral as an independent production.

1968: New costumes are purchased for degree work as Scottish Rite membership increases to 5,836.

1969: The Scottish Rite Bodies of New Mexico commence awarding four scholarships each year for students to attend the School of Medicine at the University of New Mexico.

1972: The Scottish Rite Bodies of Santa Fe salute members of the Ancient Arabic Order, Nobles of the Mystic Shrine, for their centennial anniversary.

1974: Santa Fe Scottish Rite Bodies approved a motion to award one fellowship each year to a deserving student at George Washington University.

1987: The Santa Fe Scottish Rite Temple is placed on the National Register of Historic Places.

1994: The Los Angeles Scottish Rite building is listed for sale.

1996: A special joint communication is held between the New Mexico Grand Lodge of Ancient Free and Accepted Masons and the Prince Hall Grand Lodge of Free and Accepted Masons at the Scottish Rite Temple in Santa Fe, affording Masons from each jurisdiction the rights of visitation and affiliation. Creation of the Santa Fe Scottish Rite Temple Historical Preservation Foundation.

2004: The conversion of the auxiliary dormitory above the dining room is the last major change to the Scottish Rite Temple. Originally the ladies lounge, the dormitory would become an apartment and then the development office.

2005: The wooden grid above the scenery collection is cleaned by Lou Jacobs, who removes ninety-three years of dust. This work is completed prior to commencing another phase of scenery restoration.

2007: The Scottish Rite building in Tulsa, Oklahoma, is listed for sale.

2010: The Scottish Rite building in Portland, Oregon, is listed for sale.

2012: The centennial celebration of the Santa Fe Scottish Rite includes a public presentation of the Thirty-first Degree and a parade.

2013: The Santa Fe Scottish Rite Temple is listed for sale at $8.4 million. Scottish Rite buildings in Los Angeles and in Fort Smith, Arkansas, are sold. Jo Whaley begins to photograph scenic backdrops to create historic documentation of the Santa Fe Scottish Rite Temple.

2014: On October 4, the Santa Fe Scottish Rite membership votes not to sell the building. Scottish Rite buildings in New Orleans, Louisiana, and Fort Scott, Kansas, are listed for sale.

2015: Paramount Pictures uses the Scottish Rite parking lot as a staging area during filming of *Whiskey Tango Foxtrot* in January and February. Different areas of the building are transformed to represent a variety of locations in Afghanistan. The Cleveland Scottish Rite Masonic Auditorium is listed for sale.

2016: Scottish Rite buildings in Milwaukee, Wisconsin, Moline, Illinois, Evansville, Indiana, and Charlotte, North Carolina, are listed for sale.

2017: The United Grand Lodge of England marks three hundred years since four lodges in London gathered at the Goose and Gridiron alehouse to form a grand lodge. Membership in the four Scottish Rite Bodies in Santa Fe numbers 790.

Regalia for the Fourteenth Degree worn by Scott Grant Jaquith, Thirty-second-Degree Scottish Rite Freemason and Venerable Master, Santa Fe Lodge of Perfection No. 1, 2017.

Bibliography

ARCHIVAL COLLECTIONS

Aztec Lodge No. 3 records, 1867–1967, Las Cruces, New Mexico

Collection of the Scottish Rite Temple, Santa Fe, New Mexico

Edgar L. Hewett Collection, 1891–1960, Fray Angélico Chávez History Library, New Mexico History Museum, Santa Fe, New Mexico

Great Western Stage Equipment Company Collection (PA44), Performing Arts Archives, University of Minnesota Libraries, Minneapolis

Harry Ransom Center, University of Texas at Austin
  John Rothgeb R. Papers
  Doris Moses Finks Theatre Arts Collection
  Performing Arts Collection

Holak Collection (PA049), Performing Arts Archives, University of Minnesota Libraries, Minneapolis

Montezuma Lodge No. 1, Santa Fe, New Mexico
  Minutes book, 1851–1859
  Visitors' book, 1852–1923

New Mexico State Records Center and Archives, Santa Fe, New Mexico

Territorial Archives of New Mexico
  Records of the Secretary of the Territory
  Constitutional convention of 1910 and statehood

Constitutional convention book

Performing Arts Archives, Manuscripts Division of the University of Minnesota Libraries, Minneapolis

Rio Grande Historical Collections, New Mexico State University Library, Las Cruces

Santa Fe Lodge of Perfection, Board of Directors minutes, Santa Fe, New Mexico

Scottish Rite Temple Collection, Palace of the Governors Photo Archives, New Mexico History Museum, Santa Fe, New Mexico

PUBLISHED WORKS

Adele, Lynne, and Bruce Lee Weber. *As Above So Below: Art of the Fraternal Society, 1850–1930.* Austin: University of Texas Press, 2015.

Albert Pike Scottish Rite Cathedral. *Fall Reunion Program.* Little Rock, AR: Albert Pike Scottish Rite Cathedral, 1898.

"Las Amenazas de la Masonería." *Revista Católica.* September 7, 1884, 425–26.

Ancient and Accepted Scottish Rite, Valley of Santa Fe, Orient of New Mexico, Dedication Reunion, November 17, 18, 19, 20, 1912. Tenth Reunion program. Santa Fe: Lodge of Perfection, 1912.

Anderson, George B. *History of New Mexico, Its Resources and People.* Vol. 2. Los Angeles: Pacific States Publishing, 1907.

Angulo, Diego, and Helen B. Hall. "The Mudejar Style in Mexican Architecture." *Ars Islamica* 2, no. 2 (1935): 225–30.

"Are Military Lodges Irregular?" *The New Age Magazine* 25, no. 9 (September 1917): 406.

Atkinson, Frank H. *Scene Painting and Bulletin Art.* Chicago: Frederick J. Drake, 1916.

Ávila Marcué, Felipe. "La francmasonería en México." *Ciencia UANL* 17, no. 65 (January–February 2014): 9–13.

Aztec Lodge No. 3 AF & AM. *Seventieth Anniversary, 1867–1937.* Las Cruces, NM: Aztec Lodge, 1937.

"The Beginnings of Freemasonry in New Mexico." *The New Age Magazine* 24, no. 6 (June 1916): 286–88.

Brockman, C. Lance. "A Catalyst for Change: Intersection of the Theatre and the Scottish Rite." *Heredom* 3 (1994): 121–46.

———. "Thomas G. Moses: Profile of a Scenic Artist." *Heredom* 1 (1992): 83–99.

Browne, Van Dyke. *Secrets of Scene Painting and Stage Effects*. New York: E. P. Dutton, 1913.

Bunting, Bainbridge. *John Gaw Meem: Southwestern Architect*. Albuquerque: University of New Mexico Press, 1983.

Caffey, David L. *Chasing the Santa Fe Ring: Power and Privilege in Territorial New Mexico*. Albuquerque: University of New Mexico Press, 2014.

Calkins, Helen M. *The Public Schools of Silver City (New Mexico): A History of the School from 1874 to 1928*, [1928?].

Carson, William C. *He Moved West with America: The Life and Times of Wm. Carr Lane: 1789–1863*. Bloomington, IN: Archway Publishing, 2016.

"Carta Encíclica de Leo XXI, Papa." *Revista Católica*, June 1, 1884, 256–61.

"Carta Encíclica de Leo XXI, Papa." *Revista Católica*, June 8, 1884, 268–72.

Carter, James D. *History of the Supreme Council, 33rd (Mother Council of the World) Ancient and Accepted Scottish Rite of Freemasonry, Southern Jurisdiction, USA, 1861–91*. Washington, DC: Supreme Council, 1967.

———. *History of the Supreme Council, 33rd (Mother Council of the World) Ancient and Accepted Scottish Rite of Freemasonry, Southern Jurisdiction, USA, 1891–1921*. Washington, DC: Supreme Council 33rd, 1971.

"Católico y Masón." *Revista Católica*, June 1, 1884, 255–56.

Çelik, Zeynep. *Displaying the Orient: Architecture of Islam at Nineteenth-Century World's Fairs*. Berkeley: University of California Press, 1992.

Cerza, Alphonse. *A History of the Scottish Rite in Illinois, 1846–1965*. Bloomington, IL: Pantagraph Press, 1966.

Chacón, Hipólito Rafael. "Creating a Mythic Past: Spanish-Style Architecture in Montana." *Montana: The Magazine of Western History* 51 (2001): 46–59.

Chauvenet, Beatrice. *Hewett and Friends: A Biography of Santa Fe's Vibrant Era*. Santa Fe: Museum of New Mexico Press, 1983.

Cheetham, Francis T. "Governor Bent, Masonic Martyr of New Mexico." *Builder* 9, no. 12 (December 1923): 359–61.

"Chicago Masonic Temple." *Scientific American* 70, no. 6 (February 10, 1894): 81–82.

Clawson, Mary Ann. *Constructing Brotherhood: Class, Gender, and Fraternalism*. Princeton, NJ: Princeton University Press, 2014.

Codex. "Innovation in the Ritual." *The New Age Magazine* 4, no. 3 (1906): 275–77.

———. "The Stage in Masonry." *The New Age Magazine* 4, no. 4 (1906): 379–86.

Cole, Robert G. "Ancient and Accepted Scottish Rite: Valley of Chicago 1857–1957." *Chicago Scottish Rite Bulletin* (April 1957): 95–96.

Comer, Douglas C. *Ritual Ground: Bent's Old Fort, World Formation, and the Annexation of the Southwest*. Berkeley: University of California Press, 1996.

Commission des Sciences et Arts d'Égypte. *Description de l'Égypte, ou recueil des observations et des recherches qui ont été faites en Égypte pendant l'expédition de l'armée française, publié par les ordres de sa majesté l'empereur Napoléon le grand*. 23 vols. Paris: Imprimerie impériale, 1809–29.

Consistory Bulletin (Santa Fe) 1, no. 1 (March 1913).

Consistory Bulletin (Santa Fe) 15, no. 2 (December 1933).

Correia, David. *Properties of Violence: Law and Land Grant Struggle in Northern New Mexico*. Athens: University of Georgia Press, 2013.

Cowles, John Henry. *The Supreme Council, 33rd; Mother Council of the World, Ancient and Accepted Scottish Rite of Freemasonry, Southern Jurisdiction, USA*. Louisville, KY: Standard Print, 1931.

Crawford, Charles E. *History of the Ancient and Accepted Scottish Rite in the Valley of Indianapolis, District of Indiana, 1863–1924, Northern Masonic Jurisdiction, USA*. Indianapolis: Adoniram Grand Lodge of Perfection, 1924.

DeHoyos, Art, and S. Brent Morris, eds. *Freemasonry in Context: History, Ritual, Controversy*. Lanham, MD: Lexington Books, 2004.

Denslow, Ray Vaughn. *Territorial Masonry: The Story of Freemasonry and the Louisiana Purchase, 1804–1821*. Washington, DC: Masonic Service Association of the United States, 1925.

Denslow, William R. *10,000 Famous Freemasons*. 4 vols. Independence: Missouri Lodge of Research, 1957.

Derr, Frank A. "Chronicles of the Oklahoma Scottish Rite Masonry." *Oklahoma Consistory* (February 1949): 11.

Derr, Frank A., and Robert G. Davis. *100 Years of Scottish Rite Masonry in the Valley of Oklahoma, 1899–1999, Orient of Oklahoma*. Guthrie, OK: Scottish Rite, 1999.

De Vise, Jack P. A. *Magnificent Heritage: 150 Years of Scottish Rite Freemasonry in the Valley of Cincinnati*. Cincinnati, OH: Scottish Rite, 2003.

Dille, George E., Josephine Kaye Dille, and Earl Kaye Dille. *The Dille Family: Three Hundred Years in America, 1664–1964*. Marceling, MO: Walsworth, 1970.

Duncan, Malcolm C. *Duncan's Masonic Ritual and Monitor*. New York: David McKay Company, 1866.

Edgerton, Samuel Y. *Theaters of Conversion: Religious Architecture and Indian Artisans in Colonial Mexico*. Albuquerque: University of New Mexico Press, 2001.

Edwards, Holly. *Noble Dreams, Wicked Pleasures: Orientalism in America, 1870–1930*. Princeton, NJ: Princeton University Press, 2000.

Evans, H. R. "Lodge Furnishings and Degrees." *Builder* 2, no. 7 (July 1916): 207.

Finke, Roger, and Rodney Stark. *The Churching of America, 1776–2005: Winners and Losers in Our Religious Economy*. New Brunswick, NJ: Rutgers University Press, 2005.

Ford, Richard. *Handbook for Travellers in Spain and Readers at Home*. 2 vols. London: John Murray, 1845.

Francaviglia, Robert. *Go East, Young Man: Imagining the American West as the Orient*. Logan: Utah State University Press, 2011.

Frost, Max. "Sixty Years of Free Masonry in Territory of New Mexico." *Santa Fe New Mexican*, October 19, 1907.

"El Futuro de la Masonería." *Revista Católica*, April 5, 1885, 161–62.

Garrett, Clarke. "French Missionary Clergy Confront the Protestant Menace in New Mexico, 1851–1885." *Proceedings of the Western Society for French History* 33 (2005): 292–307.

Gems of the World's Fair and Midway Plaisance: With Accurate and Valuable Descriptions of Each, Forming a Complete Panorama of the Most Magnificent Exhibition of Ancient Or Modern Times, the Whole Comprising the World's Fair in Picture and Story. Philadelphia: Historical Publishing Company, 1894.

Gleicher, Sheri Goldstein. "The Spiegelbergs of New Mexico: A Family Story of the Southwestern Frontier." *Southwest Jewish History* 1, no. 2 (Winter 1992): 1–5.

Gordon, Paul. "Freemasons on the Santa Fe Trail." *Wagon Tracks* 26, no. 3 (February 2012): 11–17.

Gould, Robert Freke. *The Concise History of Freemasonry*. London: Gale and Polden, 1903.

Goury, Jules. *Plans, Elevations, Sections, and Details of the Alhambra, from Drawings Taken on the Spot in 1834 by Jules Goury, and in 1834 and 1837 by Owen Jones; with a Complete Translation of the Arabic Inscriptions, and an Historical Notice of the Kings of Granada from the Conquest of that city by the Arabs to the Expulsion of the Moors, by Pasqual de Gayangos*. London: Owen Jones, 1842–45.

Grand Lodge of California. *Proceedings of the Grand Lodge of Free and Accepted Masons of the Jurisdiction of California, at its 62nd Annual Communication*. San Francisco: Shannon-Conmy Printing, 1911.

Grand Lodge of Illinois. *Proceedings of the Grand Lodge of Illinois*. Chicago: Grand Lodge of Illinois, 1892.

———. *Proceedings of the Grand Lodge of Illinois*. Chicago: Grand Lodge of Illinois, 1894.

Grand Lodge of New York. *Proceedings of the Grand Lodge of Free and Accepted Masons of the State of New York, 112th Annual Communication*. New York: Press of J. J. Little and Company, 1893.

Grand Lodge of Wisconsin. *Transactions of the Grand Lodge of Free and Accepted Masons of the State of Wisconsin, at Its Annual Communication*. Milwaukee: Grand Lodge, 1885.

Haines, Helen. *History of New Mexico: From the Spanish Conquest to the Present Time, 1530–1890: With Portraits and Biographical Sketches of Its Prominent People*. Santa Fe: New Mexico Historical Publishing Company, 1891.

Hall, J. Morrow. *Seven Score and Ten: 150 Years of Freemasonry in New Mexico*. Santa Fe: Montezuma Lodge No. 1, 2001.

Harris, Cyril M. *American Architecture: An Illustrated Encyclopedia*. New York: W. W. Norton, 2003.

Harris, R. Baker. *History of the Supreme Council, 33rd (Mother Council of the World) Ancient and Accepted Scottish Rite of Freemasonry, Southern Jurisdiction, USA, 1801–1861*. Washington, DC: Supreme Council, 1964.

Hendricks, Rick. *The Casads: A Pioneer Family of the Mesilla Valley*. Los Ranchos de Albuquerque, NM: Rio Grande Books, 2012.

Hendricks, Rick, and Robert D. Martínez. "A Brief Genealogy of New Mexico Governor Albino Pérez." *New Mexico Genealogist* 53, no. 3 (September 2014): 132–35.

Hill, Lawrence J. "Beyond the Scenery: Effects Used to Enhance Scottish Rite Ceremony." *Heredom* 3 (1994): 147–58.

History of St. Charles, Montgomery, and Warren Counties, Missouri. Saint Louis: National Historical Company, 1885.

Hoffmann, Stefan-Ludwig. *The Politics of Sociability: Freemasonry and German Civil Society, 1840–1918*. Ann Arbor: University of Michigan Press, 2007.

Horgan, Paul. *Lamy of Santa Fe*. New York: Noonday Press / Farrar, Straus and Giroux, 1993.

Irving, Washington. *The Alhambra: A Series of Tales and Sketches of the Moors and Spaniards*. New York: Lea & Carey, 1832.

Jaehn, Tomas. *Germans in the Southwest, 1850–1920*. Albuquerque: University of New Mexico Press, 2005.

Jeffery, R. Brooks. "From Azulejos to Zaguanes: The Islamic Legacy in the Built Environment of Hispano-America." *Journal of the Southwest* 45, no. 1/2 (2003): 289–327.

Jennings, Kohn. *Theatrical and Circus Life or, Secrets of the Stage, Green-Room and Sawdust Arena*. Saint Louis: M. S. Barnett, 1882.

Jones, Owen. *The Grammar of Ornament*. London: Day and Son, 1856.

Kalmar, Ivan Davidson. "Moorish Style: Orientalism, the Jews, and Synagogue Architecture." *Jewish Social Studies*, n.s., 7, no. 3 (2001): 68–100.

Knights Templar of Colorado. *Proceedings of the Grand Commandery, Knights Templar of Colorado*. Denver: W. F. Robinson Printing Company, 1898.

Knights Templar of the United States of America. *Proceedings of the Grand Encampment of Knights Templar of the United States of America*. Washington, DC: Grand Encampment, 1898.

Lancaster, Clay. "Oriental Forms in American Architecture, 1800–1870." *Art Bulletin* 29 (1947): 183–93.

Langston, LaMoine. *A History of Masonry in New Mexico, 1877–1977*. Roswell, NM: Hall-Poorbaugh Press, 1977.

Laos, Nicolas K. *Freemasons, World Order, and Mind Wars: The Great Reality of Memphis-Misraim Masonry*. New York: Algora Publishing, 2016.

Levenduski, Christine M., ed. *The Scottish Rite of Freemasonry in Minnesota, 1867–2001*. Duluth, MN: Scottish Rite Foundation of Duluth, 2002.

Lewis, John Frederick. *Lewis's Sketches of Spain and Spanish Character: Made During His Tour in That Country in the Years 1833–4*. London: F. G. Moon and John F. Lewis, 1836.

Lobingier, Charles S. "The Communication of the Degrees, Part I." *The New Age Magazine* 24, no. 11 (November 1916): 490–91.

———. "The Communication of Degrees, Part II." *The New Age Magazine* 24, no. 12 (December 1916): 537–38.

———. "The Communication of Degrees, Part III." *The New Age Magazine* 25, no. 2 (February 1917): 76–78.

———. "The Communication of Degrees, Part IV." *The New Age Magazine* 25, no. 8 (August 1917): 362–63.

———. "The Communication of Degrees, Part V." *The New Age Magazine* 25, no. 9 (September 1917): 409–11.

M. C. Lilley & Co. *It Takes You Back*. Columbus, OH: M. C. Lilley, January 16, 1914.

MacKenzie, John. *Orientalism: History, Theory and the Arts*. Manchester, UK: Manchester University Press, 1995.

Mackey, Albert G. and Charles T. McClenachan. *Encyclopedia of Freemasonry*. Altenmünster, Germany: Jazzybee Verlag, 2013. Kindle edition.

Major Equipment Company. *Lighting Equipment by Major: General Catalogue Number 17*. Chicago: Schmidt Printing, 1931.

Marling, Karal Ann. "Writing History with Artifacts: Columbus at the 1893 Chicago Fair." *Public Historian* 14, no. 4 (Autumn 1992): 13–30.

Marston, Richard. "Art in the Theater: The Decline of Scenic Art in America." *Magazine of Art* (April 1894):163–68.

Masonic Chronicle (M. C. Lilley) 8, no. 7 (1889): 75.

Masonic Voice Review, 27, no. 1 (July 1862): 190.

"Masons of Guthrie to Dedicate Temple." *The New Age Magazine* 31 (1923): 757.

McBride, Harriet W. "Business and the Brethren: The Influence of Regalia Houses on Fraternalism." *Heredom* 12 (2004): 163–201.

McClenachan, Charles Thompson. *The Book of the Ancient and Accepted Scottish Rite of Freemasonry Containing Instructions in All the Degrees from the Third to the Thirty-Third and Last Degree of the Rite.* New York: Macoy Publishing and Masonic Supply, 1913. First published 1867 by Masonic Publishing and Manufacturing Co.

———. *History of the Most Ancient and Honorable Fraternity of Free and Accepted Masons in New York, from the Earliest Date.* 4 vols. New York: Grand Lodge, 1888–1894.

McKevitt, Gerald. *Brokers of Culture: Italian Jesuits in the American West, 1848–1919.* Stanford, CA: Stanford University Press, 2007.

Mead, Francis H. "Costume in the Rite." *The New Age Magazine* 17, no. 4 (October 1912): 388–90.

Mehren, Edward J., Henry Coddington Meyer, and John M. Goodell, eds. *Engineering Record, Building Record and Sanitary Engineer.* Vol. 61. New York: McGraw, 1910.

Montezuma Lodge No. 1. *A Century of Freemasonry in New Mexico: One Hundredth Anniversary, 1851–1951.* Santa Fe: The Lodge, 1951.

Moody, Richard. *America Takes the Stage: Romanticism in American Drama and Theatre, 1750–1900.* Bloomington: Indiana University Press, 1955.

Moore, William D. "From Lodge Room to Theatre: Meeting Spaces of the Scottish Rite." In *Theatre of the Fraternity: Staging the Ritual Space of the Scottish Rite of Freemasonry, 1896–1929,* edited by C. Lance Brockman, pp. 30–51. Minneapolis: Frederick R. Weisman Art Museum, University of Minnesota, 1996.

———. *Masonic Temples: Freemasonry, Ritual Architecture, and Masculine Archetypes.* Knoxville: University of Tennessee Press, 2006.

Morley, Sylvanus Griswold. "Santa Fe Architecture." *Old Santa Fe Magazine* 2, no. 3 (January 1915): 278–301.

Morris, Alvin E. *To Shine in Use: A Centennial Celebration of the Scottish Rite Bodies of Wichita, Kansas.* Wichita: Wichita Scottish Rite, 1986.

Murphey, John W. *Scottish Rite Masonic Center, Santa Fe, New Mexico.* Historic American Buildings Survey (NM-228). Washington, DC: National Park Service, 2015.

New Music Review and Church Music Review 12 (December 1912): 41.

Newbury, George Albert, and Louis Lenway Williams. *A History of the Supreme Council, 33rd of the Ancient and Accepted Scottish Rite of Freemasonry for the Northern Jurisdiction of the United States of America.* Lexington, KY: Supreme Council 33rd, 1987.

Newton, Joseph Fort. *The Builders: A Story and Study of Freemasonry.* Cedar Rapids, IA: Torch Press, 1922.

Nolan, Frederick W. *The Lincoln County War: A Documentary History.* Santa Fe: Sunstone Press, 2009.

Official Catalogue of Exhibits on the Midway Plaisance. Chicago: W. B. Conkey, 1893.

Ornish, Natalie. *Pioneer Jewish Texas.* College Station: Texas A&M University Press, 2011.

Otero, Miguel Antonio. *Report of the Governor of New Mexico to the Secretary of the Interior.* Washington, DC: US Government Printing Office, 1905.

Pérez Escutia, Ramón Alonso. "El origen y protagonismo de la masonería en Michoacán, 1821–1831." *Tzintzun: Revista de Estudios Históricos* 61 (enero–junio 2015): 49–82.

Peters, Rollo. "The Newest Art." *Theatre Arts Magazine* (Summer 1918): 119–30.

Pike, Albert. *The Magnum opus, or Great Work: Pike's First Version of the Esoteric Work and Lectures of the Scottish Rite Rituals.* Kila, MT: Kessinger, 1992.

Poldervaart, Arie. "Black-Robed Justice in New Mexico, 1846–1912. *New Mexico Historical Review* 22, no. 1 (January 1947): 18–50.

Poole, Joy, ed. *Over the Santa Fe Trail to Mexico: The Travel Diaries and Autobiography of Dr. Rowland Willard.* Norman: Arthur H. Clark Company / University of Oklahoma Press, 2015.

Price, V. B. *Albuquerque: A City at the End of the World.* Albuquerque: University of New Mexico Press, 1992.

Prince, L. Bradford. *Historical Sketches of New Mexico: From the Earliest Records to the American Occupation.* New York: Leggat Brothers, 1883.

Raynolds, J. W. *Report of the Secretary of the Territory, 1903–1904, and Legislative Manual, 1905*. Santa Fe: New Mexican Printing, 1905.

Roberts, David. *The Holy Land, Syria, Idumea, Arabia, Egypt, & Nubia*. 6 vols. London: Day & Son, 1855–56.

———. *Picturesque Sketches in Spain, 1832 & 1833*. London: Hodgson & Graves, 1837.

Rosenbaum, Charles E. "Albert Pike Consistory, Little Rock, Arkansas." *The New Age Magazine* (1904): 283–91.

Royal Arch Masons. *Proceedings of the Grand Chapter of Royal Arch Masons of the State of California at Its Fifty-Sixth Annual Convocation*. San Francisco: Shannon-Conmy Printing, 1910.

Said, Edward. *Orientalism*. New York: Pantheon Books, 1978.

Santa Fe Scottish Rite Bulletin 1, no. 3 (August 1913).

Santa Fe Scottish Rite Bulletin 1, no. 8 (August 1914).

Santa Fe Scottish Rite Bulletin 1, no. 10 (October 1914).

Santa Fe Scottish Rite Bulletin 1, no. 12 (December 1914).

Santa Fe Scottish Rite Bulletin 2, no. 2 (February 1915).

Santa Fe Scottish Rite Bulletin 2, no. 6 (June 1915).

Santa Fe Scottish Rite Bulletin 3, no. 4 (April 1916).

Santa Fe Scottish Rite Bulletin 3, no. 12 (December 1916).

Santa Fe Scottish Rite Bulletin 4, no. 1 (January 1917).

Santa Fe Scottish Rite Bulletin 4, no. 3 (March 1917).

Santa Fe Scottish Rite Bulletin, 5, no. 3 (March 1918).

Santa Fe Scottish Rite Bulletin, 5, no. 4 (April 1918).

Santa Fe Scottish Rite Bulletin 5, no. 11 (November 1918).

Santa Fe Scottish Rite Bulletin 6, no. 1 (January 1919).

Santa Fe Scottish Rite Bulletin 7, no. 3 (March 1919).

Santa Fe Scottish Rite Bulletin 7, no. 7 (July 1919).

Santa Fe Scottish Rite Bulletin 14, no. 7 (July 1927).

Santa Fe Scottish Rite Bulletin 15, no. 2 (October–November–December 1933).

Santa Fe Scottish Rite Bulletin 24, no. 1 (January–February 1937).

Santa Fe Scottish Rite Bulletin 23, no. 3 (May–June 1941).

Santa Fe Scottish Rite Bulletin 26, no. 6 (November–December 1944).

Santa Fe Scottish Rite Bulletin 28, no. 2 (March–April 1946).

Santa Fe Scottish Rite Bulletin 31, no. 5 (September–October 1950).

Santa Fe Scottish Rite Bulletin 32, no. 3 (May–June 1951).

Santa Fe Scottish Rite Bulletin 33, no. 2 (March–April 1952).

Santa Fe Scottish Rite Bulletin 34, no. 3 (May–June 1953).

Santa Fe Scottish Rite Bulletin 37, no. 3 (May–June 1956).

Santa Fe Scottish Rite Bulletin 40, no. 4 (July–August 1959).

Santa Fe Scottish Rite Bulletin 41, no. 1 (January–February 1960).

Santa Fe Scottish Rite Bulletin 41, no. 4 (July–August 1960).

Santa Fe Scottish Rite Bulletin 42, no. 6 (November–December 1961).

Santa Fe Scottish Rite Bulletin 45, no. 4 (July–August 1964).

Santa Fe Scottish Rite Bulletin 50, no. 4 (July–August 1969).

Santa Fe Scottish Rite Bulletin 53, no. 6 (November–December 1972).

Sheppard, Carl. *Creator of the Santa Fe Style: Isaac Hamilton Rapp, Architect*. Albuquerque: University of New Mexico Press, 1988.

Shriners International. *Shrine Annual International Book of Reports*. Internal publication of the Shriners International. Tampa, FL: Shriners International, 2016.

"Siguen Protestando los Francmasones." *Revista Católica*, July 20, 1884, 340.

Simonson, Lee. "The Painter and the Stage." *Theatre Arts Magazine* (December 1917): 3–12.

State of Oklahoma. *Journal of the Proceedings of the Senate, Regular Session of the Third Legislature of the State of Oklahoma*. Oklahoma City: Warden Printing, 1911.

Stevenson, David. *The Origins of Freemasonry: Scotland's Century, 1590–1710*. Cambridge: Cambridge University Press, 1990.

Stoes, Henry. "Biographical sketches of members of Aztec Lodge." Freemasons Aztec Lodge no. 3 records, 1867–1967. Rio Grande Historical Collections, New Mexico State University. Microfilm.

Supreme Council for the Southern Jurisdiction. *Transactions of the Supreme Council of the 33rd Degree for the Southern Jurisdiction of the United States of America, October 1882.* Washington, DC: Joseph L. Pearson, 1882.

———. *Transactions of the Supreme Council of the 33rd and Last Degree for the Southern Jurisdiction of the United States of America.* Washington, DC: House of the Temple, 1897.

Sweetman, John E. *The Oriental Obsession: Islamic Inspiration in British and American Art and Architecture, 1500–1920*. New York: Cambridge University Press, 1988.

Tabbert, Mark A. *American Freemasons: Three Centuries of Building Communities*. New York: New York University Press, 2005.

Theatrical Scene Painting: A Thorough and Complete Work or How to Sketch, Paint and Install Theatrical Scenery. Omaha, NE: Appleton Publishing, 1916.

Toussaint, Manuel. *Arte mudéjar en América*. Mexico City: Editorial Porrúa, 1946.

Trestleboard (Amity Lodge No. 442, San Diego) 97, no. 6 (June 2010): 11.

Twitchell, Ralph E. *The Leading Facts of New Mexico History*. Vol. 5. Cedar Rapids, IA: Torch Press, 1917.

———. *Old and New Santa Fe and Roundabout*. Chicago: Atchison, Topeka and Santa Fe Railway, 1912.

———. *Old Santa Fe: The Story of New Mexico's Ancient Capital*. Santa Fe: Santa Fe New Mexican Publishing Company, 1925.

Villela, Khristaan. "More Orientalism in Santa Fe." *Pasatiempo/Santa Fe New Mexican*, October 4–10, 2013, 32–34.

———. "Orientalism in Santa Fe." *Pasatiempo/Santa Fe New Mexican*, September 20–26, 2013, 38–41.

Wallis, Michael. *Billy the Kid: The Endless Ride*. New York: W. W. Norton, 2008.

Warvelle, George W. *History of Scottish Rite Masonry in Chicago, from Its Introduction until the Semi-Centenniel Anniversary in the Year 1907*. Chicago: Rogers and Smith, 1907.

Waszut-Barrett, Wendy Rae. "Theatrical Interpretations of the Indispensable Degrees." *Heredom* 12 (2004): 141–62.

Weitze, Karen J. "Sumner Hunt." In *Toward a Simpler Way of Life: The Arts and Crafts Architects of California*, edited by Robert Winter, pp. 181–90. Berkeley: University of California Press, 1997.

White, Trumbull, and William Igleheart. *The World's Columbian Exposition, Chicago, 1893*. Boston: John K. Hastings, 1893.

Wilson, Chris. *The Myth of Santa Fe: Creating a Modern Regional Tradition*. Albuquerque: University of New Mexico Press, 1997.

———. *Scottish Rite Cathedral*. National Register of Historic Places inventory. Washington, DC: United States Department of the Interior, National Park Service, 1987.

"Winona, Minnesota." *Masonic Chronicle* 8, no. 7 (April 1889): 75.

Wright, Carroll Davidson. *Census Reports Eleventh Census: 1890, Issue 9*. Washington, DC: US Government Printing Office, 1894.

UNPUBLISHED WORKS

Cheetham, Francis T. "Pioneer Freemasons in the Winning of the Southwest." Unpublished manuscript.

DuBois, Don Carlos. "Description of Degrees." Unpublished manuscript.

Frank, Randi Givercer. "The Sosman and Landis Studio: A Study of Scene Painting in Chicago, 1900–1925." Master of Fine Arts thesis, University of Texas, 1979.

Hill, Lawrence J. "Completing the Transformation of the Sacred Space: Lighting and Special Effects." Paper presented at the Theatre of the Fraternity: Staging the Sacred Space of the Scottish Rite Symposium, University of Minnesota, Minneapolis, September 10–12, 1992.

Moore, William D. "Selling the Sacred: Masonic Lodge Rooms, Their Furnishing, and Business, 1870–1930." Paper presented at the Theatre of the Fraternity: Staging the Sacred Space of the Scottish Rite Symposium, University of Minnesota, Minneapolis, September. 10–12, 1992.

Moses, Thomas Gibbs. *My Diary and Scrapbook*. Unpublished manuscript. Theatre Arts Collection, Harry Ransom Center, University of Texas at Austin.

Murphey, John. "Scottish Rite Temple, History Section." Draft submittal to Historical American Buildings Survey, New Mexico Section, National Park Service, Washington, DC, 2015.

Stowell, Don. "Materials Supporting the Theatrical Heritage Continued through Costumes and Regalia of the Scottish Rite." Paper presented at the Theatre of the Fraternity: Staging the Sacred Space of the Scottish Rite Symposium, University of Minnesota, Minneapolis, September 10–12, 1992.

Waszut-Barrett, Wendy. "Scenic Shifts upon the Scottish Rite Stage: Designing for Masonic Theatre, 1859–1928." PhD diss., University of Minnesota, Minneapolis, 2009. University of Minnesota Digital Conservancy, http://hdl.handle.net/11299/52606.

WEBSITES

2017 Commission Report. The Commission on Information for Recognition. The Conference of Grand Masters of Masons of North America, 2004–2017. http://www.recognitioncommission.org/.

"Admiral Collingwood Lodge." Freemasons Victoria, 2017. http://www.freemasonsvic.net.au/our-lodges/lodge-directory/admiral-collingwood-lodge/.

Boudreau, W. B. Dale. "The Origin of Freemasonry in Washington." Grand Lodge of Washington, n.d. https://freemason-wa.org/grand-lodge-of-wa/history-of-washington-freemasonry/.

"A Brief History of the Origin of Masonry in the State of Washington." Genesis Lodge No. 305, n.d. http://genesis305.com/images/Good_and_Wholesome_Instruction_2.pdf.

"Catron, Thomas Benton (1840–1921)." Biographical Directory of the United States Congress, 1774 to Present. http://bioguide.congress.gov/scripts/biodisplay.pl?index=c000253.

Clapsaddle, David. "Four Foot Soldiers on the Trail: An Illinois Odyssey." Santa Fe Trail Research, n.d. https://www.santafetrailresearch.com/research/four-foot-soldiers.html.

Denslow, William R. "10,000 Famous Freemasons." Richmond, VA: Macoy Publishing & Masonic Supply Co., Inc., 1957. Phoenixmasonry, Inc., 1999–2017. http://www.phoenixmasonry.org/10,000_famous_freemasons/Volume_4_Q_to_Z.htm.

"Electric Scenic Theatre." Chicagology, January 3, 2016. https://chicagology.com/2016/01/03/electric-scenic-theater/.

"Henry and Nathan Jaffa." Jewish Virtual Library, 1998–2017. https://www.jewishvirtuallibrary.org/jsource/judaica/ejud_0002_0011_0_09940.html.

"History." Queens Masonic District, 2017. http://queensmasons.com/index.php?option=com_content&view=category&layout=blog&id=52&Itemid=155&lang=en.

"History—Ancient and Accepted Scottish Rite." Masonic Union of Strict Initiation Observance (UMSOI), 2008. http://www.umsoi.com/english/history-ancient-and-accepted-scottish-rite/.

"History of the Grand Lodge of Arizona." Grand Lodge of Arizona, 2015. http://www.azmasons.org/history.

"The History of Holcomb & Hoke Manufacturing Company." The J. H. Fentress Antique Popcorn Museum, 2015. http://antiquepopcornmuseum.com/history.php.

"Hugh N. Smith, Delegate from New Mexico: 31st Congress, First Session: Rep. No. 220." US Congress (31st, 1st session: 1849–1850), House. Houston, TX: Rice University. June 7, 2010. https://scholarship.rice.edu/jsp/xml/1911/27089/1/aa00317a.tei.html.

Khalidi, Omar. "Architecture of Islamic Inspiration in the United States: A Bibliographic Essay." Archnet, n.d. https://archnet.org/system/publications/contents/4620/original/DPC1194.pdf?1384786143(2002).

Libreria Editrice Vaticana. "Humanum Genus, Encyclical of Pope Leo XIII on Freemasonry." April, 20, 1884. http://w2.vatican.va/content/leo-xiii/en/encyclicals/documents/hf_l-xiii_enc_18840420_humanum-genus.html.

Marples, James. "Edmund G. Ross, a Masonic Profile in Courage." *Scottish Rite Journal*, March 1998. http://srjarchives.tripod.com/1998-03/marples.htm.

"Masonic Temple, Albuquerque, NM." Denver Public Library, [between 1890 and 1900?], http://digital.denverlibrary.org/cdm/ref/collection/p15330coll22/id/62129.

"Masonic Temple El Paso, Texas." Henry C. Trost Historical Organization, 2017. http://www.henrytrost.org/buildings/masonic-temple-el-paso/.

"Masonic Temple Las Cruces, New Mexico." Henry C. Trost Historical Organization, 2017. http://www.henrytrost.org/buildings/masonic-temple-las-cruces.

McAtee, W. Peter. "Masons in New Mexico." Knights Templar, August 5, 2014. http://www.knightstemplar.org/KnightTemplar/articles/nm.htm.

Meagher, Jennifer. "Orientalism in Nineteenth-Century Art." Heilbrunn Timeline of Art History, The Metropolitan Museum of Art, October 2004. http://www.metmuseum.org/toah/hd/euor/hd_euor.htm.

"Membership Totals since 1924." Masonic Service Association of North America, 2015. http://www.msana.com/msastats.asp.

"Moorish Style." Oxford Islamic Studies Online, 2017. http://www.oxfordislamicstudies.com/article/opr/t276/e624.

National Register of Historic Places Registration Form, Mosque of the El Jebel Shrine, Denver, Colorado, National Register #97001235, section 8, page 17. https://npgallery.nps.gov/pdfhost/docs/NRHP/Text/97001235.pdf.

"Orientalism." Oxford Islamic Studies Online, 2017. http://www.oxfordislamicstudies.com/article/opr/t276/e704.

"Scenery Collections Digital Database." University of Minnesota Performing Arts Archives, last modified January 2, 2009. University of Minnesota Library Digital Collections. https://umedia.lib.umn.edu/scenicsearch.

"A Short History of Chapman Lodge A.F. & A.M." Chapman Lodge, n.d. http://chapmanlodgeno2.org/history.htm.

Shumaker, T. Edward. "Hugh N. Smith, New Mexico's First Attorney General." Office of the State Historian, n.d. http://newmexicohistory.org/people/the-death-of-hugh-smith-attorney-general-of-new-mexico#_edn4.

"Survey LA: Los Angeles Historic Resources Survey." City of Los Angeles, December 2015. http://preservation.lacity.org/sites/default/files/Exotic%20Revival%2012-2-2015_0.pdf.

Tabbert, Mark A. "From a Point to a Line: Twenty Sovereign Grand Commanders." Pietre-Stones Review of Freemasonry, 1996–2017. http://www.Freemasons-Freemasonry.Com/Tabbert2.html.

T.E.C. "Famous Freemason: Bro. Lew Wallace." Midnight Freemasons, January 22, 2012. http://www.midnightfreemasons.org/2012/01/famous-freemason-bro-lew-wallace_13.html.

Tórrez, Robert J. "Rebellion of 1847 Treason Trials." N.d. http://newmexicohistory.org/events/rebellion-of-1847-treason-trials.

Acknowledgments

It is a daunting task to mention all of those who greatly contributed to the preparation and publication of this endeavor. We want to acknowledge the many Freemasons from the Valley of Santa Fe who devoted their time, talent, and knowledge to this project, especially John Adams, Sean Graystone, Don Helberg, José Montano, and Wes Thorton. We greatly appreciate the contributions of Dan Irick and George Watson, who tracked down a variety of obscure information for all the authors and acted as our historical consultants for the timeline. Thanks to Art de Hoyos and Lance Brockman, who willingly shared images from their personal collections.

We want to express our sincere appreciation to all the brave men from both the Fraternity and the Santa Fe community who endured posing in heavy antique costumes and acting as stagehands to re-create scenes from the degree productions.

For the suggestions, guidance, and patience of Lisa Pacheco, editorial director, the support of Anna Gallegos, director, and the talent of David Skolkin, art director, who transformed our ideas into book form, we acknowledge the Museum of New Mexico Press with our deep appreciation.

Two institutions have been extremely generous with their materials and time. We thank Daniel Kosharek and the staff at the Palace of the Governors Photo Archives in Santa Fe and the staff at the University of Minnesota Libraries Performing Arts Archives. Without their support and generosity, we would not have been able to present much of the visual history surrounding the Santa Fe Scottish Rite.

Special thanks to Kathryn Hjuda, assistant curator at the Performing Arts Archives and Upper Midwest Literary Archives, University of Minnesota, and Eric Colleary, Cline curator and director of the Theatre and Performing Arts Archives, Harry Ransom Center, University of Texas at Austin, for their support and for helping us access information and images from a variety of collections.

With gratitude,
Rick Hendricks, Khristaan Villela, Wendy Waszut-Barrett, and Jo Whaley

Contributors

Rick Hendricks, PhD, is the New Mexico state historian. He received his BA from the University of North Carolina at Chapel Hill in 1977 and his PhD from the University of New Mexico in 1985. He is a former editor of the Vargas Project at the University of New Mexico. After conclusion of the Vargas Project, he worked at New Mexico State University, most notably on the Durango Microfilming Project. At NMSU he also taught courses in colonial Latin American and Mexican history. He has written and lectured extensively on the history of the American Southwest and Mexico. His most recent publications include the translation of the expedition journal in Steven G. Baker's *Juan Rivera's First Colorado, 1765: Spaniards among the Ute and Paiute Indians on the Trail to Teguayo: The Comprehensive Illustrated History* (Western Reflections Publishing, 2016); *El Paso Prenuptial Investigations from the Catholic Archives of Texas, 1701–1853* (Hispanic Genealogical Research Center, 2014), coauthored with Robert D. Martínez; and *Four Square Leagues: Pueblo Indian Land in New Mexico* (University of New Mexico Press, 2014), coauthored with Malcolm Ebright and Richard Hughes. He and Ebright are completing a new book on Pueblo Indian land to be published by the University of Oklahoma Press. Hendricks is also completing a biography of the Spanish-Mexican patriot and priest Father Antonio Severo Borrajo. He and Deputy State Historian Robert D. Martínez are currently researching the Mexican governors of New Mexico and the Catholic priesthood in late colonial New Mexico.

Khristaan Villela, PhD, is director of the Museum of International Folk Art in Santa Fe. He previously served as a professor of art history and scholar in residence at the Santa Fe University of Art and Design. He specializes in the history of pre-Columbian and Latin American art and the reception of ancient American culture in the modern world. He has curated exhibitions at the Getty Research Institute, Los Angeles; the Miho Museum, Kyoto; and the New Mexico History Museum. Most recently he was consulting curator for *Miguel Covarrubias: Drawing a Cosmopolitan Line* at the Georgia O'Keeffe Museum in 2014. Villela was the founding director of the Thaw Art History Center at the College of Santa Fe, a teaching and research unit with faculty, library, and collections devoted to the arts of the Americas, ancient to contemporary. He writes frequently for publications such as *New Mexico Magazine*, *El Palacio*, *ARTNews*, and *Adobe Airstream* and has a column in the *Santa Fe New Mexican*'s *Pasatiempo* magazine. He is the author of *Ancient Civilizations of the Americas: Man, Nature, and Spirit in Pre-Columbian Art* (Miho Museum, 2011); *The Aztec Calendar Stone* (with Mary Miller; Getty Publications, 2010); and *Contemporary Mexican Architecture and Design* (with Ellen Bradbury Reid and Logan Wagner; Gibbs Smith Publications, 2002). Villela is a Past Master of Cerrillos Lodge No. 19 AF & AM in Santa Fe and is a member of the Scottish Rite Lodge of Perfection, Valley of Santa Fe.

Wendy Waszut-Barrett, PhD, is a historical consultant and artist, specializing in the restoration and replication of painted scenery for historic performance venues such as the Ancient and Accepted Scottish Rite of Freemasonry. She works as a freelance designer and scenic artist, with projects that range from animated billboards in Times Square to manual roll drops in Czech-Slovak halls. Her passion, however, is the preservation of theatrical heritage and the continued training of artists in historical scene painting techniques. Waszut-Barrett also works as a scenic art instructor, sharing her knowledge of the dry pigment paint system and the studio style used to create historical scenery at the turn of the twentieth century. Under the tutelage of Lance Brockman (now professor emeritus) at the University of Minnesota, she received a BA, MA, and PhD, focusing on the theatrical interpretation and creation of painted scenes for Masonic degree productions. She has spoken internationally to theater groups about the evolution of Scottish Rite scenery, trying to raise awareness of historic scenery collections in Masonic temples throughout North America. Her publications include numerous articles on Masonic degree productions in the Initiative Theatre Museum Berlin's *Die Verte Wand*, *TD&T*, the Scottish Rite Research Society's *Heredom*, and the *Scottish Rite Journal*. She is currently writing a book on the life and times of Thomas G. Moses, Scottish Rite Mason and final president at Sosman & Landis Studio in Chicago.

Jo Whaley infuses her photographs with the illusionary world of the theater. She received an MFA in art and an MA in visual design and photography from the University of California–Berkeley. As a young artist, she was a scenic painter for the San Francisco Opera and other Bay Area theatrical companies. With the documentary photographs of the Scottish Rite Temple in Santa Fe, she returns full circle to her roots in the theater. Her work, exhibited for more than thirty-four years, is held in the permanent collections of numerous institutions, including the Philadelphia Museum of Art; the Los Angeles County Museum of Art; the Museum of Fine Arts, Houston; and the WestLicht Schauplatz für Fotografie, Vienna. From 2008 to 2013, her exhibit *The Theater of Insects* toured museums including the National Academy of Sciences, Washington, DC, and the Museum of Photographic Arts, San Diego, concluding at the Henry Fox Talbot Museum in the United Kingdom. A monograph, *The Theater of Insects,* was published by Chronicle Books (2008). Whaley received a National Endowment Visual Artists Fellowship in 1994, as well as five grants to work with the Polaroid 20 × 24 camera in New York between 1989 and 1993. Her work is included in the traveling exhibit and book *The Polaroid Project* (University of California Press, 2017). In the Fall of 2018 an exhibition of her work will be held at the Georgia O'Keeffe Museum, Santa Fe, New Mexico.

Index

Page numbers in *italics* refer to illustrations.

 The Museum of New Mexico Press is a division of the New Mexico Department of Cultural Affairs.

Director: Anna Gallegos
Editorial director: Lisa Pacheco
Art director and book designer: David Skolkin
Composition: Set in Bembo
Manufactured in China
10 9 8 7 6 5 4 3 2 1

Library of Congress Cataloging-in-Publication Data
Names: Waszut-Barrett, Wendy, editor. | Whaley, Jo, editor.
Title: The Santa Fe Scottish Rite Temple : freemasonry, architecture, and theatre / edited by Wendy Waszut-Barrett and Jo Whaley ; essays by Rick Hendricks, Khristaan Villela, Wendy Waszut-Barrett ; photography by Jo Whaley.
Description: Santa Fe : Museum of New Mexico Press, [2018] | Includes bibliographical references and index.
Identifiers: LCCN 2017055979 | ISBN 9780890136331 (clothbound : alk. paper)
Subjects: LCSH: Scottish Rite (Masonic order)--Buildings. | Santa Fe (N.M.)--Buildings, structures, etc. | Freemasonry--New Mexico--Santa Fe--History. | Temples--New Mexico--Santa Fe--History.
Classification: LCC F804.S28 S26857 2018 | DDC 978.9/56—dc23 LC record available at https://lccn.loc.gov/2017055979
ISBN 978-0-89013-633-1 hardcover

Museum of New Mexico Press
PO Box 2087
Santa Fe, New Mexico 87504
mnmpress.org

Photographs by Jo Whaley unless otherwise noted.